WITHDRAWN
NDSU

THE COLLAPSE OF THE SOVIET EMPIRE

The Royal Institute of International Affairs is an independent body which
promotes the rigorous study of international questions and does not express
opinions of its own. The opinions expressed in this publication are
the responsibility of the authors.

THE SECURITY CHALLENGES FOR JAPAN AND
EUROPE IN A POST-COLD WAR WORLD

VOLUME 1

THE COLLAPSE OF THE SOVIET EMPIRE

MANAGING THE REGIONAL FALL-OUT

edited by
TREVOR TAYLOR

ROYAL INSTITUTE OF INTERNATIONAL AFFAIRS
and
INTERNATIONAL INSTITUTE FOR GLOBAL PEACE

We are grateful to the Sasakawa Foundation in Tokyo, which provided the principal funding for this joint project, and to British Aerospace plc, which also provided helpful support.

© Royal Institute of International Affairs, 1992

First published in Great Britain in 1992 by
Royal Institute of International Affairs
Chatham House, 10 St James's Square, London SW1Y 4LE

All rights reserved. No part of this publication may be reproduced, stored in a retrieval system, or transmitted by any other means without the prior written permission of the copyright holder. Please direct all inquiries to the publishers.

British Library Cataloguing in Publication Data

A CIP catalogue record for this book is available from the British Library.

ISBN 0 905031 54 7

Text designed and set by Hannah Doe
Cover design by Youngs Design in Production

CONTENTS

List of contributors   vii
List of abbreviations   ix
Acknowledgments   xi

Introduction   1
Trevor Taylor and Seizaburo Sato

Part I Change in the former Soviet Union

1 State and nation in the former Soviet Union   7
Neil Malcolm

2 The social and ideological consequences of the collapse of communism and the Soviet Union   30
Peter Ferdinand

3 Economic implications of change in the former Soviet Union   46
Reizo Utagawa

4 Economic and technical assistance to the former Soviet Union   58
Margot Light

Part II The regional consequences in Europe and the Far East

5 Japanese–Russian relations: issues and future perspectives   79
Hiroshi Kimura

6 The impact of changes in the former Soviet Union on the communist states of Asia   90
Yoshiaki Nakagawa

vi CONTENTS

7 The impact of changes in the former Soviet Union on
Eastern Europe 104
Yves Boyer

8 The security implications of changes in the former Soviet Union
for Western Europe 118
Trevor Taylor

9 The security implications of changes in the former Soviet Union
for Asia and Japan 139
Satoshi Morimoto

10 Disarmament and arms control in the post-cold war world 146
Ryukichi Imai

Part III Perceptions of security after the cold war

11 European perceptions of the new security situation 161
Laurence Martin

12 Japanese perceptions of the new security situation 171
Seizaburo Sato

CONTRIBUTORS

Yves Boyer, Deputy Director, Centre d'Etude des Relations entre Technologies et Stratégies (CREST), Ecole polytechnique, Paris

Dr Peter Ferdinand, Head of Asia-Pacific Programme, The Royal Institute of International Affairs, London

Ambassador Ryukichi Imai, Distinguished Fellow, International Institute for Global Peace, Tokyo

Professor Hiroshi Kimura, International Research Centre for Japanese Studies, Kyoto

Dr Margot Light, Department of International Relations, London School of Economics, London

Dr Neil Malcolm, Head of Russian and CIS Programme, The Royal Institute of International Affairs, London

Professor Laurence Martin, Director, The Royal Institute of International Affairs, London

Satoshi Morimoto, Senior Researcher, Nomura Research Institute, Tokyo

Lt.-Col. Yoshiaki Nakagawa, Senior Research Fellow, International Institute for Global Peace, Tokyo

Professor Seizaburo Sato, Director of Research, International Institute for Global Peace, Tokyo

Professor Trevor Taylor, Head of International Security Programme, The Royal Institute of International Affairs, London

Reizo Utagawa, Distinguished Fellow, International Institute for Global Peace, Tokyo

ABBREVIATIONS

ALCM	Air-Launched Cruise Missile
APEC	Asia-Pacific Economic Cooperation
ASEAN	Association of Southeast Asian Nations
C^3I	Command, Control, Communications and Intelligence
CBM	Confidence Building Measures
CFE	Conventional Forces in Europe
CIS	Commonwealth of Independent States
CPSU	Communist Party of the Soviet Union
CSCE	Conference on Security and Cooperation in Europe
EBRD	European Bank for Reconstruction and Development
FSU	Former Soviet Union
GNP	Gross National Product
IAEA	International Atomic Energy Agency
ICBM	Intercontinental Ballistic Missile
IMF	International Monetary Fund
INF	Intermediate Nuclear Forces
MIRV	Multiple Independently-targetable Re-entry Vehicle
NACC	North Atlantic Cooperation Council
NIE	Newly Industrializing Economy
NPT	Non-Proliferation Treaty
NTM	National Technical Means
SAARC	South Asian Association for Regional Cooperation
SDI	Strategic Defence Initiative
SLBM	Submarine-Launched Ballistic Missile
SS	Surface-to-Surface (Soviet missile)
SSBN	Nuclear-powered Ballistic Missile Submarine
START	Strategic Arms Reduction Talks
UNPROFOR	UN Protection Force (Yugoslavia)
WEU	Western European Union

ACKNOWLEDGMENTS

This volume and the wider project of which it is a part have been made possible by the diligent efforts of many people. Kiyoshi Araki, as a visiting fellow at the RIIA in 1991, did much to establish the project. His successor at Chatham House, Yasuaki Nogawa, has provided effective continuing support. As well as being an author, Lt.-Col. Nakagawa at the IIGP in Tokyo undertook many organizational tasks with massive efficiency, while Emma Matanle of the International Security Programme at the RIIA managed administrative matters in London. She liaised patiently with authors, and worked long and hard to ensure that texts were ready for publication. A major contribution was also made by Margaret May and Hannah Doe of the Publications staff at Chatham House. We are grateful to all of them, as we are to the Sasakawa Foundation in Tokyo, which provided the principal funding for this joint project, and to British Aerospace plc, which also provided helpful support. As ever, any responsibility for flaws in the work must lie with the editor and his partner in Tokyo.

Seizaburo Sato
August 1992 Trevor Taylor

INTRODUCTION
TREVOR TAYLOR AND SEIZABURO SATO

Politicians, officials, academic analysts, journalists and the business community, indeed all those involved with international politics, have had to grow accustomed to rapid and persistent change in the shape of world affairs. Since President Gorbachev told the United Nations in December 1988 that the USSR would unilaterally cut its armed forces by 500,000 men and 10,000 tanks, the world has been experiencing a largely positive series of changes without any new situation of stability appearing imminent. A brief list of just the most significant developments would have to include the unification of Germany, the freeing of Eastern Europe from Soviet domination, the formal ending of the adversarial relationship between the West and Moscow, substantially enhanced cooperation in the United Nations, the disintegration of the USSR, US–Russia agreements for radical cuts in the number of deployed nuclear weapons, the invasion and subsequent liberation of Kuwait, and the Maastricht Treaty with its rejection by the Danish public. The list could easily be further expanded. Many of these developments took place in and around Europe rather than in East Asia, but they were nonetheless of considerable interest to Japan, with its global economic and political interests as well as its immediate regional security concerns.

In this exciting political environment, the time seemed appropriate to establish a major academic project on the common security concerns of Western Europe and Japan. Both sides had a clear interest in the future of the former Soviet Union, both were closely involved with the United States, which was tempted towards a more isolationist posture by the demise of its central enemy, and both were drawn to take a closer interest in developments beyond their own region by the uncertainties and opportunities presented by the end of the cold war. Finally, we perceived that the two sides had perhaps neglected their political and security relationship. They had become accustomed to a regular, even intense dialogue with Washington at a variety of levels and in many fora, but they spoke comparatively little to one another.

There has been recognition of this situation at the governmental level. In particular, in the summer of 1991 an EC–Japan formal dialogue was inaugurated. Corresponding to the EC dialogues with the US and with Canada, it was agreed that the Japanese prime minister would meet annually with the presidents of the European Commission and the European Council, that another annual ministerial meeting would be held, that the EC troika of foreign ministers would meet the Japanese foreign minister twice a year and that Japan and the presidency of European Political Cooperation would keep each other informed about developments in their foreign policies. The first concrete manifestation of these steps was the 1991 United Nations General Assembly resolution to establish an arms trade register, a resolution sponsored jointly by the EC countries and Japan. The weight of political and security topics in the document establishing the dialogue was striking. For instance, the Preamble to the Joint Declaration establishing the dialogue referred to both sides' 'common interest in security, peace and stability of the world' and the importance of Japan and the Community 'deepening their dialogue in order to make a joint contribution towards safeguarding peace in the world, setting up a just and stable international order in accordance with the principles and purposes of the United Nations Charter and taking up the global challenges that the international community has to face'. On the eve of Prime Minister Miyazawa's visit to London in July 1992, the Japanese Ambassador to the European Communities, Tomohiko Kobayashi, spoke of the significance of the EC–Japan dialogue, noting that 'we need to consult each other more, not only on aid to Eastern Europe and the Commonwealth of Independent States but also in other areas. Japan welcomes the EC's growing political role in the world, and wants to impress on the EC the need to consider the problems of security worldwide, paying more attention to Northeast Asia and the Asia-Pacific region'.[1]

To link academics and other researchers, during 1991 the International Institute for Global Peace in Tokyo and the Royal Institute of International Affairs in London set about the organization of a two-year research project which would address security issues on a global scale. The two institutes were attracted to work together by their academic expertise, their independence from home governments, and their range of contacts with official and unofficial bodies. Their initial aim was to have a security dialogue, to explore each side's concerns, so that more ambitious possibilities for cooperative action could perhaps be identified over the longer term.

This volume represents the outcome of the project's initial discussions, held in Tokyo during June 1992 as the Japanese Diet voted to permit Japan to contribute to UN peace-keeping forces, a symbol of Japan's growing concern with international security matters. The focus of the papers is on the former Soviet Union and the multi-dimensional consequences of its collapse for the security of its eastern and western neighbours.

The initial chapters in this volume deal with change within the former Soviet Union (FSU). Neil Malcolm surveys the shape and depth of the collapse of the communist government, and Peter Ferdinand discusses the problems of the cultural foundations of political life in the FSU. Reizo Utagawa looks specifically at economic collapse, warns against reliance on the approach of the Chicago school of economics, indicates a role for the state, and makes suggestions on aid issues. Margot Light then brings a European perspective on the aid issue and, among other points, stresses the need to secure cooperation among the successor states of the FSU.

The second section of the volume is concerned explicitly with the relations of the FSU with the outside world, and Hiroshi Kimura highlights some possibilities as regards the Northern Territories dispute, a major obstacle to the normalization of Japan–Russia relations. Yoshiaki Nakagawa analyses the impact of the Soviet collapse on relations among communist states in Asia, while Yves Boyer looks at the consequences of the same phenomenon for relations among the ex-communist states of Europe. Trevor Taylor and Satoshi Morimoto survey the security consequences of change in the FSU for Western Europe and East Asia respectively. Finally in this section Ryukichi Imai clearly illustrates the links between Japanese and European security, focusing on disarmament and arms control issues.

The two final papers in the collection, by Laurence Martin and Seizaburo Sato, adopt the widest perspective and discuss the impact of the collapse of the USSR on broad perceptions of security in Europe and Japan respectively, taking into account also the Gulf war and the Yugoslav crisis. As well as concluding this volume, these papers lead on to the concern of the second volume in this series, to be published early in 1993, on the international and regional order after the end of the cold war.

The papers and discussions from this first meeting did not, indeed could not, lead to any firm conclusions but illuminated the dimensions of the problems in Europe and the Far East presented by the demise of the FSU. Increasingly, Japan and Europe, as well as the US, face a security agenda with many common items, which Yukio Satoh of the Japanese Foreign Ministry has clearly outlined.[2] The former British Foreign Secretary, now Lord Howe, has argued that 'partnership and openness ... are the best ways for the United States, Japan and Europe together to maximise and constructively deploy their influence in the world'.³ Partly as a consequence of the end of the USSR, the world is facing a mass of political problems with a potential for violence, as states, governments and borders come under question. The successful management and control of such issues will constitute a major challenge and their resolution may well take years.

Notes
1 'Tokyo looks for closer ties with a stronger Europe' (interview with Ambassador of Japanese Mission to the European Communities, Tomohiko Kobayashi), *The Financial Times*, 3 July 1992.
2 Yukio Satoh is Director-General of the North American Affairs Bureau in the Japanese Foreign Ministry. See his 'Japan and NATO: Agenda for Political Dialogue', *NATO Review*, June 1992, pp. 18–22.
3 Sir Geoffrey Howe, 'Japan and the United States – a European perspective', *The World Today*, Vol. 48, No. 7, July 1992, p. 129.

PART I
CHANGE IN THE FORMER SOVIET UNION

CHAPTER 1

STATE AND NATION IN THE FORMER SOVIET UNION

NEIL MALCOLM

What has happened in Russia since 1985 has gripped the watching world's attention so forcefully partly because it has been so unexpected, almost at every step. Like the collapse of the imperial order in 1917, it has contradicted the accepted view of a ruthless, all-powerful bureaucratic state confronting a helpless, atomized society. The long-predicted revenge of the bureaucracy, the coup attempt of 1991, now appears as a feeble last spasm of resistance.

It would be equally misleading, however, to imagine that Russian society, released from its bonds, can now emerge swiftly, with some help from the advanced countries, onto the sunlit uplands of parliamentary democracy and market-based economic prosperity. Russian society, and the role in it of the Russian state, has been and continues to be 'exceptional' in a European context. To put it crudely, society and state have *both* been weak, and these weaknesses are connected. Imperial and communist governments alike, substituting regulation for self-regulation, tended to intervene far more actively in social and economic life (and indeed in the cultural and 'private' spheres) than their Western contemporaries. For this they paid the price of vulnerability to the effects of overload and isolation from society. Their policies were often inflexible and ineffective, and they lacked support at moments of crisis.

It would be wrong to exaggerate this exceptionalism as apologists for autocracy have in the past, arguing that the Russian people cannot cope with freedom, and need a 'firm hand'. It would in particular be wrong to accept that Russia, as one of its political scientists asserted during the period of perestroika, 'has no civil society even in embryo'.[1]

Before 1917 the absolutism of the tsars, which had earlier crushed clerical and aristocratic autonomy, had softened sufficiently to permit the emergence of an independent intelligentsia, a developing market economy and merchant class, and even representative institutions.² Stalin's despotism was followed by three decades during which, as social differentiation, levels of education and institutional specialization increased, officials and intellectuals became gradually more confident about using the state organizations they worked in as vehicles for forwarding sectional interests.³ Some Russian economists now argue that by 1980 the old administered economy had already metamorphosed into a 'bureaucratic market' based increasingly on barter and private interest.⁴

Under Gorbachev this process accelerated. The old cardboard cut-out fake democratic institutions came disconcertingly to life – local councils, republic parliaments, academic and cultural bodies, the press. Factory directors paid less and less attention to instructions from the centre, and struck deals with the new private 'cooperative' companies. Even the Communist Party began to break up into more and more independently acting fragments.

Yet after 1985 a smooth transition to democracy and the market could never have been expected. Gorbachev refused to face this: he seemed to believe, as he hung on to the Party and condemned the 'neo-Bolshevism' of his democratic critics, that institutional continuity could be preserved, that the anarchy of previous 'times of the troubles' could be avoided, and that the festival of destruction and violence initiated in 1917 need not be repeated; in other words, that there could be reform rather than revolution. Clearly he took the view, which some Western political scientists had expressed, albeit earlier on, that the Soviet Union had succeeded in building strong political institutions, embedded in society, and essential for maintaining what Samuel Huntington described as 'consensus, community, legitimacy, organization, effectiveness'.⁵ There was indeed a desperate need to renovate and democratize the system, but existing structural elements could be put to use in the rebuilding process.

This was not, as it turned out, a viable strategy. Gorbachev encouraged new political and social institutions to grow up alongside the old ones. He permitted the flourishing of glasnost, 'informal' political groups, popular fronts, 'cooperative' private enterprise, joint ventures, and eventually, as even he became more disillusioned with the inflexibility of the bureaucracy, the emergence of independent parties and increasingly assertive representative institutions at the centre and in the republics. But the old and the new structures were hostile to and corroded one another. The new challenged the legitimacy of the old, and threatened to displace them. The old tried to marginalize and criminalize the new. In the economy, for instance, the growth of private enterprise was obstructed at every turn: it developed as a semi-legal institution feeding on and encouraging the disintegration and corruption of the state sector. In relations between nationalities, liberalizing and centralizing tendencies fought each other and encouraged the very cynicism and 'extremism' which Gorbachev was so anxious to avoid. In political life in general, democratic institutions, deprived of real power, tended to act irresponsibly, and found it difficult to preserve public credibility.

By 1991, despite Gorbachev's repeated calls for compromise, tolerance and the building of a legal state, the Soviet Union seemed to be closer to Huntington's 'praetorian' pattern than to his civic polity. Conflicts were being expressed less through a network of respected institutions, in accordance with generally accepted laws and rules, and more through the direct use or threat of use of force – strikes, demonstrations, military manoeuvres, trade embargoes, and violent interventions by the forces of order: 1917 seemed to be repeating itself, with power apparently falling into the streets. As it turned out, the process of building parliamentary authority had advanced far enough by August to avert a military takeover, but the new regime was left with a daunting legacy of chaos and mistrust.

It is no accident that 'strengthening Russian statehood' has become one of the central issues in Russian public life. Lacking the dense network of parties, movements and associations which organize social support, coordinate action, facilitate recruitment and channel communications for the state in well-established industrial democracies, the new leaderships of the post-Soviet republics find themselves floating in a void. The 'rules of the game' remain to be invented, and then it will take a long time for them to be internalized by the players. Centuries of arbitrary rule have given little encouragement to the Russians and their subject peoples to develop a respect for the rule of law. Gorbachev's campaign to establish a law-governed state was discredited by the charade of the 'war of laws' in 1990–91. The programmes of the proto-parties that exist tend to extremes: the area of consensus is very limited. There is a widespread belief that governments will have to use authoritarian methods if crime and ethnic conflicts are to be brought under control, and if their decrees and administrative decisions are to have any effect.

Enormous and at the same time delicate tasks are facing the post-Soviet states: to nurture the social institutions which are to take over state functions; to devolve and decentralize while retaining sufficient levers to control the process and to cope with large residual responsibilities; and to maintain the momentum and flexibility that will be needed over a period of decades. It is thus a matter of some importance to try to set aside myths and stereotypes, and to look at what concrete evidence is available, in order to estimate the depth and nature of the problems. For the sake of manageability, the pages which follow will concentrate principally on the key case of Russia. Comments on its former partner states in the USSR will be made by the way. We shall look in turn at the political, economic and military spheres, and at relations among the former Soviet republics.

Politics
National questions

As time passes it is becoming increasingly clear what an important part was played by nationalism in the destruction of Soviet communist rule. This was not just in the European non-Russian republics, where local parliaments rested their right to seize power on an inseparable combination of electoral endorsement and their national leadership role. It was also the case in Moscow, where Yeltsin successfully snatched the patriotic card from the hands of the conservatives, presenting his battle against Gorbachev as part of a struggle for Russian national emancipation. By promoting the idea of self-determination for all, he was also able to build the coalition of all the republics against the centre which achieved the dissolution of the USSR in December 1991.

It is clear in 1992 what a dangerous weapon nationalism can be. In Armenia and Moldova, with their worsening ethnic frictions, governments are under increasing threat from more 'patriotic' oppositions, as the balance of legitimacy shifts from electoral to national-populist. In Azerbaijan two presidents have recently been toppled after military setbacks. In Russia itself, the leadership is forced into uncomfortable manoeuvres, as the (neo-communist) opposition propagates extreme variants of nationalism which challenge its more enlightened version.

The most pressing aspect of the current 'crisis of Russian statehood' concerns the very geographical definition of the state. Like the other European empires, the disintegrating Russian empire has left, firstly, a pattern of borders which frequently (and in many cases intentionally) ignore ethnic boundaries and, secondly, communities of marooned settlers from the metropolis. Around 25 million Russians live, as they express it, in the 'near abroad', elsewhere on the territory of the former Soviet Union. They make up approximately 20% of the population of Ukraine, in Kazakhstan they constitute 38%, in Estonia 30%, and in Latvia 34%. In Estonia and Kazakhstan there are clear-cut zones inhabited mainly by Russians and located near the Russian border. The Transdnestrian region of Moldova, dominated by the local Russians, declared itself a republic in 1991, and has been fighting a low-level war with the rest of the country for months. Crimea, handed over to Ukraine by Khrushchev in 1954, has a majority Russian population. Its leaders, like those in Transdnestria, have close links with neo-communist and other 'patriots' in Moscow. In the first half of 1992 their calls for independence or reunion with the motherland injected an explosive element into relations between Moscow and Kiev.

Defining Russia

The effect of all this is that in Russian politics different groups use the concept 'Russia' with quite different meanings. Many consider the Russian Federation (coterminous with the old RSFSR) to be an administrative invention – for them Russia is the area populated by Russians. Such uncertainty feeds a morbid sensitivity on national issues. There are calls for a state which will assert its authority, 'protect' Russians abroad and stand firm against any further encroachments on 'Russian' territory.

There is an internal dimension to the problem too: only 82% of the population of the Russian Republic itself are Russians. Many of the minorities live in some 20 'autonomous republics' and a smaller number of autonomous regions and districts, and some have aspirations to independence. These entities typically are situated in underdeveloped (but often resource-rich) parts of Russia, have no borders with other states, and have a population in which the titular nationality represents a minority. As such they have not represented a great challenge to Moscow. On 31 March 1992, 18 out of 20 of the republics initialled the Russian Federal Treaty. The two outstanding cases, the Chechen Republic and Tatarstan, however, have provoked a great deal of trouble in the Kremlin.

The 6.5 million Tatars constituted the sixth largest ethnic group in the old USSR, and the only one to make up a clear majority in their own autonomous republic. Gorbachev's government deliberately stoked up nationalist assertiveness in Tatarstan in order to embarrass Russia, but Yeltsin's policy of political and economic concessions ('Take as much independence as you need') seems to have been effective in keeping the temperature low. Just before the Tatars voted for 'independence' in a referendum in March 1992, the event was declared illegal by the Russian Constitutional Court, but the government decided to turn a blind eye. Bilateral negotiations are currently under way with President Mintimer Shaimiev to build a special relationship between Moscow and Kazan.[6] While General Dudaev, the leader of the small Caucasian Chechen Republic, is more intransigent, the problem there is generally regarded as a local one susceptible to manipulation from Moscow. Needless to say, however, such Fabian tactics do nothing to calm the fury of Yeltsin's nationalist critics.

The issue of the autonomous republics is only a special case of the general problem of Russia's geographical integrity. In the past the three powerful vertical structures – the Communist Party, the KGB and the industrial ministries – which held the Soviet Union together were counterbalanced by strong local networks maintained by party bosses and industrial managers. In the last twelve months the centralizing elements of this system have been virtually swept away.

Yeltsin's policy has been to accept the reality of devolution. Local authorities have been allowed a bigger share of tax income and have been given larger spending responsibilities. Enterprises have been left to find their own suppliers and customers. At the same time a new system is in the making. 'Governors' have been appointed by Moscow in the regions, and 'prefects' in districts. Units of the armed forces needed for preserving order inside the country are being reinforced and given higher status. Control over money emission and credit is being strengthened, to replace the old 'planned economy' levers.

But in the middle of a chaotic and confused process of transition, it is difficult to predict exactly where the new balance will come to rest. With opportunities to gain possession (for use or profitable resale) of valuable state assets, local cliques have every incentive to combine to resist central inspection and control. Some regions have rich natural resources which they can sell for hard currency or barter with neighbouring states. Although not on the scale observable in the Caucasus, irregular armed detachments, for example of Cossacks, have been set up in some southern regions of Russia. Even regular troops, deprived of basic supplies from the centre, have become more dependent on local authorities to feed and clothe them, and are thus less responsive to orders from above.[7]

Problems in the administration

President Yeltsin has consistently affirmed the CIS line on the inviolability of existing borders and has been a devolutionist in Russian Federation matters. Yet government policy has remained disturbingly ambiguous since the moment when, in September 1991, Yeltsin's press secretary made a statement, later officially disavowed, implying that borders could be open to revision if the Soviet republics separated completely.

In the months which followed, the Russian Vice-President, Aleksandr Rutskoi, repeatedly contradicted Yeltsin's declared policy. An Afghan veteran, Rutskoi began his career in politics in the 'patriotic' Fatherland group, but condemned the Soviet intervention in Lithuania in January 1991, and in March set up the pro-Yeltsin Communists for Democracy. As vice-president, however, he demanded a harder line towards the Chechen Republic than parliament would accept. In December he predicted that the Russian Federation 'will fall apart just as the Soviet Union has'. Subsequently he recommended to the Constitutional Court that a law should be introduced 'to imprison national careerists and separatists for a term of 10–15 years, otherwise we shall still have the Dudaevs and the Shaimievs'.[8] In April 1992, Rutskoi visited Crimea and Transdnestria, declaring that Crimea was 'part of Russia', and proposing that the CIS (effectively Russian) 14th Army, located in Transdnestria, should be given the task of protecting the Russian population there.

Some see this behaviour as part of a plan by Yeltsin to appeal to nationalist feeling without compromising his own progressive image: Rutskoi was joined on his excursion to the south by Sergei Stankevich, one of the president's close advisers. Certainly Russian democrats talk a great deal about the danger of being outflanked by the 'patriots', and they choose their words carefully on national issues. Yet Rutskoi is not just a political lightning conductor. He repeatedly attacked the Russian government, of which Yeltsin was Prime Minister, in the most damaging terms. In December 1991 he stated that there was 'no governing power and no democracy in Russia' – it was 'in a state of chaos'. On 9 February he appeared at a Congress of Civic and Patriotic Forces organized by the opposition, and described the stabilization policy of his own government as 'economic genocide'.[9]

It is difficult to avoid interpreting this as evidence of Yeltsin's political weakness. As in the final years of Gorbachev, it is the forces of order and their spokesmen who have been able to insist on a hearing.[10] (Rutskoi reportedly has widespread support in the armed forces, and his support was vital in defeating the August coup.) As a result there emerged a damaging rift at the highest level of power. Rutskoi has since been publicly reconciled with Yeltsin, but continues to cause trouble.

Relations with the legislature

The executive/legislature balance, like the centre/regional balance, is still being fought over. A large proportion of the deputies and Ruslan Khasbulatov, an old ally of Yeltsin and speaker of the Supreme Soviet, have been fighting to defend the idea of a parliamentary republic in which the powers of the president and his ministers would be closely restrained. However the experience of two years of paralysing conflict between soviets and executives at all levels has increased support for limiting parliamentary powers. Not surprisingly, these constitutional questions have become hopelessly entangled with policy issues. The Russian parliament, elected in 1990 and packed with apparatchiks, now appears conservative and out of touch with the public mood. Most democrats and reformers look instead to the president and the government.

At the sixth session of the Russian Congress of People's Deputies (the expanded version of the parliament) in April 1992 Yeltsin faced a frontal challenge. His opponents demanded that he relinquish his special powers to rule by decree, that he compromise on economic policy, and that he abandon his post as Prime Minister. But the opposition turned out to be disunited and irresolute. The president was able in the end to gain their reluctant support at the price of small concessions. Their refusal to discuss a new constitution, to accept the reality of the end of the union (it was not even possible to find a two-thirds majority to remove references to the USSR from the existing constitution) and to accept the need for macroeconomic discipline made them appear simply irresponsible.[11]

This made it easier for Yeltsin to call subsequently for the dissolution of the Congress. His supporters are now gathering the one million signatures needed to trigger a referendum on the issue. It is calculated that the process will be completed by December 1992, when the current special powers of the president are due to expire.[12] A new parliament, of course, would enjoy the kind of electoral legitimacy that the current Congress does not, and it would doubtless reflect the enormous popular resentment caused by the now impending unemployment and other hardships. If the dissolution plan appears to be working, a useful six months with a lame-duck legislature will have been bought, but the underlying problem will remain – how to construct a new, democratic constitution in the absence of consensus, in the midst of national conflicts inside the country and across its borders, and in conditions of steadily dwindling popular support for the government.

Political movements and forces

It has been argued in the democratic press that the April Congress, for all its farcical aspects, served as a valuable demonstration of the virtues of parliamentarism and the separation of powers: it provided a legitimate forum in which discontent could be expressed, constructive criticism formulated, compromises forged and policy adapted. Certainly it was the occasion for one very public deal whereby in exchange for voting support from the centrist, business-backed 'Bloc of Creative Forces' Yeltsin undertook to appoint more industrial managers and business people to his government, and to loosen credit policy somewhat. But there was in fact little scope for deal-making, or indeed any kind of decision-making, since apart from the centrist 'industrialists' (a particularly well-organized lobby) there were few coherent groups with which to bargain.

Of the three blocs into which the thirteen 'factions' registered in the Congress divided themselves, Creative Forces was the smallest, with 165 members (72 from the Industrial Union, 41 from the Workers Union of Russia, 52 from the Change (*Smena*) faction). The largest was the oppositionist Russian Unity bloc, with 311 deputies (54 from Communists of Russia, 54 from the 'Russia' faction, 54 from 'Fatherland', and 121 from the Agrarian Union (collective and state farm directors)). The Bloc of Democratic Factions contained 248 deputies (46 Radical Democrats (small-business), 67 from the (social-democratic) Left Centre, 72 from (Yeltsinite) Democratic Russia, and 66 from Rutskoi's Free Russia). The rest of the over 1,000-strong body of deputies belonged either to one of the two non-aligned factions ('Non-Party Deputies' – 44, Sovereignty and Equality – 53) or to no group. On a 'unanimity scale' where 100% represents all members of a faction voting the same way on all occasions at the Congress, and 0% represents a 50:50 average split, no faction scored more than 70%, and only 4 over 60%.[13]

These groupings were somewhat artificial: their composition partly reflected the parliamentary rules about minimum sizes for registered factions. They did not correspond in any consistent way to the political parties outside parliament, which are themselves relatively small and uninfluential. Russian political scientists express concern that the parties and factions, unanchored in popular constituencies and mass movements, are at the mercy of well-organized lobbies with bases in the bureaucracy and the regions. They fear that political life is likely to be overshadowed by powerful personalities, and that parliament will find it difficult to resist pressure exerted by direct action on the streets or in the factories.[14]

Apart from the naturally unformed state of democratic politics in Russia, the crystallization of 'real' parties is hampered by the rapidity with which the political agenda has been changing. In 1991 the dominant issue was what was to happen to the old Party-managed 'command-administrative system'. It was in relation to this issue that political groups defined themselves as more or less 'socialist' or 'democratic'. In 1992 'democrats' find themselves splitting along new lines: (1) they do not necessarily agree among themselves on the national question or on how federal the Russian state should be; (2) they hold different opinions about how rapid the pace of transition to a market economy should be, and what sacrifices can be demanded from the population; (3) finally, and in ways affected by their stances on the first two sets of questions, they disagree over how power should be distributed between executive and legislature.

The first substantial fissure in the Democratic Russia movement (the coalition of groups which helped to propel Yeltsin to the presidency) occurred last November, when Nikolai Travkin's Democratic Party of Russia (DPR), the Russian Christian Democratic Movement and the Constitutional Democratic Party walked out over what they saw as the movement's anti-Union stance and formed the Popular Concord bloc. Rutskoi's People's Party of Free Russia was reported in May to be in negotiation with the DPR to form an alliance of *gosudarstvenniki* (supporters of a strong Russian state). This alliance of the two largest political parties in the country has now been joined by the industrialists' Renewal movement in a Civil Union bloc, which looks set to displace Democratic Russia.

The rise of this alliance corresponds to the political shift inside the government represented by the appointment of the former director of the Krasnodar engineering works, Vladimir Shumeiko, as first deputy prime minister, and of two other industrialists to leading posts. It also parallels the adjustment in policy during May and June towards a slackening of the monetary squeeze and a more positive industrial policy. One Moscow newspaper predicts the rise of 'strong men personifying the realism of state capitalism, as opposed to the romanticism of liberal capitalism'. At the founding meeting of Renewal, Shumeiko himself declared, 'There is a need for a class of owners, and it should be stated that all who are now concerned with production are entitled to a high rank in this class.'[15] Yeltsin and Gaidar, who has in a balancing move been promoted to acting prime minister, appear to be taking the change of course relatively philosophically, and it has slowed up, rather than torpedoed, negotiations with the IMF. Arkady Volsky, head of the Union of Industrialists and Entrepreneurs, states that reform is irreversible and that Gaidar and his team should remain in charge of strategy, assisted now by more competent 'tacticians'. Yet there are fears among liberals that, just as on the national issue, compromises with men whom they perceive as representatives of the old order threaten a replay of 1991.

The extreme right (Pamyat, and Zhirinovsky's 'Liberal Democratic Party'), by contrast, has not so far shown the capacity to gather substantial support, despite all the fears of a 'Red–Brown Alliance'. Neither have the elements of the parliamentary 'right', who seem to be too much associated in the public mind, fairly or unfairly, with the old regime (some are hostile to private enterprise, some are in favour of it; they unite on non-economic issues). This is even more of a handicap to those socialist movements, such as Roy Medvedev's Socialist Party of Labour, which are trying to build support among the industrial workers.

A peculiar feature of the current situation is that the industrial managers, who have so far held back from shedding labour, are able to act as spokesmen for the interests of their workforces. This is a powerful argument for Yeltsin, who shows great sensitivity to the public mood.

Public opinion
The amorphous nature of politics in Russia means that public opinion is particularly volatile and unpredictable. However there are certain persistent features. The first is mistrust of communism. As early as 1990 a provincial poll showed that only 20% of respondents wished to preserve socialism.[16] Now only a small minority (15% in one survey) can imagine that the old regime has any chance of being restored in the country.[17] Private enterprise is no longer rejected as 'speculation', and 13% of Muscovites questioned recently declared that they wanted to start their own business.[18] Although they say that they want 'firm rule', Russians nevertheless claim to prefer democracy (albeit dimly understood, according to the findings of one survey) to dictatorship.[19]

At the same time the population are disillusioned with the results of perestroika, and not enthusiastic either about the recent economic policy measures which mean that 72%, by their own account, can no longer afford to feed their family. Most say they would never have backed the changes begun in 1985 if they could have foreseen the outcome.[20] Yet the predominant mood seems to be one of despairing acceptance. For all the apprehension about popular reactions to 400% or 500% price rises in January and February

1992, there has been remarkably little public protest so far. One poll in February even reported that 40% of Muscovites supported the government's economic policy.[21] According to another, while only 12% of Russians were prepared to 'give full support and assistance' to the government's efforts, and 54% were 'critical of its shortcomings', only 18% were inclined to demand its resignation.[22]

One paradoxical effect of the most recent market reforms is to strike at those groups which have been Yeltsin's most consistent supporters, namely state-employed and industrial professionals, groups which have always enjoyed relatively good salaries, high status and job security. Hyperinflation, savage cuts in public spending and the prospect of radical industrial restructuring put all these at risk. Key industrial workers, by contrast, have had their wages protected, and the conservatively-inclined rural areas, where money has tended to play less of a role in the economy, seem to have suffered least of all from the price increases. But perhaps material factors are less important than the fact that there is for the present no perceived alternative to something like current policies. If a political movement were to appear which was able to put forward such an alternative with conviction, the situation could be transformed very quickly.

Economics

The Soviet legacy is a uniquely difficult one for a government determined to establish a working market economy. For decades the message was repeated that the state could control economic processes and ensure reasonable equality of reward, job security, and a steadily rising standard of living. Current efforts to detach economic from political power not only threaten the interests of large sections of employees and bureaucrats. They also face the obstacles posed by sheer incomprehension and unfamiliarity with the conventions of what the rest of the world regards as 'normal' economic behaviour (an unfamiliarity which indeed predates the revolution of 1917). For the time being capitalism enjoys high public prestige, but that is on the basis of a fairly hazy understanding of its operation, and there could be a rebound of discontent as things progress.

More immediately there is the problem of how to forward real marketization in an environment where political leaders instinctively (and to meet popular expectations) seek to extend their economic powers, and economic elites act on the assumption of continued political patronage and subsidy, albeit in different forms from before. This is especially evident at a local/regional level, where the basic requirements for independent business activity – security of person and property – are often not present. Far more important than the strict legality of a particular deal involving, say, privatization or foreign currency dealings (even if anyone could be certain of the law or confident in the probity of the courts) is the assurance of protection against prosecution, or indeed 'mafia'-supplied protection from extortion.

It is argued by some that elemental, *nomenklatura* privatization is better than no privatization. Yet, quite apart from the bad effects on public opinion, the market culture that these old/new elites bring with them is a far cry from the ideal types of Western capitalism. They have grown up in a society where profits are made not by improving products and making them more cheaply but by restricting supply and terrorizing competitors out of the market place. Previously this was done openly and justified in the language of socialism. Now more covert and less subtle methods are used. The black economy which has existed for decades has come out into the open, but it stubbornly refuses to turn 'white'. Here the general weakness of the government's ability to enforce its will risks provoking a vicious circle of declining public respect and authority, at a time when a series of unpopular economic policies have to be pushed through. More generally what is happening is a reminder that economic transformation in Russia and the CIS will be a task of decades, not years.

The Russian recovery programme
Because of the urgency of the economic decline in 1991, and particularly the loss of faith in the rouble, the government's young economic policy team, led by Yegor Gaidar, resolved to launch out on immediate (from 1 January 1992) macroeconomic stabilization and price liberalization. In contrast to the 1991 budget deficit for Russia of approximately 20% of GDP, the first quarter of 1992 was intended to be deficit-free. But tax collection was inefficient, especially at first. Certain autonomous republics and regions refused to pass on tax takings at the required level. Interest rates were raised, but remained low relative to the rate of inflation, and the Central Bank of Russia continued, especially at first, to supply loans to enterprises and commercial banks at a generous level. The government's programme for the remainder of 1992, adopted on 27 February, talked of reducing the budget deficit from around 10% in the first quarter to zero in the last quarter of the year; it later announced a zero budget deficit for the first quarter, but its calculations are disputed.

Retail prices were freed in two stages, leaving only certain basic services and commodities, including fuel, controlled. But the still largely state-owned retail enterprises continued to react sluggishly to market signals, and local authorities imposed price controls and restrictions on the flow of goods. More importantly, the (almost entirely state-owned) producers raised prices to a level which produced a severe downturn in retail trade, and kept them high, anticipating further inflation. Confident that the government would not enforce bankruptcies and mass sackings when it came to the crunch, they showed little inclination to rationalize and find other ways of lowering prices. Official retail price inflation figures were 24% in February and 21% in March.[23]

The outcome of these processes and of the other problems in the economy has been a sharp decline in output. This can be seen in the tabulation below, which shows first quarter 1992 economic results in Russia as a percentage of first quarter 1991, using comparable prices.[24]

Industrial output	87
Capital investment (all sources)	56
Monthly cash wages	600
Retail prices (March/March)	1300
Wholesale prices (March/March)	1300
Retail sales	49
Oil and gas condensate production	87
Exports	80

The solid achievements of the period should not be neglected, however. A huge monetary overhang has been soaked up, and the slide of the rouble against the dollar has been brought under control. Russia and a number of the other CIS states have been accepted into the IMF, with whose principles the reform plan was indeed designed to accord, and a $24 billion assistance package has been promised by the G7. The Russian government has been able to move ahead with its programme for the next stages of reform which, although it is scarcely likely to stick to the original timetable, nevertheless now carries a measure of credibility.

Prospects
The main elements of the second phase are further liberalization of prices (principally those on energy, which will be raised step by step to world levels over the next two years), further tightening of money and credit, a unification of foreign exchange rates for current account transactions (at present exporters

have to sell dollars for roubles at half the market rate), accompanied by an export tax and a general freeing-up of foreign trade, more detailed social security provisions and incomes policy measures. There will be an immediate start on mass privatization of small enterprises, mainly by auction, immediate commercialization of large enterprises, followed by their privatization on a huge scale, mainly from 1993. Employees will receive 25% of the shares free, without voting rights, and privatization vouchers will be distributed to the population in the autumn. Foreign investors will be able to participate, at a special exchange rate.[25]

All these measures face enormous political and technical obstacles. Most immediately, it is proving difficult for Yeltsin to persuade parliament to pass the most fundamental laws necessary to create a framework for marketization and attracting foreign investment. The package of measures prepared in the run-up to the G7 meeting in July 1992 represented in large part decisions promulgated by presidential decree because the legislature refused to back them – on the private sale of land, on the transformation of state firms into joint stock companies, and on bankruptcy.

An extra R200bn of credit was promised at the sixth Congress in April, simply in anticipation of industrial crisis, and the government has tended to yield to pressure from groups of workers for pay rises in a reactive way. But the problems are only beginning. One Russian economist estimated at the end of March that 80% of large enterprises were already insolvent. Inter-enterprise debt had reached R1.43 trillion by 1 May.[26] It may be difficult to stop any process of allowing a few exemplary bankruptcies from snowballing into catastrophe. Estimates of the employment implications of determined restructuring vary enormously. The government predicts 2.5 to 3.5 million out of work by the end of 1992, its critics 7 to 15 million. How quickly the private sector can soak up the extra workers and how the population will react to the quite novel phenomenon of mass unemployment remains to be seen.[27] It is not surprising that Yeltsin keeps insisting in public that he does not take orders from the IMF.

As the experience of other countries shows, privatization is a slow and complicated process, even with the help of a large network of established financial institutions, which Russia does not have. Employment in the private sector has been growing (the state sector lost 8% of its workers in 1991), but mainly in new businesses: only just over 200 enterprises were privatized in the first two months of 1992.[28] A great deal of discretion is left to local authorities in small business privatization and to state and collective farm managements in allotting land for private farms. Yet these are the strongholds of the remnants of the communist *nomenklatura* least sympathetic to reform; delay also helps to keep up the going rate of bribes.

International aspects introduce further unpredictability. It is, for example, by no means clear how long it will take to put the various elements of G7-sponsored assistance in place, what impact it will have on the rouble and on the level of consumption, and how trade and inward investment patterns will develop over the coming years.

More immediately, the prospects for economic policy cooperation and free trade with the other ex-Soviet states are difficult to judge. While states continue to issue credit in roubles with little regard for the wishes of the Central Bank of Russia (CBR), plans for stabilization of the money supply and of the value of the currency remain quite theoretical. By the middle of 1992 agreement seemed to be emerging that Russia's partners must either follow Estonia and Ukraine in setting up their own currencies, or accept CBR discipline, but it would be rash to predict that matters will be settled promptly or smoothly.

The non-Russian states are all profoundly dependent on Russia for supplies of underpriced fuel and for many other industrial inputs. Only Azerbaijan, Turkmenistan and Kazakhstan have significantly developed oil and gas deposits, and they too form part of a highly specialized division of productive labour constructed by successive generations of Soviet planners, far deeper than the Comecon one whose break-up has provoked economic near-disaster in parts of Eastern Europe. Few ex-Soviet producers are fit to compete on world markets, and without cheap Russian oil they would be at an even greater disadvantage. Apart from the Baltic states, which had already started on reforms, the others have been forced to trail along behind Russian innovations. As a rule strong ex-communist bureaucracies have been able to block efforts at marketization, often by diverting debate along nationalist lines. Whereas the Asian republics have frankly acknowledged their dependence and argued for cooperation, while making few internal changes (with the partial exception of Kazakhstan and Kyrgyzia), in the European republics inflamed national feeling has blocked any far-reaching coordination of policy and collaboration in the CIS. The tendency has been to 'protect' local markets by preventing exports, and to cherish unrealistic hopes concerning rapid integration into the world market.[29]

Military and international (CIS) aspects

If adjustment to the end of the cold war is uncomfortable for arms suppliers and the military in the NATO countries, it is traumatic for their counterparts in the former Soviet Union, where the defence effort took a much larger share of national resources. One indicator of the sharpness with which policy has changed is the slump in planned arms production in 1992 to around one third of its 1988 level (and half of the 1991 level).[30] The producers concerned are struggling to increase their output of civil goods to compensate. No such openings are available (at least legally) to the military themselves. By early 1992 it was obvious that their morale was at a very low point. Despite the humiliatingly rapid withdrawals from Eastern Europe which left hundreds of thousands of officers not only functionless but also homeless, and despite the abrupt lowering of status brought about by Gorbachev's cultural and political changes, the army and air force withheld wholehearted cooperation in the August coup attempt. This temporarily raised their prestige in society, but no solid rewards were to follow for the majority, only further deprivations and humiliations.

Probably largely in deference to the sentiments of the generals, the Minsk summit of the CIS in December 1991 agreed that the (broadly-conceived) strategic forces of the former Soviet Union would be kept under single command. It was assumed that the setting up of the now permitted national forces would be a gradual process. Already in January, however, Ukraine, Belarus and Azerbaijan began to solicit oaths of allegiance from troops serving on their territory. In Kiev, President Kravchuk continued to maintain his republic's right to control the Black Sea fleet. This situation provoked scenes of near disorder at an 'officers' assembly' held in Moscow on 17 January, with speakers claiming that the army was being destroyed and that there was no fatherland left to defend. On 16 March, after weeks of rumour and hesitation, Yeltsin resolved the uncertainty by announcing that Russia would have its own Ministry of Defence. The Russian armed forces are to be reduced to 1.5 million and conscription will gradually be phased out. Forces in Germany, Poland, Mongolia and Cuba had already been transferred under Yeltsin's control. Subsequently units in the Transcaucasus, Moldova, the Baltic states, and the Caspian and Black Sea fleets were declared to be under Russian command.

This was small consolation to those stationed in the first two of these areas (specifically in Nagorny Karabakh and Transdnestria), who found themselves in the crossfire of local conflicts, their comrades shot at and kidnapped and their weapons stolen, yet under orders not to retaliate. The Russian government's policy has been to pull forces out from areas of fighting, but the withdrawals already under way mean there are few resources to spare for this purpose. In any case, the morale of men left inactive, poorly paid and badly housed, as many now find themselves in the Kaliningrad region, for instance, is likely to be almost as bad. One symptom of this is rampant corruption at all levels, based on diverting funds and on selling off equipment, for which there is a ready market in areas like the Transcaucausus and Moldova. Another is insubordination, and in particular unauthorized participation in local wars by deserters and by the forces themselves. In Nagorny Karabakh, for instance, both the Armenian and the Azerbaijani sides complained bitterly about CIS/ Russian forces fighting for the opposition, or selling them weapons. In Moldova, Rutskoi's suggestion that the 14th Army should officially be given the task of protecting Transdnestria seems to have been partly stimulated by the fact that it was already beginning to do so unofficially. Yeltsin announced in June 1992 that this army too was to be withdrawn, but statements from the military themselves have tended to be much more hardline. The Russian troops in Georgia are also in danger of being drawn into internal political conflicts surrounding the region of South Ossetia.[31]

Concern in the outside world initially centred on the future of Soviet nuclear forces. Although the states which set up the CIS undertook to observe arms control agreements signed by their predecessor, these covered only a part of the strategic nuclear weapons and none of the non-strategic ones, which accounted for the bulk of the USSR's 27,000 nuclear warheads. Kazakhstan refused to join Ukraine and Belarus in undertaking to become nuclear-free, and Ukraine subsequently announced it was suspending transfer of tactical nuclear weapons to Russia. However, international pressure had its effect, and on 28 May 1992 NATO was able to announce that it was satisfied all these weapons were now on Russian soil. The strategic missiles are effectively controlled from Moscow. Measures have also been taken to provide additional employment opportunities for unemployed Russian military technology experts. A more serious after-effect of the military rundown is likely to be an expansion of arms exports. Yeltsin's adviser on conversion of the military-industrial sector to civil production has repeatedly stated that only large-scale arms sales can provide the hard currency needed for retooling.[32] This is indeed a major consideration in squabbling over the division of military equipment between the ex-Soviet states.

At the CIS summit on 15 May Russia, Uzbekistan, Kazakhstan,

Turkmenistan, Tajikistan and Armenia signed a collective security agreement. There were hints that Belarus and Kyrgyzia might join later.[33] Although now that the dictator Gamsakhurdia has gone and Shevardnadze has taken over as leader, Georgia is eligible for CIS membership, it has chosen not to apply. The domestic situation in Ukraine makes it impossible for Kravchuk to sign security agreements with Russia, even if he wished: the opposition Rukh movement, whose support he now counts on, demands that the country leave the CIS itself. In any case it would probably be regarded as a breach of Ukraine's principle of 'neutrality'. Azerbaijan is at war with Armenia, and sees the treaty as an anti-Azeri alliance in the Transcaucasus. As for Moldova, its president declared the country 'at war with Russia' on 22 June, as battles raged around the town of Bendery on the Dniestr.

So far Russian nationalism has failed to fulfil the fears of pessimistic observers of the collapse of Soviet power. But the Yeltsin government is likely to face an excruciatingly difficult task in responding to national resentments without aggravating them, as Yeltsin's opponents strive to exploit growing sensitivity to the fate of the 25 million-strong diaspora. In Estonia millions of Russians who entered the country after 1938 look likely to be deprived of full citizenship until they have learned the local language and waited until the end of a transition period, during which they will be excluded from participation in referendums on the constitution and from the privatization process. Latvia is taking similar measures to reassert its national identity. There are 200,000 Russian troops in the Baltic states.[34] In Transdnestria Russian regular troops are already becoming involved in the fighting, alongside irregular Cossack volunteer detachments from the Don area of South Russia.

Cossack groups are helping to stir up Russian separatist feeling in North Kazakhstan. They are also present in Russian-populated Crimea. Here the local parliament finally backed down in May 1992 from its declaration of independence, yielding to pressure from Kiev and from the local Ukrainian minority, but the Russian parliament subsequently complicated matters by voting on 21 May to declare illegal the 1954 transfer of Crimea to Ukrainian jurisdiction. The Crimean question is unhelpfully entangled with the dispute between Moscow and Kiev over the division of the Black Sea fleet, which is based in Sebastopol. Since February 1992 there has been poll evidence of growing polarization of Russian and Ukrainian opinion about the conflicts between the two countries.[35]

Smaller Russian communities inhabit other areas of potential ethnic strife, in which they would not necessarily be initial participants, but which would eventually threaten them. The Caucasus and Central Asia contain a seemingly endless number of potential conflict zones of this kind. For the time being Russians are valued for their key functions in the economy of the less developed CIS states, but it is quite possible that nationalist passions could come to outweigh such prosaic considerations.

Conclusions
Whether the Russian people will rise to the nationalist bait is one of the three big unknowns on which the future of the ex-Soviet Union hangs. The second is how long their patience will endure in the face of material hardship and economic upheaval. The third is what quality of leadership and what alternative political programmes the political class in Moscow will offer them.

Such is the gelatinous state of Russian civil society that it is very difficult to gauge political moods and tendencies. Constitutional arrangements and the legal framework of economic activity are in a state of flux. We can be certain of some elements in the equation: the advanced industrial countries will continue to exert pressures for market reforms and control over arms movements, and they will tend to favour Western-oriented democratically-minded groups; some kind of marketization and integration in the world economy will continue to be seen by the Russian informed public as the only long-term solution to the country's problems; there will be a long period of painful adjustment for the productive structures, and poverty and psychological stress for most of the population; and the other post-Soviet states will remain in varying degrees economically dependent on Russia. But these factors could combine to produce a whole range of scenarios: rapid marketization under authoritarian rule, temporary reversion to a system containing important command-economy features, a fairly prolonged period of isolationist 'red–brown' dictatorship, a more or less democratic 'muddling through' to the market, and so on.

There are points of international comparison. Hungary, Poland and, most ominously, Yugoslavia demonstrate the variety of paths that post-communist evolution can take. Already we can see emerging in the former Soviet Union political patterns characteristic of dependent, developing countries, where the government is forced to balance between external forces pushing for liberalization, monetary discipline and restructuring, and internal forces pushing for protection and more cautious change. But the peculiar history of Russia and its ex-Soviet partners means that a much wider (and more dangerous) range of outcomes is possible than in many other countries. A great deal will depend on good judgment and leadership, backed up where necessary and possible by the right kind of support from the outside world, if the present period of instability is to be successfully traversed and if the states which have emerged from the Soviet Union are to forge a more constructive relationship with their societies than the one which took shape over the previous 70 years.

Notes
1 Andranik Migranyan, in *Literaturnaya gazeta*, 16 August 1989.
2 Barrington Moore draws parallels between the Russian experience and that of Germany and Japan; see *Social Origins of Dictatorship and Democracy* (London: Penguin, 1967), pp. 416–18, 438, 445. See too G. Hosking, *A History of the Soviet Union* (London: Fontana, 1985), pp. 19–20.
3 For a recent perspective on this see C. Merridale, 'Perestroika and political pluralism: past and prospects', in C. Merridale, C. Ward, eds., *Perestroika: The Historical Perspective* (London: Edward Arnold, 1991), pp. 14–33. M. Lewin eloquently evokes 'a civil society operating in the fortress of statism' in the Brezhnev period, in *The Gorbachev Phenomenon* (London: Hutchinson Radius, 1988), p. 80.
4 O.Vite, 'Stagnation era as the precursor to the market', *Moscow News*, 1992, no. 25, p. 11.
5 *Political Order in Changing Societies* (New York: Yale UP, 1968); 'Political Development and Decay', *World Politics*, April 1965.
6 See the interview with Shaimiev in *Moscow News*, 1992, no. 18, p. 14.
7 According to Alexei Pankin, deputy editor of *International Affairs* (Moscow), the 'Union of Independent States', which Gorbachev's union treaty sought to create on the territory of the Soviet Union, now exists *de facto* inside the Russian Federation. See also A. Migranyan, 'State and Society: a Delicate Balance', *Delovye lyudi*, 1992, no. 23, pp. 12–14.
8 *Moscow News*, 1992, no. 18, p. 14; *The Times*, 1 January 1992.
9 *Nezavisimaya gazeta*, 19 December 1991; *The Times*, 1 January 1992; *The Financial Times*, 10 February 1992.
10 S. Kordonsky, 'Bedevilled with Problems', *New Times*, 1992, no. 1, p. 18; M. Shakina, 'The Rutskoi Riddle', *New Times*, 1992, no. 12, pp. 9–12; and A. Rahr, 'Winners and Losers of the Russian Congress', *RFE/RL Research Report*, 1 May 1992, pp. 6–7. Shakina paints a more 'democratic' picture of Rutskoi. The Vice-President was also accompanied on his visit to Crimea by General Boris Gromov, Pugo's deputy as Minister of the Interior in the Pavlov government which launched the coup attempt.
11 A public opinion poll taken during the Congress gave 60–70% support for

the government; see Rahr, op. cit. p. 92. 20,000 Muscovites demonstrated in support of Yeltsin in Manezh Square on 19 April; see *Moscow Times*, 21 April 1992.
12 *Moscow News*, 1992, no. 19, p. 2.
13 See the report by Igor Yakovenko, *Nezavisimaya gazeta*, 24 April 1992; also J. Steele in *The Guardian*, 21 April 1992.
14 H. Diligensky, 'Yeltsin's Game in Mittelspiel', *New Times*, 1992, no. 5, pp. 4–6; L. Shevtsova, 'Struggles under a Roof without Walls', *New Times*, 1992, no. 16, pp. 6–8; A. Migranyan, op. cit. pp. 12–14; and O. Bychkova in *Moscow News*, 1992, no. 17, p. 7.
15 *Moscow News*, 1992, no. 24, pp. 6–7.
16 L. Gordon in *Moscow News*, 1991, no. 41.
17 VTsIOM Report (All-Union Central Institute of Public Opinion) in *Moscow News*, 1992, no. 10, p. 16.
18 Ivan Bunin in *New Times*, 1992, no. 8, p. 14.
19 Diligensky in *New Times*, 1992, no. 5, p. 6. See Boris Grushin's survey of conceptions of 'democracy', in *Moscow News*, 1992, no. 4, p. 7.
20 VTsIOM in *Moscow News*, 1991, no. 38; 'Russians dissatisfied but coping', CRCE Press Release, 15 May 1992 (survey by CSPP, University of Strathclyde). The standard of living survey is in *Moscow News*, 1992, no. 20.
21 *Delovye lyudi*, 1992, no. 23, p. 49.
22 VTsIOM in *Moscow News*, 1992, no. 10, p. 16.
23 B. Granville, *Price and Currency Reform in Russia and the CIS* (RIIA Post-Soviet Business Forum Special Paper, 1992); *Ekonomika i zhizn'*, 1992, no. 13; *Delovye lyudi*, 1992, no. 23, pp. 3, 48–9; G. Yavlinsky, 'Spring '92 Reforms in Russia', *Moscow News*, 1992, no. 21. pp. 6–7; and *The Financial Times*, 27 March 1992 and 14 May 1992.
24 *PlanEcon Business Report*, vol. 2, no. 11 (27 May 1992).
25 M. Wolf in *The Financial Times*, 13 May, 1992, supplement, p. IV; *The Economist*, 25 April, 1992, pp. 19–21.
26 *The Financial Times*, 27 March 1992 and 14 May 1992.
27 C. Bohlen in *International Herald Tribune*, 29 May 1992; 'The Russian Economy in 1992', *Delovye lyudi*, 1992, no. 23, p. 48.
28 Yavlinsky in *Moscow News*, 1992, no. 21, p. 7; *International Herald Tribune*, 29 May 1992.
29 Granville, op. cit. ; D. Dyker, *After the Soviet Union: the International Trading Environment* (RIIA, Post-Soviet Business Forum Special Paper, 1992); *Moscow News*, 1992, no. 21, p. 9.
30 *Delovye lyudi*, 1992, no. 23, p. 49. Figures are for all the (ex-)Soviet republics taken together.
31 For accounts of corruption, see *Moscow News*, 1992, no. 17, p. 8; *The*

Financial Times, 2 and 10 March 1992; and S. Kordonsky in *New Times*, 1992, no. 1, pp. 16–18.
32 Mikhail Malei, reported in *The Financial Times*, 2 March 1992. On Ukrainian nuclear ambitions, see *Moscow News*, 1992, no. 18.
33 *Guardian*, 18 May 1992.
34 *Moscow News*, 1992, no. 17, p. 16.
35 Yury Levada in *Moscow News*, 1992, no. 10, p. 16. In February 1992 46% of Russians and 50% of Ukrainians considered the other side to be at fault.

CHAPTER 2

THE SOCIAL AND IDEOLOGICAL CONSEQUENCES OF THE COLLAPSE OF COMMUNISM AND THE SOVIET UNION

PETER FERDINAND

It used to be said that the future of communist regimes was clearly known; it was only their past which was constantly changing. Whether or not they would actually achieve communism, the ethos of five-year plans was that achievable targets were set into the medium-term, and even long-term, future. The collapse of first the Soviet Union and then communism since the attempted coup of August 1991 has destroyed that reassuring predictability. Not only will the past of Russia continue to be rewritten, as new information is released from previously secret archives, but the future will also be unpredictable, as traditional institutions, personalities and policies come to be discarded.

Since the failed coup, almost all existing political institutions in Russia and most of the other former republics of the USSR have disintegrated. It is no exaggeration to describe this as a revolution, even though there has not as yet been the same degree of physical violence that normally accompanies revolutions. Surviving institutions have been left in an extremely precarious situation.

This has two consequences. Firstly, existing bases of authority for political actors have been undermined. The legitimacy of individual politicians has been greatly weakened. It is now much more difficult for any individual political leader to retain support.[1] As difficult decisions and choices continue to have to be made by political leaders, the risk of making one which definitively destroys the support that an individual had previously enjoyed is much increased. In addition, there will be a sustained pressure to 'purge' individuals associated with the old communist regime, particularly those from the *nomenklatura* who have taken advantage of their old positions to build new, and possibly corrupt, wealth.[2] Even if the files of the KGB remain closed to citizens, unlike the files of the former State Security Police in East Germany which are now being opened, with all the opportunities for recrimination and suspicion which this provides,[3] there is still likely to be some selective manipulation of KGB files to discredit political opponents.[4] And the prospect of a protracted trial to determine whether the CPSU operated illegally will bring into the open increasing amounts of information which will discredit those who rose to power through its ranks, perhaps even including Yeltsin. All of this means that the next few years are likely to see a succession of newcomers become leaders in Russia and elsewhere, as older, more familiar figures lose public confidence. The new Russia will greedily devour politicians.

At one level this might seem desirable since it means that Russia and elsewhere will have become more 'democratic', if 'democracy' means that politicians are more responsive to the popular will, however expressed. The scope for a political leader, or at least a civilian one, to ignore public opinion and impose his or her own decisions upon the people over a protracted period of time will be much diminished.

On the other hand, it also means that political leaders will be likely to be less sophisticated, less 'street-wise', more prone to mistakes, and more likely to antagonize social groups. In this sense they will themselves contribute to the disorder which will surround decision-making over public policy. On the international level, diplomacy will be more difficult to practise. As new politicians and new diplomats come to grips with all the problems of Russian foreign policy and Russia's international role as, for example, one of the five permanent members (P5) of the UN Security Council, they will stumble and err. They will also disagree publicly amongst themselves. Russian Vice-President Rutskoi and Foreign Minister Kozyrev, for example, have been advocating very different policies towards some of Russia's neighbours, and they have vied in trying to implement them.[5] This will make the coordination of policy among P5 members more difficult than before. Traditional alliances with Russia may be jeopardized as much out of inadvertence as intent. And although Russia, as the inheritor of the superpower role of the USSR, might naturally have been expected to play a significant role in the search for solutions to world problems and crises, it will find it difficult to coordinate its policy with that of its partners. In this sense Russia is unlikely to be a reliable international partner for years to come. Above all, international statesmanship from Russia may at best be intermittent.

The second consequence of the collapse of traditional political authority in Russia is the undermining of confidence in political institutions as well. Even with the increase in democracy, elected institutions will continue to have to prove themselves vis-à-vis the population. A residual mistrust will persist for a considerable time. And this is in addition to the unpopularity provoked by the introduction of radical market-reform measures.

All of this means that politics in Russia will continue to be swayed by unpredictable popular passions. They will be unpredictable in the sense that the ebb and flow of the popular mood in Russia will be difficult for outsiders to chart, let alone predict. But they will also be unpredictable in that the belief systems of Russians and other nationalities are changing rapidly in response to the collapse of communism. To take one example, there is the rapid upsurge in popular interest in religion, oriental as well as Christian, and in the occult, which has resulted from the collapse of atheistic communism. What popular opinion will accept in terms of new policies, therefore, may be extremely difficult to predict, and may in any case fluctuate from one period to another.

Collectivism versus individualism

Soon after the failure of the coup in Moscow, the newly-reinstalled Boris Yeltsin declared that henceforth individual interests would be the guiding principle in society. This seemed to mark a historic break with the class politics and collectivism of the Soviet past, and indeed with the socialist traditions which predated the revolutions of 1917.

Since then the old communist institutions of collective social policy have been rapidly undermined or abolished, certainly in the cities. The attempt to organize a large-scale demonstration by communists on May Day largely failed. Support for old-style communist views has been put at five per cent at the maximum,[6] and there are at least five parties vying for the communist mantle. For the moment, despite the rising prices and increasing poverty, there seems to be no sign of a collective response to defend collective rights and values. Instead the response seems to have been in many cases to resort to crime and corruption, with increasing signs of violence breaking out. Egocentric individualism seems to be triumphing. Society, in other words, has continued to implode.

The one exception has been in the countryside. One of the curious features of Russian history since the 1970s has been a revival of interest in the traditional Russian village, and the values associated with it. Starting with the 'village writers' (*derevenshchiki*), it then developed into a Russian patriotic movement, which still saw the village, and the people who continued to live in it, as the moral basis of Russian society. Despite the decades of suppression of traditional peasant values in the collectivization system, and the widespread complaints about the erosion of morality in general in society, there continued to be people who regarded the village as providing the basis for a moral revival. Whether or not they were religious believers, these villagers were supposed to embody self-sacrifice and cooperation in their relations with neighbours. Life in the villages was supposed to be more 'healthy', certainly on a moral level. These attitudes have continued to hinder a full de-collectivization of agriculture (although it must be admitted that pressure from old members of the rural *nomenklatura* has also contributed to this).

There is a certain similarity here with the views of Slavophiles of the nineteenth century, which in turn might have a bearing upon Russian foreign policy today. Nostalgia for pan-Slavism remains quite potent, as seen, for example, in the criticism in the Russian parliament of the government's acceptance of the UN policy of sanctions against Serbia.[7] Yet there is one major difference, in that there have recently been major disputes between Russia and other Slav states, such as Ukraine, Poland and Czechoslovakia, as well as a marked distaste among some of the latter for continued close cooperation with Russia. For the moment it is difficult to envisage a significant international Slavophile movement catching on in Russia.

Democratization versus fascism
One estimate in March 1992 suggested that 20–25 per cent of the Russian population had for the moment accepted Western liberal values and supported government reforms.[8] This is not a large proportion of the population, and the possible fragility of even that support is reinforced by the estimate that only 5–7 per cent were actually enjoying an improved standard of living. Another survey carried out in 18 cities of Russia, also in March, showed that 21 per cent had no confidence in the government, whilst 43 per cent did not trust it very much. Only 6 per cent had complete trust.[9]

The problem has been compounded by the proliferation of new parties. With the arrival of spring, new parties continued to appear like mushrooms. In the Russian Congress of People's Deputies there are thirteen factional groupings, and three blocs, which tend to vote together, but certainly not all of the time.[10] Outside parliament a dizzying array of new parties has been created, ranging from communist to fascist.

So as to create a distinguishable identity, each of these new organizations needs to criticize its opponents and the government, usually virulently. This in turn preserves the image of parties of opposition rather than government. This frequently grates on the public, who become frustrated by what they regard as the antics of the leaders of many of those parties. It frequently happens that the leader of a party makes a declaration which is then contradicted by a significant number of its members. There is great scope for personalized politics – all too often the 'voice of the party' is in practice the voice of a dozen office-holders living in Moscow.[11] Even within the government there are opposing voices, the most extreme example being Vice-President Rutskoi condemning his government's own market reforms. And in Georgia, ex-President Gamsakhurdia never came to terms with being in power, continuing to behave as a dissident, and stigmatizing imaginary 'enemies' and 'agents' from the Kremlin and the KGB.

One consequence of this is an exasperation with the practice of 'democracy', and a greater readiness on the part of commentators to suggest that the firm hand of the state needs to save the country for democracy later.[12] Indeed at the end of April the Gaidar government did threaten to resign in the face of criticism from the parliament, thereby provoking a confrontation which, at least for the time being, the government won. Yet popular support for the government was not in any way increased.

Meanwhile the economy continues to decline rapidly, and dissatisfaction grows. Increasingly in political life 'the idea of revenge takes hold of the minds of hundreds of thousands, if not millions, of people' and with that comes an increased threat of fascism.[13] A number of fascist-type organizations sprang up during the winter of 1991–2, and some of them, such as the Officers for the Regeneration of Russia, have explicit links with the military. Parallels are increasingly drawn in the press with Germany in the early 1930s. One Russian academic who has worked previously on Nazism remarked recently that the chances of avoiding fascism in Germany in the 1930s were greater than in Russia now, because in Germany democratic parties had been in control of political life for the preceding ten years, whereas they have only just come to power in Russia, and the 'totalitarian mode of thinking' still exercises a strong hold on the minds of many Russians.[14] For the moment writers suggest that the threat of fascism can only be averted if all groups opposed to it combine forces. Since society seems to be still disintegrating rather than uniting, this is not encouraging, although maybe a cause is needed for reintegration to start again, and perhaps anti-fascism just as much as fascism could serve as that cause.

Religion

A recent survey of religious beliefs in Russia suggested that a growing proportion of the population was coming to believe in some kind of supernatural force, if not necessarily Orthodox Christianity. One recent survey suggested that a majority of respondents believed not in God, but in various kinds of supernatural forces. Only 5–12 per cent of the population went regularly to Orthodox Church services and prayed every day. But 25 per cent believed in heaven and hell, and 44 per cent in the devil. The largest concentration of traditional religious believers is still to be found in the countryside. On the other hand, rural dwellers now represent only 20–30 per cent of the population. In large cities of the Russian Federation up to 20 per cent were attracted by Buddhism and Hare Krishna.[15]

For the moment neither religion nor the Orthodox Church seems to play a major role in Russian political life, although clearly Yeltsin and other political leaders have sought to win the backing of the church so as to increase their own legitimacy. But religion is important in other former republics of the USSR, as their peoples seek to rediscover the historical roots of their nationhood. Catholicism plays a major part in the life of the Baltic states, and increasingly in the Ukraine. The Georgian church is playing an important part in the national revival there. And Central Asia is witnessing a revival of Islam, as seen in the popular protests which forced President Nabiyev of Tajikistan to resign in May 1992.

In itself this rediscovery of religious roots to national identity might be entirely beneficial, were it not for the fact that the rediscovery of those roots will also bring out historical conflicts between religions and thereby exacerbate already troubled relations, as in the conflict between Armenia and Azerbaijan over Nagorny Karabakh.

Russian national identity
Clearly Russians and the other peoples of the former Soviet Union are rediscovering and re-establishing their national identity. One element in that is obviously history. With what national experiences should Russians today identify? The most obvious sources which were suppressed under communist power and which are now reasserting themselves are religion (the Russian Orthodox Church) and the monarchy. Whether or not there are significant numbers of people who want to see a restoration of the monarchy, as an institution it is now attracting a considerable amount of attention. Films are being made about the Tsar, the fate of the royal family in 1918, and so on. A revisionist school of history is beginning to emerge which presents the monarchy and its achievements in a more positive light. For two years the Soviet, later Russian, army has been identifying with the symbols of the Tsarist army.

All of this means that if President Yeltsin should cease for whatever reason to be head of state, and if there could be no agreement on a natural successor, then it is not inconceivable that the monarchy, or some descendant of the royal family, might come to play a leading role.

Then there is the Orthodox Church. However weakened this may have been by the Soviet past, it still survives as a potent symbol of national identity, and even Yeltsin has attended services carrying a candle.

All of this suggests that, as Russians build their future, it will be at least with one eye on the past. In one respect that is natural, since peoples with long-established national traditions naturally draw inspiration and new ideas for public choices from their past, especially a past which is regarded as 'respectable'. One suggestion has been that the Russian state should seek to draw its strength from the traditional principles of *derzhavnost'* (state-ness), *religioznost'* (religiousness) and *narodnost'* (people-ness), which still resonate in the minds of the people,[16] and which do not require democracy. Another variant of this would be the principles of orthodoxy, autocracy and nationalism which were associated with the era of Nicholas I.

This could be worrying. However it is now presented, the monarchy before 1917 operated in a repressive, often narrow-minded way. The principles of autocracy which proved such a constraint on the thinking of even a reforming Tsar such as Alexander II greatly hindered Russia's adaptation to new ideas from the outside, and held it back from competing with other European states.

The Church too, before 1917, robustly defended the autocracy, and never came to terms with attempts to establish a democratic political system. Worse, the Church, as well as the monarchy, in part condoned racist attacks on minorities, such as the anti-Semitism of the Black Hundreds.

Yet although Russia seems to be restoring links with its past, in other respects it is trying to break new ground by establishing links with the present and the future, as well as with ideas in the world which are more associated with other countries. Let us take, for example, decentralization.

Decentralization

Throughout its history, at least since the defeat of the Mongols, the Russian state has been associated with a high degree of centralization. Despite the enormous size of the Russian empire and, later, the Soviet Union, the state remained one of the most centralized on earth. Partly this was the result of the struggle to overthrow the Tatar yoke, and partly the impact of the memory of

Russian disunity leading to Mongol domination. Partly it was associated with the doctrine of autocracy, under which no institution or obstacle should come in the way of the 'little father' in Moscow or St Petersburg. Also, according to one argument, it was in part a reaction to the attempts at decentralization during the Provisional Government of 1917 – the experience being so traumatic that even decades later the Soviet government maintained a high degree of centralization so as to prevent a repeat of the chaos which ensued.[17]

The consequence has been that it was above all the state that served as the most important hoop which would bind all Russians together. The fear that Russian society is incapable, independently of the state, of cohering naturally together in a single community has obsessed Russian leaders.

Now, however, that principle of centralization is coming under attack from two quarters. Firstly there is the pressure from non-Russian ethnic minorities who live inside Russia. The most potent and vociferous group are the Tatars in the former Tatar autonomous republic, now redesignated Tatarstan. Many Tatars have begun stridently to demand parity of treatment with the (mostly) larger nationalities in the former union republics who have now achieved full sovereignty, and even independence. Since, for example, Tatars outnumbered Estonians in the old USSR, and Estonia is now independent, whilst Tatarstan is not, the people in the latter are tending towards demands for full independence themselves.

This is not a phenomenon which is confined to the Tatars. In the far east, for example, the Yakuts have voiced demands for full sovereignty over the economic wealth which their territory possesses. In general this pressure from minorities for fully equal treatment will require a new and imaginative response from Moscow if the existing Russian state is to be held together. Will Russia itself, for instance, become a genuinely federal state?[18]

But the demand for greater rights from the periphery is not confined to non-Russians. The Russians in Siberia, for example, now complain openly about the way in which they were treated in the past by Moscow. A recent congress of deputies from Siberia was held in Krasnoyarsk, and this witnessed repeated accusations that Moscow had extracted the wealth from Siberia, whilst giving very little in return in terms of quality of life for the inhabitants there. Moscow allegedly took three-quarters of the taxes collected in Krasnoyarsk in the first quarter of 1992, whilst, according to one estimate, Siberians had a standard of living 47 per cent below that of European Russia. At the very least the people there want a greater control over the region's mineral and other forms of wealth, so that they can extract greater benefits for themselves in return.[19] As the economy of Russia as a whole disintegrates during the process of adaptation to market methods and the world economy, the eastern part of Russia will probably find that it may achieve greater prosperity by aligning itself to the more dynamic economies of East Asia.

Indeed it is no longer inconceivable that Russia itself might fragment into two or more states, with one west of the Urals more oriented towards Europe, and one east of the Urals more oriented towards the Asia-Pacific region. It was already striking that during the referendum in the Baltic states a significant number of Russians there voted for independence, even though that would mean they became minorities in a state outside Russia. The Russian Foreign Minister, Kozyrev, admits that many Russians in other republics of the former Soviet Union are indeed prepared to accept this.[20] If that fragmentation of the Russian self-consciousness should be replicated in other parts of Russia, clearly this would increase the likelihood of the disintegration of Russia. At the congress in Krasnoyarsk, the demands for independence from Moscow were not as strident as had been expected or feared, but nevertheless the deputy chairman of the Kemerovo regional council, Sterligov, declared: 'We can do without Russia. Russia cannot do without us!' The opposition will clearly not go away, although they cannot but be aware of the problems caused by the small size of the population in Siberia and the Russian far east.[21]

Ethnic relations

Clearly one of the factors which will profoundly affect the cohesion of Russians is the relationship which develops with other nationalities of the former USSR. If this is relaxed, then the sense of a need for national unity will be diminished. If there is perceived to be a major threat from the outside, then this will encourage Russian unity – in one form or another.

One striking feature of developments in what is now the CIS has been the rapidly worsening relations between Russia and Ukraine since August 1991. The disputes over the Black Sea fleet and control of nuclear weapons have escalated to a point where any kind of Slav ethnic solidarity seems very tenuous in the foreseeable future. Relations with the states in the Caucasus also remain extremely tense, with allegations of Russian interference in the Transdnestrian region of Moldova, and of Russian partiality in the dispute between Armenia and Azerbaijan. In fact there is a weariness in Russia proper about entanglements with other ethnic communities, and voices have been heard advocating that Russia should pull its troops out of contested areas.[22] They say that if this leads to further ethnic strife, then it should be the primary responsibility of the rest of the world to resolve it, e.g. through the United Nations. If such a view becomes widely accepted, however, the rest of the world will necessarily become more fully involved in trying to solve bloody ethnic disputes. Already, for example, we have seen Russia cooperating with Turkey in trying to bring an end to the fighting between Armenia and Azerbaijan.

It cannot be excluded, of course, that disputes over the territorial boundaries of former Soviet republics will in places lead to conflict – and according to the then Deputy Foreign Minister of Russia, Fedorov, in autumn 1991, 80 per cent of the administrative boundaries within the former USSR had no official legal basis. That in itself will cause continued concern in other countries.

Then there is the question of the status and treatment of Russians in now independent states of the former USSR. If they suffer repression, will the government of Russia feel obliged not merely to intercede on their behalf, but also to take action if it receives no satisfaction? Even democratic and liberal-inclined voices argue that a democratic Russia must defend Russians against discrimination in former Soviet republics.[23] This will make it difficult for Russia to treat, say, the Baltic states on equal terms, and will leave open the possibility of renewed conflicts all round its borders. And even developments among Russians which are not primarily linked with Central Asia can cause a reaction there. For example, the re-creation of Russian Cossack units to defend Russian minorities has in turn been said to be stimulation for the formation of the Kazakh nationalist opposition party, Alash, which claims that the whole of Kazakhstan should be for Turkic-speaking peoples.[24]

But the ethnic problem which will preoccupy Russian leaders most of all will be relations with Muslims. At a time when religion is part of the renewed national identity of Russians, Central Asians, Azeris and Tatars, the fear of an Islamic revival sweeping across Russia is currently tangible in Moscow. For the moment, according to President Nazarbaev of Kazakhstan, there is no conception in Russia of how to coexist with the Muslim world.[25] There seem to be attempts to provoke a confrontation between the Russian leadership and the Islamic states, whilst popular articles belittling Islam abound.[26] Within Russia itself there are increasing independence demands for Tatarstan, and the Islamic Renaissance Party recently held a regional conference in Saratov, which was a Muslim city three hundred years ago. For the moment Islamic groupings tend to be quite wide-ranging in their concerns, some concentrating upon cultural and educational activities, whilst others are more inclined towards religious fundamentalism.²⁷ But Central Asia is also the part of the former Soviet Union where outside countries may be most inclined to try to play a part. Whilst today Russia and Turkey seem to be cooperating in trying to defuse the conflict between Armenia and Azerbaijan, President Ozal gave a warning that if Armenia continued to attack Azerbaijan, Turkey would send in troops on the latter's side. This provoked the Russian Defence Minister, Marshal Shaposhnikov, to respond that this could lead to a Third World War.²⁸ There are growing fears in Russia about the ambitions of Turkey and Iran to expand their own territory, and to cause trouble for Russia.²⁹

The consequences for Russia's place in the world

It is a geographical truism to describe Russia as a land bridge linking Europe and Asia, and Russians have in the past drawn ideas for their national development from their close associations with both. Yet, it will be argued, there has hitherto been a fundamental difference between their relations with Europe and those with Asia. With regard to Europe there have been alternate periods of superiority and inferiority. With Asia there have been occasional bouts of fear, largely stemming from the relative sizes of the Russian and Asian populations, as well as a lingering memory of the period of Tatar domination, but in terms of ideas about social organization, Russia has not been inclined to feelings of inferiority towards Asia. If anything it has tended to be attracted by the idea of becoming an agent for the Westernization of Asia, in other words acting as a bridge with a tilt towards Asia. It has found it very difficult to treat Asia and Asians as equal.

Russia and the West

Historically speaking, after the defeat of the Mongols in the seventeenth century, Russia deliberately turned westward. The predominant preoccupation of the various rulers and their governments was with Europe. Following Peter the Great's decision, in the words of Pushkin, 'to cut a window through into Europe' with the foundation of St Petersburg, Russia became preoccupied with the possibilities for learning technology and systems of government that would help to prevent a return of the Mongols, or any equivalent threat from the East.

Of course this did not mean that Europe to the west was necessarily peacefully disposed towards Russia, as the Napoleonic invasion demonstrated. Nor did it mean that Russians as a whole saw themselves as Europeans just as much as Germans, Italians or the French did. There remained a sense of Russia's different past and its different social institutions. The fact that Russia was an Orthodox rather than a Catholic or Protestant country obviously set it apart from Western Europe. And for most of the nineteenth century, for example, social reformers and political conservatives alike cited the village commune as a basic difference from the social order of Western Europe, and some extrapolated from the values apparently embodied within it a natural Russian tendency for Slavophile collectivism, which they contrasted favourably with the increasing individualism of Western Europe. Most of the debate over social reform within Russia in the nineteenth century could be cast in an argument between Slavophilism and Westernism.[30]

These values of collectivism greatly resembled Asian patriarchal traditions which stressed the importance of the family and the village rather than the individual. Yet they were not presented as 'Asian' values. Rather they were seen as differences within a basically common set of 'European' values. For good or ill, and whatever the differences between Orthodoxy and Catholicism, Christianity was seen as a fundamental set of values which bound together European countries, including Russia, and set them apart from the peoples of Asia.

Then the victory of the communists in Russia led to a reassertion of 'Western' values. This, of course, had nothing to do with religion, except insofar as many adherents espoused an atheistic doctrine with a kind of religious fervour. Such values had more in common with the values of the Enlightenment, held with a romantic fervour. Even though they came to be implemented by a set of leaders under Stalin who were far from 'Europeanized', they were seen as the product of the most advanced societies in the world which, at that time, were exclusively Western.

The emergence of Gorbachev and perestroika opened a new phase of 'Europeanization'. On an international level this led to the concept of the 'common European home', in which the USSR would occupy a prominent place. And domestically, after 1987, the most important element of perestroika was democratization: the attempt to establish a Western-type political system, with a democratic political culture to go with it. The collapse of the USSR in one respect intensified the reliance of Russia upon Western factors, in that Yeltsin and others became convinced that without Ukraine, there would be no possibility of rebuilding a state of the size of the USSR. So a preoccupation with Ukraine overshadowed attention directed towards, for example, the former Central Asian republics, which did want to preserve an alliance with Russia.[31]

Russia and Asia

Russia's attitude towards Asia was traditionally one of superiority. It was Russia's 'manifest destiny' to bring civilization and economic development to the Asian peoples, especially those near or inside its (expanding) imperial frontiers.[32]

It is true that individual Russians came to identify more with 'Asian' values, and indeed on occasion to glory in them. For example, the poet Blok at the beginning of the twentieth century declared that Russians were Asians, and that they should be proud of their Scythian ancestry. Yet by and large, if Russians used the term 'Asian' to describe themselves as a whole, or to designate any particular group, it was intended in a pejorative sense. Lenin's virulent criticisms of the 'semi-Asiatic mentality' of Bolshevik officials from an early stage of the revolution are typical of this. There was little sense that Russians had anything new to learn from Asians. They had already absorbed more than enough characteristics of Asian-ness.

Of course the world has changed since then. Asia is now more of a factor in world affairs than it was at the time of the collapse of Tsarism. The resurgence of Islam in the Middle East and Western Asia also produces circumstances which make Russian foreign policy more complicated than before, and which challenge the leaders to come up with new thinking. There is again now an 'Eastern question' to preoccupy Russia's leaders as it did in the nineteenth century. But this time it is Russia which, for the moment, is the declining power, and its southern neighbours which are gaining strength.

In one respect the growing divergence of interests between Russia on the one hand, and other western states of the former USSR, especially Ukraine, on the other hand, means that the CIS increasingly consists of two blocs. One, oriented around Ukraine and Belarus, looks westward, and in security as well as economic terms seeks minimal integration with the rest of the CIS. The other, centred on Russia and the Central Asian states, but also including Armenia, proclaims the need for greater integration. Most of the existing regimes in Central Asia wish to maintain a close link with Russia because, apart from being dependent upon Russian markets, they also wish Russia to guarantee the existing frontiers between them. Without that guarantee, there is a strong possibility that ethnic and nationalist forces might appear which would demand the redrawing of frontiers. This could lead to fighting similar to that in the former Yugoslavia. In this respect, Russia is necessarily being forced to turn towards Asia.[33] On the other hand it is difficult to believe that Russian popular opinion will support any significant involvement by Russia in settling disputes in that region if fighting breaks out, given the general weariness of the Russian population with international commitments, and the continuing exodus of Russians who have felt themselves discriminated against, even persecuted, in Central Asia. Yet if relations with Muslims in Central Asia worsen, so too will relations with Muslims inside the Russian Federation, for instance in Tatarstan.

On an international level, both Tsarist Russia and the Soviet Union enjoyed quite good relations with at least some countries in the Middle East.[34] It seems unlikely that this will continue for the new Russian state. On the one hand Russian support for the coalition forces in the Gulf war has destroyed the support which it might have enjoyed from radical, secular Arab regimes. On the other hand the antagonisms within the former USSR between Christians and Muslims, between Russians and Central Asians, could well worsen relations between Russia and Muslim states in general. For all of these reasons, Russia's relations with the Middle East will probably be more turbulent than they have been for decades.

As for relations with countries on the Pacific rim, above all Japan, the recent decades of economic development there mean that, at least for some Russians, especially those east of the Urals, there is an increasing sense of the need to cooperate with and learn from eastern neighbours. Even the former minister of economic reform under Gorbachev, Abalkin, has written recently of the need for Russia to learn lessons from Japan's economic success.[35] Were this view to become widely established, it would in itself represent a major change in Russian national identity, although it has to be said that there still seems to be a popular reluctance in Sakhalin to contemplate new political concessions to Japan over the Northern Territories. And it might be that preoccupations with Central Asia will divert attention from East Asia, especially if Russia's concerns and policies coincide with those of West European countries and the United States about the Middle East.

Nevertheless, given the pressures on the Russian leadership and people, it is no exaggeration to say that their ability to surmount their difficulties may in large part depend upon their ability to develop a new set of attitudes towards Asia, i.e. to treat Asians as equals, and even to accept that they can learn from Asian experiences. Were they to be able to achieve this, it would turn Russia into a much more evenly balanced bridge between Europe and Asia. It might facilitate a thicker set of relationships between Europe and East Asia. Not only would this be a historic change for Russia, it would also be a historic change for the rest of the world. It might assist not only Russia to cope with the twenty-first century. The alternative, for both Russians and the rest of the world, is more bleak.

Because there are so many uncertainties about developments in Russia and the rest of the former Soviet Union, other countries will not be able to make a decisive impact upon events there. Wariness will be only prudent in policies towards Russia. But so too will patience and positive, persistent goodwill, especially from countries on Russia's borders. Given the instability and volatility within the territory of the former USSR, an unfriendly external world, or one that was perceived to be so, might be the factor which provokes large-scale confrontation, even conflict. And if that were to occur, it would be likely to spread. The consequences would be felt far beyond the boundaries of the former Soviet Union.

Notes
1. For a poll showing an apparent fall in support among Muscovites for all Russian leaders, including Yeltsin, see *Nezavisimaya gazeta*, 30 May 1992, p. 2.
2. Vasily Lipitsky, *Nezavisimaya gazeta*, 27 March 1992, p. 2.
3. See, for example, Ulrich Greiner, 'Die Falle des Entweder-Oder', *Die Zeit*, 24 January 1992; *Der Spiegel*, 24 February 1992, pp. 26–39.
4. Vasily Lipitsky, *Nezavisimaya gazeta*, 27 March 1992, p. 2.
5. *Nezavisimaya gazeta*, 21 May 1992, p. 2.
6. Mikhail Maliutin, *Literaturnaya gazeta*, 25 March 1992, p. 11.
7. Marina Pavlova-Sil'vanskaya, *Nezavisimaya gazeta*, 25 June 1992, p. 5.
8. Maliutin, op. cit.
9. *Nezavisimaya gazeta*, 30 April 1992, p. 1.
10. For an account of voting patterns in the Russian parliament, see Igor' Iakovenko, *Nezavisimaya gazeta*, 24 April 1992, p. 2.
11. Sergei Stankevich, *Literaturnaya gazeta*, 11 March 1992, p. 11.
12. Aleksei Kiva, *Literaturnaya gazeta*, 11 March 1992, p. 10; cf. Maliutin, op. cit.
13. Vladimir Iliushenko, *Literaturnaya gazeta*, 19 February 1992, p. 11.
14. Lev Gintsburg, *Nezavisimaya gazeta*, 28 April 1992, p. 5.
15. Liudmila Vorontsova and Sergei Filatov, *Nezavisimaya gazeta*, 21 April 1992, p. 6.
16. Kiva, op. cit.
17. M.I. Piskotin, *Sotsializm i gosudarstvennoe upravlenie* (Moscow, 1984), pp. 214–15.
18. Radik Batyrshin, *Nezavisimaya gazeta*, 7 March 1992, p. 2.

19 *Izvestiya*, 30 March 1992, p. 2.
20 Andrei Kozyrev, *Izvestiya*, 30 June, p. 3.
21 Vladimir Toders, *Nezavisimaya gazeta*, 2 April 1992, p. 2.
22 'Nashi interesy v Zakavkaz'ie', *Nezavisimaya gazeta*, 4 March 1992, p. 3.
23 Iliushenko, op. cit.
24 Aleksei Malashenko, *Nezavisimaya gazeta*, 2 July 1992, p. 3.
25 *Nezavisimaya gazeta*, 6 May 1992, p. 5.
26 Aleksei Malashenko, *Nezavisimaya gazeta*, 21 March 1992, p. 3.
27 Aleksei Malashenko, *Nezavisimaya gazeta*, 8 May 1992, p. 3.
28 *Nezavisimaya gazeta*, 25 May 1992, p. 1.
29 Asal' Azamova and Viktor Kuval'din, *Nezavisimaya gazeta*, 15 May 1992, p. 5.
30 See, for example, Leonard Schapiro, *Rationalism and Nationalism in Russian Nineteenth Century Political Thought* (New Haven: Yale UP, 1967).
31 Aleksei Bogaturov and Mikhail Kozhokin, *Nezavisimaya gazeta*, 26 March 1992, p. 4.
32 For example, see Milan Hauner, *What is Asia To Us?* (London: Unwin Hyman, 1990), Chapters 2, 3 and 4.
33 *Nezavisimaya gazeta*, 19 May 1992, p. 1.
34 For an account of recent relations between Russia and the Middle East, see Galia Golan, *Moscow and the Middle East: New Thinking on Regional Conflict* (London: RIIA/Pinter, 1992).
35 Leonid Abalkin, *Nezavisimaya gazeta*, 20 June 1992, p. 2.

CHAPTER 3
ECONOMIC IMPLICATIONS OF CHANGE IN THE FORMER SOVIET UNION

REIZO UTAGAWA

Politically, the transformation of the former Soviet Union (FSU) is a relatively simple matter: democracy is emerging from the rubble of a collapsing authoritarian state. There are many precedents for this type of change; Japan and Germany after the Second World War are perhaps the best-known examples.

But the economic transformation, from a centrally planned to a market economy, is unprecedented. We have no assured results or reliable models and we cannot foresee the outcome. The Soviet economic reforms now in progress are designed to convert a command economy that prohibited virtually all private economic activity to a market economy. Part of that process involves the privatization of previously state-owned enterprises.

The world has ample experience in the creation of socialist economies: the history of Eastern Europe after the Second World War is a veritable textbook. At the peak of their acceptance, one-third of the world's population lived under socialist economic systems. Creating a centrally planned economy from the ruins of a market economy is relatively easy, although creating an efficient economy is another matter altogether. Going the other way, from a centrally planned to a market economy, is not so simple. That the first leads to the second with relative ease by no means guarantees that the process can be reversed with similar nonchalance.

A convincing analogy can be made with reference to ecology. It is easy to destroy an environment in order to construct a building. It is virtually impossible to recreate the original environment from the ruins of the building. In this sense, the creation of a market economy is like rebuilding such an ecology.

Capitalism has developed organically. Its present-day characteristics are historical outgrowths of the subtle relationship between contract and credit.

The republics of the FSU are now trying to establish a capitalist, market economy in a very short time, like trying to ferment vodka overnight. While this process is difficult and fraught with uncertainty, they must proceed. They have burned their bridges and cannot retreat. During the cold war era, the 'Soviet problem' was a security or political question, not an economic one. From the international economist's perspective, the Soviet Union was of negligible concern, since Soviet leaders had opted out of the world economy, choosing isolation over interdependence. They pursued autarky within the socialist economic zone.

The Soviet Union's collapse has dramatically diminished the weight of military factors within international policymaking. Concomitantly, the significance of economic considerations has risen. Thus there is an inverse relationship between politico-military and economic factors. The FSU's economic reforms create two tremendous issues: Can the former Soviet republics successfully manage their economic transformation? And can they then be integrated into the world economy? Answers to these questions will be central to the future stability and growth of the world economy.

If it is successful in its efforts, the FSU, with its large land mass and sizeable population, and well endowed with natural resources, will be a real asset for the global community. Failure, on the other hand, threatens the entire world economically, politically and militarily. The future is murky but it is difficult to be optimistic. Indeed, pessimism prevails: there is widespread fear of waves of economic refugees and the FSU eventually defaulting on its loans. The FSU is commonly viewed as a threat to the international economy.

The spectre of capitalism
A spectre is haunting the FSU – the spectre of capitalism. All the powers of the Western economy have entered into a holy alliance to encourage this spectre.

The leaders of the former Soviet republics are enticed in the early 1990s by the siren song of the Chicago school of economics, with its laissez-faire extremism and the notion of a common economic space. But a mad rush towards capitalism will not create a stable and thriving economic order. Unfortunately, it seems that President Yeltsin and other Russian economic policymakers have embraced the view that it will. Prime Minister Gaidar's economic plan, which reads like pages from a Chicago school textbook, calls for the axe, not the scalpel.

Sceptical of any government role in the economy, the Chicago school's libertarians go too far in their respect for the effectiveness of the 'invisible hand'. They believe market mechanisms can and will sort out any difficulties, that the market is a veritable panacea. Liberalize your prices and ye shall be free. But extremism in the pursuit of laissez-faire is no virtue: the invisible hand sometimes misses the ball.

In January 1992, President Yeltsin introduced his bold price liberalization policy to encourage the rapid development of the market economy. The most optimistic scenario was as follows: (1) price liberalization would lead to immediate sharp price increases, after which prices would stabilize; (2) this would permit the realization of the market economy espoused by the libertarians; (3) market mechanisms would allow the Russian economy to allocate resources rationally and efficiently; and (4) normal production processes would resume.

Things have worked out otherwise. Thus far, prices have not yet even stabilized. Hyperinflation prevails and there is no sign of a market economy emerging. Instead, barter reigns in the grey market. The economy seems to be moving towards the worst-case scenario, involving a long-term deterioration of productive activity.

A second will-o'-the-wisp is haunting the FSU, that of the common economic sphere. In 1991, President Yeltsin declared the termination of the Soviet Union and announced the formation, with the leaders of Belarus and Ukraine, of the Commonwealth of Independent States (CIS). The CIS decided to use the rouble as the single currency among the 11 republics to maintain a common economic area, the first step in the eventual formation of an economic commmonwealth. From the Western perspective, this type of commonwealth, which would be open to other countries, is highly desirable, yet it is but a dream, an illusion.

The CIS is destined to fail for two reasons. The first is political: the republics want to be fully independent and establish themselves as nation-states. The second is economic: The collapse of the central, Moscow-based financial mechanism has deprived the Commonwealth of its economic glue. The two interact. Complete independence requires economic freedom. That forces each nation to have its own currency. A common economic area is not impossible; it is impossible at present. It may be realized in the next century, but certainly not next year.

Power in the Soviet Union, ruled from the centre, was exercised through the political equivalent of centripetal force. But the vacuum created by the collapse of the ruling authority reversed the flow of power and now the FSU is like a giant centrifuge, with different regions spinning wildly away, drawn towards other poles of economic power. Russia and Ukraine feel the pull of the European Community, the Central Asian Republics are drawn to the emerging Islamic economic zone, while Siberia is attracted to the Far East. In the words of Robert Scalapino, 'natural economic territories (NETs) are being formed, cutting across political lines.'[1]

A new economic strategy: from market socialism to the mixed economy
The most important thing for the FSU is stimulation of the supply side of the economy, a sadly neglected component of economic policy, and Gaidar's policies have lost precious time. In my judgment, the Shatalin–Yablinsky plan of 1990 was a better policy. The so-called '500 Days Plan' was not driven by the two illusions just discussed. Rather, it aimed first to cut the fiscal deficit and then to absorb excess money circulating in the economy. The second stage envisioned gradual price liberalization. The plan aimed at creating an economic alliance among the republics through economic mechanisms. Shatalin thereby aimed to finesse the inevitable disputes created by the terms of a treaty or any document that artificially established rights and obligations. In other words, he aimed to disconnect politics from economics. Regrettably, the Shatalin plan is dead.

The economies of the former Soviet republics are now moving into uncharted waters and Western nations have no assured guides to offer. The recent decision by the IMF to provide credits with some conditions attached treats only the symptoms of the FSU's economic malaise and does not get at the cause of the problem. The IMF package calls for severe restrictions on demand to curb inflation. This treatment does not address the supply-side problems: it does not restore productivity. At worst, this cure could worsen the economic turmoil and force even harsher austerity upon the population.

The IMF expects money supply to be tightened, thus stabilizing prices, which in turn would restore the productive sectors of the economy. But seventy years' absence of economic rationality dooms the IMF plan. It is unrealistic to expect the idealized market economy to develop in Russia, springing like Athena from the head of some economics textbook writer.

There is an alternative path from the socialist command economy to the capitalist model: the mixed economy. China, for example, is moving towards a less centralized economy and calls this strategy a two-track economic policy. This divides the economy in two: one part driven by market forces, the other centrally planned. In 1979, the agricultural sector was reformed and free enterprise zones were established to encourage foreign investment with land reform, market incentives and new distribution mechanisms spurring productivity. After 1984, small, private industries and banks were born. Foreign investment in the special economic zones flourished. The traditional command economy remains in the heavy industry sector, but the new market economy now creates more than half of China's GNP. According to the Chinese economist Gao Shangquan:

> Through price reform, currently in place for prices of consumer commodities and prices for the means of production, state-set prices for commodities now make up less than 30 per cent and prices formed through the market have reached more than 70 per cent. The market is playing an increasing regulatory role.[2]

The Chinese experience shows how market socialism can lead to the mixed economy that one finds in non-socialist countries. In the near future, the remaining sectors of the economy controlled by the centre may be liberalized as well.

This example could serve the former Soviet republics well. Russia desperately needs human resources, but not only the entrepreneurial talents of the businessman. There is also an urgent need for bureaucrats with the knowledge and morale to manage a mixed economy. Western economic texts have played an important role in the destruction of the centrally planned economic systems but that role is over. Laissez-faire is no cure-all from this stage forward.

In addition, the Japanese experience of rebuilding its economy in the aftermath of the Second World War provides a powerful example of a mixed economy and the leading role a government can play in setting economic priorities and structuring the development process. At the end of that war, Japanese industrial productivity was one half the prewar figure, there was hyperinflation and the population was on the brink of starvation. From 1947 to 1949, Japan received economic aid from the United States equivalent to 3 per cent of Japanese GNP.[3] These monies were not used for private consumption, but were invested in the economic infrastructure. Although the Japanese government understood the crying need for immediate aid to its own people, it recognized that its first priority had to be sparking the dynamism of the Japanese economy so that it could eventually meet those needs on its own. In short, the government pushed a supply-side economic policy, which developed three basic industries: coal, steel and fertilizer. To stimulate their growth, the government pursued *keisha-seisan*, a means of pushing the development of the basic materials sectors. *Keisha-kinyu* provided finance for these industries with low interest rates. Thus the Japanese mixed economic policy evolved, not as a substitute for market economics, but as a supplemental stimulus for the market.

The FSU should draw upon the Chinese model now being used or on the Japanese model of 45 years ago to construct its own mix of public and private economies.

A Marshall Plan for the FSU?

Many Western economists find the Marshall Plan analogy seductive. From 1948 to 1950, the United States provided some $10 billion of economic assistance to European countries to speed their economic reconstruction. This investment totalled roughly 2 per cent of the receiving nations' annual GNP. A similar level of assistance today for the FSU could reach $30–50 billion per year. Should we offer the FSU these monies? It is too early to say, but there are three reasons for not offering large-scale assistance immediately to the private sector. First, immediately after the war Western Europe had a traditional market that could be stimulated by US seed money. The FSU does not: it has only the grey market and wild capitalism. Second, there are no bureaucrats capable of guiding the private sector towards economic dynamism. Finally, there are no mechanisms within the FSU to accumulate capital. So, even with the seed money, there is no soil within which it can take root and produce fruit. Thus far, the FSU has had no opportunity to enter the enlarged production cycle. As a result, there is no immediate need for an aid package along the lines of the Marshall Plan. We are confronting a situation expressed best by the old proverb: give a man a fish and he eats for a day; teach him to fish and he eats for a lifetime.

Thus, rather than strewing money carelessly across the length and breadth of the FSU (money, incidentally, that we do not have), it is a far wiser use of our limited resources to pursue two types of investment in the petroleum industry and in small demonstration projects at the local level. Assistance to restore the petroleum industry is urgent, as many Western economists have pointed out. In this paper, I want the stress the importance of relatively small projects at the local level. These seed projects will serve as models for the larger projects that follow.

The socialist ideology, the glue that once bound the fifteen disparate Soviet republics, is gone. As Moscow no longer has the power to direct and manage trade among the republics, such trade is deteriorating. Some republics are being pulled towards other economic poles, like the EC, the Islamic countries or the Far East. The industrialized countries must appreciate and utilize this phenomenon as they formulate their response to the FSU's difficulties. The recentralization of economic authority within the CIS is very unlikely.

Consider what is unfolding in the Far East. Russia is eager to see the realization of an East Asian economic zone. This zone would use private companies and official government assistance to build the region's infrastructure. Technology transfer would follow. This is the way in which Taiwan, South Korea, Hong Kong and Singapore became NIEs (Newly Industrializing Economies). This pattern has been employed in Southeast Asia, in Thailand and Malaysia, and in the southern Chinese provinces; it will hopefully be extended to Vietnam as well. This phenomenon of passing on successful growth strategies has been dubbed the 'flying geese' model by economist Kaname Akamatsu. The result is a horizontal division of labour in the region.

In the near future this concept will be extended to Northeast Asia, with Japan, Korea, the northeastern part of China and probably Russia joining this network. Russia offers mineral and other natural resources, while China will provide agricultural goods and labour. Korea has chemical products, medium-level industrial technology and capital. Japan has high-technology goods, managerial know-how, information and capital. The Japan Sea will serve as the transportation conduit for all these assets. The resulting new economic territory could be Russia's doorway to the prosperous Asian economy. Perhaps by the time those parts of the FSU west of the Urals get into their own economic stride, the Russian far east will have become the last of Asia's 'flying geese'.

While the FSU should not be too hasty in its economic designs, local projects should be studied and pursued. The ultimate result may be a reversal of the traditional information flows: economic success may flow from the periphery – the far east – to the west.

Oil, the immediate concern

The economy of the FSU is being influenced by three mistaken therapies: (1) over-hasty liberalization of the market, premised on blind allegiance to the free-market ethos; (2) the imposition on Russia, by the G7 countries and the IMF, of an economic package that overly restricts demand without stressing the need for stimulating the supply side of the economy; and (3) drawing the wrong lessons from 70 years of economic mismanagement under communist rule: the FSU policymakers have left no role at all for government industrial policy initiatives.

If capable bureaucrats are available, there must be some room for a government-led programme, not to dictate economic development, but to structure and nurture growth. This gives rise to an interesting paradox: in China, where political power is still effectively centralized, bureaucrats can direct market liberalization – the centre can direct the market to work its magic. In Russia, there is no power centre capable of stimulating the market. Political decentralization has given way to economic anarchy.

Without a radical change in the FSU and in Western attitudes, deterioration will continue and the complete collapse of the FSU economy is a real possibility. At this juncture, what are the global implications of that deterioration?

In the short term, the direct impact on the world economy is not likely to be large. The Soviet economy has experienced a declining growth rate for 50 years. A Soviet monthly magazine stated that from 1928 to 1985, the Soviet government announced a 90-fold increase in national income; in reality, growth was up only 6.5 times.[4] The CIA had assumed the scale of the Soviet Union's economy was 50 per cent of that of the United States, based on purchasing power. It has since revised the figures to 15–20 per cent. In the last two years, national production has fallen sharply, by some 10 per cent per year. The FSU economy is much smaller than it ever appeared. Therefore, the shrinkage of the domestic economy should not have a great impact on the international economy save for the oil trade issue.

Previously, the Soviet Union had been considered an oil superpower with abundant underground resources. But in the past five years its oil production has sharply declined because of ageing and obsolete equipment and because shortages of funds prevent maintenance of old facilities and slow the development of new projects. Oil production peaked in 1987, when total annual output was 12.5 million barrels per day. Exports went primarily to Europe (some 3.9 million barrels per day). Now the situation has changed dramatically. In 1992, total production of oil in the FSU is estimated at 9 million barrels per day, a decline to 1975 levels. Its ability to export crude oil to Eastern Europe has decreased dramatically. In 1991, *Pravda* warned that if this deterioration continues unabated, the FSU will become a net oil importer. Within the CIS itself, Russia has begun to cut its oil exports to Ukraine and other republics: Ukraine already faces petrol shortages.

To generate hard currency, Russia is targeting production for eventual export to Western Europe, but exports are still declining. In 1991, Russia exported 1.6 million barrels per day, but that figure was expected to fall 300,000 barrels during 1992. That shortfall is being filled by Middle East countries. This shift firms up oil prices, so the deterioration of FSU oil output has prevented oil prices from falling.

According to estimates from a Japan-based oil research institute, by 1995 FSU oil production will decline to 7 million barrels per day.[5] This is the Institute's more pessimistic scenario, but the one it considers most probable – in fact, almost inevitable. This 2-million barrel decline is equivalent to 9 per cent of OPEC's production. Thus, the impact of declining FSU production has already been felt within the international economy and, in the medium term, will become a very important issue in the oil economy. Furthermore, if the FSU becomes a large oil importer, it will become a serious problem for the world economy.

The coming capital crunch

In the medium term (3–5 years), the world economy will face a real shortage of capital. As a result, interest rates in the international markets will rise. At this moment, the international impact of capital inflows to the FSU is very small compared with the case of the former East Germany. One estimate puts the total amount that the German government has spent on the former East Germany since reunification at $100 billion, and these outlays will continue for several years. But no country at this stage is interested in investing a similar sum in the FSU, nor are there expectations that it will reach a similar level of growth.

The IMF and the G7 have decided to provide $24 billion in monetary assistance to the Russian Republic but the major part of those funds is in the form of stand-by credits, a rouble stabilization fund and export credits. New money is a very small part of the entire package. In the short term, the capital shortage issue is almost negligible.

However, a worldwide capital shortage – a possibility regardless of developments within the FSU – will be a real concern in 3–5 years. The situation in the FSU will increase the demand for capital on the margin. When the FSU begins its turn, Western countries, including Japan, will need to provide aid, not merely as a bandaid (in the form, say, of debt relief or food assistance), but as a vitamin to strengthen its economic recovery. In this scenario, how much money will be required? There is no way of knowing, but using the Marshall Plan as an analogy, it is likely to require 2 per cent of the FSU's GNP, roughly $30 billion per year.

Regardless of the eventual success or collapse of the FSU's efforts to create a functioning economy, there will be a real crisis in world money markets. Even now, with the impact of the FSU minimal or non-existent, there is an international shortage of funds. Putting aside the needs of the FSU and Eastern Europe, the total demand for funds already outstrips supply. Many economists, bankers among them, say that real demand and supply are always in equilibrium. This is true, but irrelevant.

The issue is one of potential demand and real supply. That shortfall has grown in the last three years. The Japanese Economic Planning Agency estimates a shortage of $54 billion in 1991 and expects the deficit to reach $103 billion in 1992. Total demand for funds is put at $3.496 trillion (OECD countries $2.63 trillion, developing countries except the FSU and Eastern Europe $866 billion), with available funds of $3.393 trillion (OECD countries $2.56 trillion, developing countries except the FSU and Eastern Europe $833 billion). In 3–5 years, the FSU is expected to stretch that gap by roughly $30 billion each year.[6] This will increase international interest rates by one percentage point per year. Developing countries will be particularly hard hit since they will be obliged to pay the one percentage point plus to compete with preferred borrowers from the industrialized world. In 1991, the world economy accommodated the capital needs of East Germany through a recession in the United States and other English-speaking countries. The total GNP of the G7 countries is $15 trillion. Mathematically the world can offset the shortage of funds through a mere one per cent drop in the G7 investment rate, but in 1992 the situation is complicated by the economic recovery in the United States and Western Europe (the Japanese economy remains stagnant, with a large gap between its investment and savings balances). Thus only Japan has an economy with room to assist the FSU. This situation will result in a real reluctance among Western capital exporters to provide funds to the FSU. Credit will be kept in balance with the expected capital surplus in the industrial economies to avoid sacrificing their own growth. The industrial economies will be very selective in where they direct their funds for projects in the FSU.

In the long run, the failure of the FSU economy to recover will have incalculable costs. Thus, the dilemma that seems to be emerging for the industrialized nations is whether to leave the FSU to fend for itself or to cut their own growth rates.

Dark shadows on the world economy

If FSU economies fail to take off, the risk of civil wars in 14 republics, each split into smaller enclaves and threatening to spill over national and international borders, is very high. That situation – compounded by the presence of thousands of nuclear and other weapons of mass destruction – is perhaps the gravest threat posed by the protracted collapse of the FSU economy.

There are still other areas of concern for the world economy. The first is the massive outflow of people from the FSU. There are millions of potential refugees. Obstacles exist: shortages of hard currency and the low value of the rouble prevent many from moving abroad. A Japanese research institute has estimated that with the removal of these economic barriers, 50–70 million refugees might migrate westward by the year 2000.[7]

A second concern is the outflow of highly educated scientists and technology engineers. It is estimated that in 1991 4–600,000 emigrated, of whom two-thirds had received an advanced education. A recent concern is the emigration of nuclear scientists to Iraq, Iran, Pakistan and other countries desperate to develop nuclear weapons capability. Even if the FSU economy recovers, the income of such professionals will remain below that of their counterparts in the West. The FSU has more than one-third of the world's doctorates in science and engineering. An FSU littered with broken building blocks, the legacy of the socialist past, and devoid of its highly educated professionals, will be unable to reconstruct itself.

The third concern is the problem of integrating the FSU's economy within the international economic system. At this moment, that integration is virtually non-existent. As I write, Russia and a few other republics have joined the IMF. The five Central Asian Republics will soon have the opportunity to join the World Bank and to receive development assistance from the industrialized world. These are ultimately small moves towards participation in the international division of labour with only a limited capacity to renovate the economies of these economies, particularly their stunted productive capacity.

Joining international economic organizations like GATT is not a pressing concern. Before they do that, the FSU republics have to recreate working economies within their own regions. Otherwise there is a real danger they will engage in 'beggar thy neighbour' policies or even in trade wars. They must focus on issues closer to home.

Finally, there is the peace dividend. The real significance of the successful management of the political and economic transformation of the FSU will be the substantial reduction in defence expenditures throughout the world. The industrialized economies now spend roughly $500 billion per year on defence. Economic recovery and stabilization in the FSU should permit world defence outlays to be cut by $100 billion per year. But no one can predict if and when the world economy will taste the fruits of this peace dividend, and the FSU still has the ability to deploy its strategic nuclear arsenal within 30 minutes if it so decides.

There is as yet no visible or convincing solution to the problems the FSU faces. While the former Soviet republics have been blinded by the light of the free-market ethos, the rest of the world is blinded by the dust rising from the ruins of the shattered Soviet economy.

Notes

1 Robert Scalapino, 'The United States and Asia: Future Prospects', *Foreign Affairs*, Vol. 70, No. 5, Winter 1991/1992, pp. 20–21.
2 Gao Shangquan, 'The Process and Basic Experience of China's Economic Reform'. This is a background paper for the UN Department of Economic and Social Development, Transnational Corporations and Management Division's international seminar, 'Linkages of Micro-economic Reforms and Macro-economic Adjustment in Transitional Centrally Planned Economies', held in Beijing, 21–25 April 1992.
3 Yukitsugu Nakagawa, *Reflections on Restoring the Former Soviet Union: Can the Japanese Experience Help?*, International Institute for Global Peace publication 92E, May 1992.
4 *New Community*, February 1987.
5 Toyoaki Ikuta et al., 'Konmei suru Dyu-Soren no Sekiyu Jousei wo Dou miruka', internal report by the Energy Research Institute of Japan, Tokyo, 26 March 1992, p. 34.
6 *World Economic Report 1991*, Japan Economic Planning Agency.
7 *Reclamation of the Former USSR Towards the 21st Century*, Nomura Research Institute, 1992.

CHAPTER 4
ECONOMIC AND TECHNICAL ASSISTANCE TO THE FORMER SOVIET UNION*

MARGOT LIGHT

Introduction

When Mikhail Gorbachev began to talk about the need for perestroika, his avowed aim was to restructure the centrally planned economy which had been performing increasingly poorly since the 1970s. Apart from making the economy more efficient, he wanted the Soviet Union to join the international economy from which it had been separated by the October Revolution, the subsequent industrialization and centralization and the consequent political division of Europe and the world. His initial diagnosis, that the Soviet economy was in a perilous stage of pre-crisis, turned out to be optimistic; it had already entered a state of crisis. It soon became clear that tinkering with details would not help. A wholesale reform, up to and including the introduction of market principles, was required if the Soviet Union was to emerge from its precipitous decline. Gorbachev was faced with two insuperable tasks: finding a reform programme that had sufficient political support to enable its implementation and to ensure its success; and persuading the external world to give the financial and technical assistance required to execute it.

Gorbachev's failures in both these endeavours were related and they led to the disintegration of the Soviet Union. On the one hand his search for an 'acceptable' formula for reform led to half-hearted plans which the Party bureaucracy had no difficulty in obstructing. As a result, the economy continued to deteriorate.[1] On the other, his irresolution made the governments of the countries to whom he turned for help sceptical of his intentions. Although Western leaders were impressed by the domestic political changes

---

*I would like to thank Edwina Moreton, Suzanne Crow and Sergei Manezhev for their generous help, and the Joint Technical Assistance Unit and the Economic Relations Department of the Foreign and Commonwealth Office for their ready assistance with statistics.

which he had brought about and by his foreign policy, they insisted that effective reforms should precede the commitment of aid. His response to their strictures – that assistance was required *in order to* reform – did not convince them. They were prepared to offer some technical assistance, but insisted on a reform programme of which they approved before they would consider extensive aid.

At home Gorbachev was pleasing neither radical reformers nor the conservative wing of the Communist Party of the Soviet Union (CPSU). Moreover, his domestic political changes – glasnost and democratization – served to exacerbate the economic crisis. When economic decline turned into catastrophic free-fall and life became increasingly difficult for Soviet citizens, his domestic popularity evaporated. By the middle of 1991 he owed his position more to the absence of a credible replacement (Yeltsin, already president of the Russian Federation, did not aspire to the presidency of the USSR) and to his still solid international reputation than to domestic support. Yet when he returned from the Group of Seven (G7) meeting in London in July 1991 with little substantive aid, he no longer seemed such a convincing international emissary for the Soviet Union.[2] The attempted right-wing coup which took place in August was defeated, but Gorbachev no longer had sufficient legitimacy to resume effective leadership.

The coup seemed to convince the leaders of the industrialized countries that their backing was a prerequisite for reform, rather than something to be proffered as a reward for the successful introduction of a market economy. Serious efforts by the industrialized world to assist the former Soviet Union (FSU)[3] only really began, therefore, after August 1991. This chapter will assess the efforts and consider some of the problems and pitfalls of future aid programmes.

Since an assessment of the effectiveness of assistance only makes sense in terms of what the donors hoped to achieve, the first section of the chapter considers the motives of donor countries. Various types of assistance that have been offered are examined in the second section, which also looks at the way in which assistance has been organized. The special problems of defence conversion are considered next. The chapter ends by pointing out why it is difficult to assess whether assistance is effective and by making some suggestions about the way forward.

Donors' motives: altruism and enlightened self-interest
I have suggested that the attempted coup in August 1991 seemed to support Gorbachev's contention that unless external aid was offered, there could be

no economic reform. The coup itself, however, would not have been enough to convince potential donors if the CPSU, its authority totally undermined by its implication in the coup, had not been suspended when it ended. The main obstacle to reform seemed to have been removed. There appeared to be a new, firmer commitment within the Soviet Union to the introduction of a market economy. But these were not the only reasons why donors changed their minds about the timing of assistance. As the inexorable disintegration of the USSR proceeded, it became clear that the industrialized countries should offer aid not only for disinterested, altruistic reasons or because they were committed to the idea that a market economy was both more efficient and morally superior to central planning; there were (and are) sound self-interested motives for coming to the assistance of the successor governments.

A major aim of economic assistance is to buttress the new democracies of the former Soviet Union, to prevent political instability and a possible reversion to authoritarian rule which, even if it is not communist, is unlikely to be in the interests of neighbouring states or of Europe as a whole.[4] A related goal is more directly connected to security. If the political instability of a disintegrating great power is a threat to international security, the danger is that much greater when the great power possesses nuclear weapons. In the case of the FSU it is not just a case of ensuring that the successor states accept responsibility for, and implement, the arms control agreements which the Soviet government had made and of preventing nuclear proliferation as a result of the disintegration. There is the added problem of disabling, moving and dismantling the warheads that are supernumerary to the START agreement and disposing of the fissile material which remains. Assisting in the conversion of conventional defence industries and finding gainful employment for nuclear scientists to prevent them from seeking jobs elsewhere are other aspects of assistance which arise directly from the security interests of the donors.

There are also sound economic reasons for coming to the aid of the FSU. For one thing, the countries of the now defunct Council for Mutual Economic Assistance would benefit greatly in the short and medium term (at least until their industries are able to compete with Western products) from the revival of trade and the restoration of their traditional markets. In other words, the assistance that has already been given to East Central Europe will be more effective if economic recovery takes place in the FSU. A second reason is the danger that political instability and economic chaos could cause mass migration into East Central Europe, destabilizing the fragile democracies and weak economies of those countries and possibly 'spilling over' into the rest of Europe. The dislocation and migration that have resulted from the civil wars in Yugoslavia are indications of the problems that could result from serious conflict in the FSU.

But there are also potential direct long-term economic benefits for donors who assist the FSU now. It has a huge unsatisfied consumer market of approximately 280 million people, rich (although not easily accessible) raw material reserves and a labour force which, while not yet accustomed to the work habits and ways of capitalism, is relatively skilled and well educated. The domestic economies of the countries that participate in the economic revival of the successor states to the Soviet Union stand to reap great profits in the future – if assistance is effective and revival takes place.[5]

Types of assistance

The first thing to say about the aid that has gone to the FSU is that the term 'assistance' is more accurate than aid, since few of the offers correspond to a strict definition of aid (the Development Assistance Committee of the OECD restricts the term to resources that include a grant element of at least 25 per cent). A second important point is that there has been more talk than action. In other words, promises abound – for humanitarian aid, technical assistance, credits for imports – but deliveries lag far behind offers of assistance. From press reports, for example, it might seem that vast sums have already been sent. Most of the reports, however, refer to pledges rather than deliveries. Moreover, the amounts promised sound less substantial when they are compared either with the requirements for economic transformation, or with the amounts the industrialized countries spend on other budgetary allocations. There is scarcely any follow-up reporting on what happens to the pledges. Some of the reasons for the discrepancy between pledge and delivery will be discussed in the section on the effectiveness of assistance, but it is important to note that, first, virtually none of the offers have been unconditional, and, second, that part of the delay between recognition that assistance is vital on the one hand, and delivery on the other, has to do with the fact that although donors are convinced that the end-product of economic reform in the former Soviet Union should be a functioning market economy, none of them has been sure about the best way to achieve it.

Although there was some transfer of resources to the Soviet Union before the coup,[6] serious international concern about the situation only really began in August 1991. In May 1991 Yevgeny Primakov and Grigory Yavlinsky, reformist advisers to Gorbachev, and a group of Harvard economists had submitted an ambitious appeal for a 'Grand Bargain' (Western aid in return for Soviet reform) to the G7.[7] Initially it met with considerable enthusiasm in the West, but by the time Gorbachev addressed the G7 in July, Soviet reform plans had been watered down and the Western response had become more cautious. After the coup, the new Russian government and its advisers pleaded with the international community as a whole for a 'Marshall Plan', but the plea fell on deaf ears.[8] The first sign that a multilateral effort might be feasible was a conference on emergency aid to the former Soviet Union called by the American government in Washington in January 1992.

The background to the Washington conference on 22–23 January 1992 was the sudden realization by James Baker, the American Secretary of State, that assistance to the successor states to the USSR was a matter of urgency. The American administration had also begun to fear that the USA might be expected to foot the assistance bill, so hoped to create a coalition of donors on the model of the coalition formed to support and fund the Gulf war against Iraq in 1990–91. While the European Community suspected that the American initiative was an attempt to undermine the lead the EC had taken in providing aid, the German government, overwhelmed by the unexpectedly high cost of reunification, was reluctant to continue carrying the main burden of assistance. Thus it was vital to find new offers of help.[9]

Sixty potential donors were invited to Washington (47 of them attended, together with the representatives of five international financial institutions) to discuss how aid to the FSU could be streamlined and coordinated. The recipients themselves were not represented. Although it was not meant to be an aid-pledging event, a number of countries, including the United States, used the occasion to make widely publicized offers of aid.[10] However, the hope in Russia that the conference (or the Russian–American summit which took place soon afterwards) would produce a comprehensive aid package was disappointed. The only firm commitment was that the United States would, like Britain and the rest of the EC, support Russian membership of the International Monetary Fund (IMF). Nonetheless, there were two useful outcomes of the Washington conference. The first was the decision that the five specialized working groups set up to deal with food aid, energy, medical aid, shelter (housing for returning military personnel) and technical assistance in preparation for the conference should remain in existence to investigate what was required in their fields and coordinate bilateral assistance to prevent duplication of effort. The second useful outcome was the commitment to hold two further conferences, sponsored by the EC and Japan in turn.

The G7 and other official creditors agreed collectively to defer repayments of principal on the debts of the former Soviet Union until the end of 1992 but emergency humanitarian aid and technical assistance continued to be offered bilaterally. Tables 4.2 and 4.3 at the end of the paper indicate the amounts and various types of assistance that have been pledged. After a long period of negotiation, the IMF finally endorsed Russia's economic reform programme at the end of February. Yegor Gaidar, deputy prime minister and architect of the programme, then pleaded with the G7 for a rouble stabilization fund of $5b, as well as $6b in emergency food and humanitarian assistance, $6b in credits to fund imports and further relief on debt service.[11] Despite the general agreement among Western economists that macroeconomic stabilization was essential if hyperinflation was to be avoided,[12] the G7 still could not agree on the details of a comprehensive aid package.

At the beginning of April 1992 the IMF finally accepted Russian membership with a 3 per cent stake in the fund (the formal vote which incorporated fourteen of the fifteen former republics of the USSR took place on 27 April) and two weeks later the World Bank recommended incorporating the former Soviet republics with a 5.05 per cent of its shares (of which Russia would get 2.92 per cent). Immediately after the IMF acceptance, the details of a rescue package for Russia, to be adopted by a World Economic Summit in Munich in July, were announced: it was to consist of a $6b stabilization fund and $18b of aid and trade credits, which would include $4b from the IMF, $1.5b from the World Bank and the rest from the European Bank for Reconstruction and Development (EBRD) and bilateral export credit guarantees and food credits. The entire package depended upon an adjustment programme agreed between the IMF and the Russian government which would be monitored at quarterly intervals by Western governments and the IMF.[13]

The seriousness of the IMF conditions was demonstrated almost immediately: when the Russian government announced changes in its economic programme in an attempt to encourage economic growth, Gaidar was summoned to Washington to explain and the IMF threatened that the package would be placed in jeopardy. To stiffen Russian resolve, G7 finance ministers spelt out the conditions Russia would have to fulfil to ensure receipt of the loans: the budget deficit had to be reduced to stabilize the economy; monetary growth had to be curbed to bring inflation under control and encourage the closure of unviable industries; a legal framework necessary for privatization and private ownership had to be established; agriculture and energy had to be reformed to promote increased production and the earning of foreign exchange; a payments system had to be set up between the fifteen former republics to enable them to meet their foreign exchange obligations; and a unified and market-determined exchange rate set at a realistic level had to be introduced.[14]

The April package concerned Russia alone, but agreement was also reached on a framework for cooperation with the other successor states to the USSR. The IMF estimated that a further commitment of $20b a year would be required to assist the other fourteen states but they too would have to adopt adjustment programmes approved and monitored by the IMF.[15]

The first follow-up conference on aid to the former Soviet Union was held in Lisbon on 25 May 1992, this time with CIS participation. On the eve of the conference the five working groups, each with multilateral chairs, reported on their progress since the Washington conference in setting up missions to investigate needs, coordinating assistance and keeping a record of bilateral offers and deliveries of assistance. Several of the working groups had adopted a plan of action on which to base their future work.[16] The participants at the Lisbon conference agreed that the time had come to shift from emergency aid to longer-term assistance, aimed particularly at helping the recipients to increase their capacity to absorb aid effectively. A third conference was planned for the autumn, to be held in Tokyo.[17]

The IMF/G7 aid package announced in April was formally adopted by the G7 meeting in Munich in July. It remained unclear, however, who the donors would be. Moreover, IMF aid depended upon the American Congress agreeing to an increase of $12b in the US quota, a task that proved difficult for President Bush to achieve in an election year. The Japanese government agreed reluctantly to participate in multilateral aid but it was determined to link its own bilateral contribution to a settlement of the territorial issue of the Kurile Islands. There were also disagreements between the IMF and the Russian government in the run-up to the G7 meeting about Russia's fulfilment of the conditions set by the IMF. Under pressure from the G7, Mr Michel Camdessus announced on the eve of the meeting that $1b would be made available to Russia immediately. However, the money was to be held as reserves and could not be spent. In return the Russian government agreed to reduce its budget deficit sharply, to bring inflation down from 20 per cent to 10 per cent per month by the end of 1992, and to reduce state subsidies further. The release of further tranches of the $24b package was made conditional on a single rouble exchange rate, strengthening fiscal policy, maintaining tight constraints on monetary policy and continuing structural reforms (including land reform, bankruptcy legislation and a faster privatization programme).[18]

Yeltsin, like Gorbachev a year before, made a personal appeal to the G7 for assistance and a two-year deferral of loan repayments. And, like Gorbachev, he left the G7 meeting virtually empty-handed. The G7 agreed to support his request for debt deferral and the EC undertook to raise $700m for an emergency programme to make Soviet and East European nuclear reactor plants safe. But the leaders of the G7 countries insisted that Russia would have to fulfil all the IMF conditions before the rest of the $24b package would be released.

The special problem of defence conversion
The idea of funding economic reform by reducing military expenditure and using defence expertise in civilian production is as old as perestroika itself. By 1989 a long-term programme of conversion was being formulated and at the end of 1990 it was approved by the USSR Council of Ministers.[19] It has long been clear, however, that conversion is an expensive undertaking and that, in financial terms at least, it is more rational to shut down excess defence capacity and build new industries to expand civilian production than to convert existing defence plants. In 1990 2 billion roubles were allocated to defence conversion and it was predicted that the cumulative amount required would reach 40 billion roubles by 1995.[20] The decline in the economy, inflation and the budget deficit mean both that the costs of conversion are likely to be much higher than predicted and that the necessary investment is unlikely to be available.[21]

The high economic costs of conversion are not the only obstacle to transforming the defence industries and reducing military production. There are heavy social and political costs which make the enterprise hazardous. In 1988 the defence industries employed 7.5 million people.[22] Falling military production and the closure of defence industries will lead to massive unemployment which will be exacerbated by the fact that in some areas the entire community is involved in defence production or services to support it. In other words, in these areas there is no alternative employment for either defence workers or those who work in related service industries. Although the problem is worse in Russia than in the other republics, the geographic distribution of the defence industries in the former Soviet Union means that all the successor states will face some problems.[23]

However compelling the economic arguments are for shutting down defence plants and establishing new civilian industries, there are equally persuasive economic and social reasons for investing in conversion. There are also strong political arguments in favour of conversion and the retention of some defence capacity: while the military-industrial complex has lost a great deal of influence, it remains a powerful pressure group with the capacity to destabilize government and society. In 1990 it was sufficiently strong to influence Gorbachev's policies and in 1992 it still appeared capable of making Yeltsin's government modify its reforms.

From the very beginning of the attempt to convert defence industries, the Soviet leadership sought international cooperation in the endeavour both from foreign governments and from private business. A number of joint projects were launched, particularly in the field of aerospace.[24] While private investment and joint projects are useful, the scale of the problem and the extent to which reduced military production is tied up with international security interests indicate that this is an area in which international governmental assistance is required. The temptation for the governments of the successor states to use military production as a means of earning foreign currency will be extremely strong.

While conventional arms have aroused some concern in the international community,[25] the governments of the industrialized nations have taken the danger of nuclear proliferation far more seriously. Assistance has been offered in the form of special containers and lorries to transport nuclear warheads, expertise in the dismantling of the warheads and disposing of the nuclear fuel and guidance on dealing with pollution.[26] The danger of nuclear scientists seeking employment abroad and undermining nuclear non-proliferation by assisting aspiring governments to obtain nuclear weapons has also worried both the Russian and foreign governments. After many months of negotiation, the EC, USA, Japan and Russia initialled an agreement at the Lisbon conference on assistance to set up an International Science and Technology Centre in Moscow to provide employment for nuclear weapons specialists.

It is clear from this brief discussion that although military conversion and the demilitarization of the former Soviet Union are important for security reasons, far from producing savings to invest in reform, their cost will contribute to the economic problems of the successor governments.

The effectiveness of economic and technical assistance

What is effective assistance? At one level, the motives of the donors suggest what the answer should be: if the assistance contributes to political stability and a prosperous, open economy, it will be seen as effective. However, this answer raises a number of problems. First, it is too soon to judge whether the former Soviet Union will be politically stable. Second, the experience of economic reform in East Central Europe suggests that economic prosperity (or even growth) will take longer to achieve than was initially hoped. Third, there is a danger that the measures which must be implemented to embark upon the path to potential prosperity might threaten the fragile political stability which exists at present.

In the case of East/Central Europe, it has been suggested that the long-term aim of assistance is 'to enable the recipients to help themselves to build a viable civil society and a self-sustaining market economy'. In the short term, the goal is to ensure that the transition to democracy and a market economy is maintained. And the immediate requirement to begin the transition to a market economy is macroeconomic stabilization and the reduction of inflation.[27] These aims clearly apply equally to the former Soviet Union.

It is far too soon to assess whether the short- and long-term aims have been achieved in the successor states to the USSR, since the immediate requirements, macroeconomic stabilization and the reduction of inflation, are only now being put into place. All that can be said with assurance is that while many features of democracy appear to be absent in a number of those states, there has been no attempt since August 1991 by conservative forces to re-create a central government. Moreover, in the Russian Republic, Boris Yeltsin's government and his presidency appear to be relatively secure for the moment. The commitment of that government to market reform has been tested: the government threatened to resign *en masse* when the Russian Congress tried to water down the reform programme in April 1992.[28] The commitment of the industrialized countries to the stability of Yeltsin's government and the introduction of its particular economic programme has been demonstrated by the timing of the April aid package and the promise of the release of $1 billion in August. The announcement, and the firmness with which it was linked to the programme negotiated by Gaidar, was designed with the obvious intention of deterring the Congress from deviating from the reform.[29] Since then, however, the government has been forced by domestic pressure to modify its programme. The complete liberalization of energy prices has been postponed and two members of the industrial old guard have been included in the government. Moreover, a week after the G7 reiterated its stringent conditions for aid in Munich, the Russian parliament voted a budget that would increase the deficit to $700m roubles this year.[30]

The brief time that has elapsed since assistance was first offered is one reason why it is difficult to evaluate its effects. But there are other factors that make it remarkably difficult to assess what the impact is of different forms of assistance. A combination of too little data and confusing information makes it almost impossible to judge who has given what and how it is being used. Since donors have domestic and international political aims which do not relate directly to the assistance they are offering, they tend to announce their pledges rather than their disbursements. This can indicate to domestic publics that, while they are responding to humanitarian needs, they are not squandering national resources, for example, or can show other donors that they are participating in the international assistance effort. While it may be possible to assess how much has been promised, therefore, it is far harder to find out how much has been delivered and how it has been used.[31] Moreover, in announcing their pledges, donors frequently omit the conditions attached to them. As a result it is difficult to judge whether the discrepancy between pledges and disbursements is solely a problem of slow absorption by the recipient or whether, in fact, the conditions attached to the pledge make it impossible for the offer to be accepted (for example because the terms will raise external debt to unacceptable levels).

Assessment is also made difficult by a form of double counting. Pledges are sometimes publicly announced which turn out, on closer examination, to include commitments already made. The $24 billion of the grand G7/IMF plan, for example, is not composed of entirely new money but incorporates existing pledges by various countries. It should also be reduced by the amount of money that the new members of the IMF and World Bank have to invest in those organizations in order to become members. It has been suggested that an Assistance Coordination Council should be established for Central and Eastern Europe to coordinate aid and include the recipients as full partners in the decision-making processes about assistance. Part of its function would be the collection of accessible data.[32] Assistance to the FSU similarly requires permanent coordination, the involvement of the recipients and the collection of reliable and easily accessible data.

As far as the effectiveness of future assistance is concerned, three vitally important general points are worth emphasizing. First, the East Central European experience suggests that bureaucratic procedures must be simplified in both donor and recipient states so that the problems of effective absorption can be tackled as a matter of urgency. The second general point concerns cooperation among the successor states of the USSR. While it may not be the case that the success of individual reform programmes in the former Soviet Union requires the success of all the programmes, there is general agreement by donors that cooperation among republics is an essential ingredient of economic recovery. It is important to re-establish inter-republic trade (and also trade between the former Soviet Union and East/Central Europe). At present, however, the political difficulties of establishing cooperation are overwhelming. They are likely to increase as the wrangling continues about the division of the property and responsibilities of the former central government, and as some states introduce their own currencies. Dissolving the Commonwealth of Independent States will not resolve the difficulties and may even exacerbate existing conflicts and retard economic recovery further. The effectiveness of any future economic assistance, therefore, requires a coordinated effort by donors to persuade the governments of all the successor states that their individual interests will be best served by economic and political cooperation.

The third and most important general point centres on the link between economic reform and democracy. If assistance is intended to ensure political stability, it is essential that donors consider carefully the conditions attached to their pledges. While it is understandable that donors want to be assured of the commitment of the recipients to democracy and market-oriented reforms, if conditions are dictated without due regard for the domestic political and economic fragility, and if they threaten the viability of the government, assistance will undermine political stability rather than supporting it. This is one reason why the recipients should be involved in every stage of the decision-making about assistance. It is also why flexibility may be required in the timing and implementation of adjustment programmes. The IMF tends to use economic criteria exclusively in assessing reform and prescribing austerity programmes. It cannot be emphasized too strongly, however, that if austerity produces social and political instability, the future of economic reform will be doomed.

The security of the post-cold war world requires stable democratic government in the former USSR. It also requires that the people in the successor states should perceive that the international community is striving to alleviate the very real difficulties involved in moving from a command economy to a functioning market. Effective aid must be based on an ideal model of the correct economic route from socialism to capitalism which is modified by our security needs and the welfare of the citizens of the former Soviet Union.

Table 4.1: Assistance to the former Soviet Union, 1991/92

	US$ billion
Humanitarian (food/medical) assistance	14.93
Technical assistance	2.80
Bilateral credits	33.53
Balance of payments	3.10
Debt deferral	7.00
Total	61.36

Table 4.2: Humanitarian (food/medical) assistance to the former Soviet Union, 1991/92

Donor	Commitment ($ billion)
EC	2.640
United States	5.820
Canada	1.640
Italy	1.200
Germany	0.905
Japan	0.678
Thailand	0.500
Turkey	0.468
France	0.370
Austria	0.359
Finland	0.108
Hungary	0.100
Netherlands	0.072
Britain	0.039
Sweden	0.010
Denmark	0.007
India	0.005
Switzerland	0.004
Norway	0.003
Greece	0.002
Others	0.001
Total	14.931

Table 4.3: Technical assistance to the former Soviet Union, 1991/92

Donor	Commitment ($ billion)
EC	1.052
IBRD	0.030
EBRD	0.144
United States	0.510
Germany	0.242
Oman	0.205
Britain	0.158
Switzerland	0.113
Canada	0.093
Norway	0.090
France	0.083
Finland	0.030
Sweden	0.022
Japan	0.006
Netherlands	0.006
Australia	0.005
Austria	0.002
Belgium	0.002
Others	0.003
Total	2.796

Table 4.4: Balance of payments/credits for the former Soviet Union, 1991/92

Donor	Commitment ($ billion)
G7 debt deferral	7.00
Germany	14.40
Italy	4.56
Korea	3.00
Japan	2.00
Turkey	1.91
France	1.90
Spain	1.75
Saudi Arabia	1.50
Kuwait	1.10
United States	1.00
Netherlands	0.53
Britain	0.50
UAE	0.50
Australia	0.40
Belgium	0.40
Switzerland	0.33
Canada	0.30
Norway	0.27
Greece	0.12
Oman	0.10
South Africa	0.03
Portugal	0.03
Total	43.63

Source: Economic Relations Department, Foreign and Commonwealth Office, 28 July 1992.

Notes

1 The pre-coup economic reforms and the economic predicament in 1990 are analysed in a report commissioned by the G7, *The Economy of the USSR: Summary and Recommendations* (Washington, DC: The World Bank, 1990).
2 Gorbachev pleaded for an invitation to address the meeting. Despite an impassioned plea for assistance, he returned to Moscow from the meeting virtually empty-handed.
3 The term 'former Soviet Union' is used in preference to the 'Commonwealth of Independent States'. The two are not coterminous, of course, since the Baltic states and Georgia did not join the Commonwealth. In fact, most of the aid referred to in this paper has been offered to and disbursed in the Russian Republic.
4 Douglas Hurd, British Foreign Secretary, while insisting on self-help as well as assistance, has no doubt that international security depends upon political and economic stability in the former Soviet Union. See his article in *The Observer*, 1 March 1992.
5 The managing director of the International Monetary Fund, Michel Camdessus, calculates that if growth in East/Central Europe and the former Soviet Union reaches 4 per cent in the medium term, 1.8 percentage points will be added to world economic growth. See the report of his speech in *The Financial Times*, 26 May 1992.
6 Kuwait, for example, offered a loan of $1b in May 1990 and, after the Gulf crisis began, Saudi Arabia, Kuwait and the United Arab Emirates offered a total of $7b in loans. South Korea offered $3b in tied loans in January 1991 and a further $500m for joint projects in March 1991. The British Know-How Fund was extended to the Soviet Union in November 1990 while the European Community offered ECU 750m in food and medical aid and ECU 400m in technical assistance in December 1990.
7 A summary of the Yavlinsky–Primakov appeal was published in *The Guardian*, 31 May 1991. It called for $150b in trade credits and investments over five years.
8 For an example of the case made for international aid by an adviser to the Yeltsin government, see the article by Richard Layard in *The Independent*, 15 January 1992. Most of the calls for aid have asked for three elements: emergency food aid to prevent social unrest, foreign exchange to support the import of essential food and industrial equipment, and a stabilization fund to underpin the rouble when it is made convertible.
9 According to the European Commission, 75 per cent of all aid to the Soviet Union between September 1990 and January 1992 came from the European Community, 57 per cent of it from Germany alone. See *Keesing's Record of*

World Events, Volume 38, Issue 1, February 1992. The United States had provided only 6.5 per cent of the $80b aid and credits supplied by the West by January 1992. See the report in *The Guardian*, 24 January 1992. Germany's aid contribution to Moscow is discussed in S. Crow, 'Russian Federation faces Foreign Policy Dilemmas', *RFE/RL Research Report*, Vol. 1, No. 10, 6 March 1992.

10 The US pledged $645m in new humanitarian aid and 54 emergency airlifts of food and medicines left over from the Gulf war (worth $61m, about 2 per cent of the humanitarian aid sent by Germany in 1991), while South Korea offered $800m in loans, Thailand offered $450m for food, and Oman offered $200m for Azerbaijan's oil industry. See *The Independent on Sunday*, 26 January 1992.

11 See his article in *The Financial Times*, 4 March 1992.

12 Gaidar based his reform closely on the ideas of the Harvard School, but there seemed to be general agreement amongst economists, even those in favour of slower reform, about the order in which reform should take place and the purposes of external assistance. See, for example, the contributions in William C. Brainard and George L. Perry, eds., *Brookings Papers on Economic Activity*, No. 2, 1991.

13 An analysis of the package can be found in *The Financial Times*, 2 April 1992. The announcement was carefully timed to give political support to Yeltsin on the eve of a crucial session of the Congress of People's Deputies of the Russian Republic. The $18b of loans and credits sounded more generous than it was since it included money that had already been granted in debt deferrals and pledges that had been made at the Washington conference in January. Gaidar responded to the package and gave his view of the progress of reform in an interview given to *The Economist*, 25 April 1992.

14 Russian plans for the second stage of the reform were reported in *The Financial Times*, 21 April 1992. For the IMF response and the G7 conditions, see *The Guardian*, 24 April 1992 and 28 April 1992.

15 See the report of a press conference by Michel Camdessus, managing director of the IMF, in *The Guardian*, 16 April 1992.

16 The Medical Working Group, for example, adopted a 'health care partnership programme', while the Food Working Group adopted the World Bank's Review of Food Policy Options and Agricultural Sector Reforms; see USIA Wire Service, 28 May 1992.

17 A report of the Lisbon conference was published in *The Financial Times*, 26 May 1992.

18 *The Financial Times*, 7 July 1992.

19 For details of the plan and the difficulties of implementing it, see Julian Cooper, *The Soviet Defence Industry: Conversion and Reform* (London: RIIA/Pinter, 1991), Chapter 4.

20 Daniel Nelson, 'The costs of demilitarization in the USSR and Eastern Europe', *Survival*, Vol. 33, No. 4, July/August 1991, pp. 312–26.
21 In March 1992 the Russian atomic energy minister, Viktor Mikhailov, maintained that Russia was spending $100m per annum on converting military to civilian production. See the report in *The Guardian*, 12 March 1992.
22 Cooper, *The Soviet Defence Industry*, p. 13.
23 For the geographic distribution of the defence industries, see Julian Cooper, 'The Defence Industries of the States of the Former USSR', unpublished paper presented at the BASSEES Conference, Birmingham, April 1992.
24 For details of some of the schemes, see Cooper, *The Soviet Defence Industry*, Chapter 7.
25 In April the EBRD announced a 'swords-into-ploughshares' funding package for Eastern Europe, for example, with loans at less than market rates. See the report in *The Guardian*, 13 April 1992.
26 The UK, for example, offered £30m assistance in the form of special containers and transport for nuclear weapons.
27 Raymond Barre, William Luers, Anthony Solomon and Krzysztof Ners, *Beyond Assistance: Report of the IEWS Task Force on Western Assistance to Transition in the Czech and Slovak Federal Republic, Hungary and Poland*, Institute for East-West Studies, European Studies Center, New York, Prague, May 1992, pp. 16–17.
28 For a report of the proposals and the threat to resign, see Jonathan Steele in *The Guardian*, 14 April 1992.
29 See *The Financial Times*, 2 April 1992.
30 On the faltering of the reform, see *The Economist*, 11 July 1992. The budget is reported in *The Guardian*, 18 July 1992.
31 With regard to Czecho-Slovakia, Poland and Hungary, for example, the disbursement rates for 1990 were 4 per cent, 27 per cent and 16 per cent of pledges respectively. See *Beyond Assistance*, p. 3. As far as the former Soviet Union is concerned, much of the assistance pledged at the Washington conference had not been delivered or taken up by the time the Lisbon conference took place. See *The Financial Times*, 26 May 1992.
32 See *Beyond Assistance*, pp. 69–76.

PART II
THE REGIONAL CONSEQUENCES IN EUROPE AND THE FAR EAST

CHAPTER 5
JAPANESE–RUSSIAN RELATIONS: ISSUES AND FUTURE PERSPECTIVES

HIROSHI KIMURA

The relations between Tokyo and Moscow are among those that have been least affected by the dramatic, revolutionary changes initially triggered by Gorbachev's perestroika, new political thinking, and their partly expected and partly unintended consequences. If one accepts this general observation, the question is why it is so. The next question is whether there is any likelihood that bilateral relations between these two neighbouring countries will improve in the near future. This paper addresses these two related questions.

Changes in territorial dispute since Yeltsin
Bilateral relations between Japan and Russia take place in many fields and on many dimensions – political, military, economic, cultural and others. But nobody disagrees that the most formidable obstacle to improved relations is the dispute over the Northern Territories off the coast of Hokkaido, the northernmost of the four main Japanese islands – the islets of Habomai and the islands of Shikotan, Kunashiri and Etorofu. The Tokyo government has requested the return of these islands to Japan, but the Russians have adamantly rejected this request since the Soviet Union under Stalin seized them at the end of the Second World War. The major reason why the Northern Territories issue has remained a thorny conflict between Japan and Russia is the fact that the dispute tends to be a 'zero-sum game' in which one side gains only at the expense of the other. In contrast, the negotiation between the United States and the FSU and Russia on disarmament and arms control can reach an agreement relatively easily because it is a positive-sum game in which both sides gain from agreement, which enhances the security of each and may even enable them to devote their resources to the civilian sectors of their economies. Mikhail Gorbachev's conduct of foreign affairs, guided by the new political thinking, failed to solve this long-standing conflict with Japan.[1] During his

visit to Tokyo in April 1991, Gorbachev did not change the USSR's traditional position enough to solve this question, though he made some concessions, including his official acknowledgment of the existence of such a dispute.[2]

Since the advent of Boris Yeltsin, first as *de facto* political leader of the Soviet Union after the abortive coup in August 1991 and later as head of the CIS and the Russian Federation, some changes over the territorial dispute with Japan have been taking place. Yeltsin has come up with a new guiding principle in solving this dispute with Tokyo. Previously, the Soviet government had taken the position that national boundaries, having been set on the battlefield, are not determined by legal norms and that the Northern Territories were thus the spoils of the Second World War.[3] The Soviet position might be summarized by the maxim of a German geopolitician, Karl Haushofer, who once said: 'Boundaries are fighting places rather than legal norms of decision.'[4] During his visit to Tokyo in September 1991, Ruslan Khasbulatov, the acting Speaker of the Russian Supreme Soviet at that time, and currently the Speaker, handed a message from Russian President Boris Yeltsin to the Japanese Prime Minister, Toshiki Kaifu. Yeltsin's message underlined that the Russian Republic, which intended to become an active member of the international community, would put an end to the Soviet doctrinaire approach of regarding relations with Japan as those between a victorious and a defeated nation. Explaining the substance of Yeltsin's letter, Khasbulatov proposed that the Northern Territories dispute now be resolved on the basis of 'law and justice' (*zakonnost' i spravedlivost'*). Since that time 'law and justice' has become a catchword for the Yeltsin government's approach to the territorial dispute with Japan. The shift in the yardstick from battlefield results to 'law and justice' constitutes a revolutionary change in the guiding principle of the Russian leadership on the issue.

Unfortunately for the Japanese, however, the Russian leadership under Yeltsin has not gone any further. It has changed the principle of foreign policy, but this does not necessarily mean that Russia is ready to yield to Japanese insistence on regaining sovereignty over all four disputed islands. When the USSR disintegrated in December 1991, the Russian Federation declared that it had inherited all the international rights and obligations of the defunct USSR. This would oblige the Russian government to hand over the two islands of Habomai and Shikotan to Japan upon the signing of a peace treaty, since such an obligation was clearly stipulated in Article 9 of the Soviet–Japanese Joint Declaration in 1956, which was both signed and ratified by the

Soviet government and the Supreme Soviet. Yeltsin's associates argue, though, that it is not yet clear that the Russian Federation is also obliged to return the two other islands, Kunashiri and Etorofu. Yeltsin's advisers are divided over this question. Some of them have argued that Russia does not have to give these islands to Japan, because Tokyo relinquished the right of sovereignty over the Kurile islands in the 1951 San Francisco Peace Treaty. Others, however, think that Russia should return all four islands to Japan, since they had never been Russian territory and Russia did not sign the San Francisco Peace Treaty. Considering that neither Japan nor Russia has unquestionable legal grounds to claim Kunashiri and Etorofu, some Russian Japanologists conclude that both countries should make 'a mutually acceptable' (*vzaimopriemlemyi*) compromise.[5]

However, such a compromise is difficult to find, particularly because Japan has not shown any flexibility on the number of islands it wants the Russians to return. This leads to the conclusion that eventually the Russian side must give way. Some Russian Japanologists argue that, once the Russian government dares to make a political decision to give up all four islands, wider Russian political forces will not oppose such a choice.[6] There are several reasons why one might expect such a concession from the Russian side. First, the military-strategic value of these islands for the Russians has decreased with the end of the cold war. Second, in its efforts to pursue radical economic reforms at home the Russian government under Yeltsin badly needs money from Japan, one of the most economically powerful states in the Group of Seven (G7) Western industrialized countries. Third, gradually prevailing in Russia is the sober recognition that the failure to build a good, 'full-blooded' (*polnokrovnye*)[7] relationship with Japan over the past 47 years has been due to the Soviets' uncompromising attitude towards the Northern Territories. Let us now examine the changes which have been taking place on the Japanese side.

Flexibility on Tokyo's side
Tokyo's position on the Northern Territories was for a long time very simple: all four islands, regarded as inherent territory of Japan from both a legal and a historical point of view, must be returned *immediately as a group*. Sometime after Gorbachev's ascent to power, Japan's rigid position began to show slight flexibility, for at least two reasons. The first involved developments in the Soviet Union. Perestroika and its unexpected consequences, such as the disintegration of the USSR, required Tokyo to relax somewhat its policy

towards the former Soviet Union. Japan had to demonstrate its readiness to help Russia and the other former republics, all of which were and are facing serious economic and other crises. Otherwise Japan would have been perceived and criticized as too egocentric a nation, whose virtually sole concern towards Russia was the territorial claim. Second, the recent changes in Moscow's attitude and flexibility towards Tokyo in turn influenced Japan's attitude. Thinking that the golden opportunity to regain the lost islands might be approaching, the Tokyo government seemed to have decided that, from a tactical point of view, it was appropriate and even necessary to soften slightly its approach towards Russia.

Certainly, Tokyo began to modify its traditional Soviet policy, summarized in the principle of 'inseparability of economics and politics' (*seikei fukabun*). Tokyo regarded the solution to the political issue, i.e. the reversion to Japan of the Soviet-held Northern Territories, as a precondition for further cooperation in economic and other fields between both countries – that is, the so-called 'entrance' (*iriguchi*) approach. Moscow, in contrast, argued that developments in economic and other fields might help lead to a solution to the political issue – that is to say, the so-called 'exit' (*deguchi*) approach. Japan's principle of linking economics with politics tended to produce deadlocks, in which both political and economic improvements became marginal and did not go beyond a certain point. During his visit to Moscow in May 1989, Sosuke Uno, then Foreign Minister of the Nakasone administration, advocated a policy of 'enlarged balance' (*kakudai kinko*) or 'expanded equilibrium' (*sbalansipovannoe rasshirenie*). In an attempt to overcome the deadlock, Uno proposed a sort of middle way between the 'entrance' and 'exit' approaches based on simultaneous improvements in both political and economic areas. The Kaifu administration was the first to make humanitarian aid to the collapsing Soviet Union an exception to Japan's traditional policy of linkage between politics and economics. The current Miyazawa administration went one step further in loosening the linkage policy. In a gesture to demonstrate that Japan understands the necessity of helping the former Soviet Union in its transition to a market-oriented economy, the Japanese government accepted that economic aid to Russia and other former republics was an obligation of each member state of the G7.

As for the Northern Territories, the Miyazawa administration has demonstrated a more flexible approach by declaring, for instance, that Tokyo would no longer cling to the traditional formula of the 'immediate return of all four islands *in toto*' (*ikkatsu sokuji henkan*). Instead, Prime Minister Kiichi

Miyazawa and Foreign Minister Michio Watanabe officially acknowledge that, provided Moscow recognizes Japan's sovereignty over all four disputed islands, Japan would accept 'a two-stage formula' (*nidankai henkan ron*) for solving the issue: the return first of two islands, and then of the two others at a later stage. In April 1992, Watanabe went so far as to remark: 'If Russia acknowledges Japan's sovereignty over the four islands, Tokyo may allow Moscow to continue governing the islands of Kunashiri and Etorofu for a certain period after the other two (Shikotan and the Habomai islet-group) are returned.'[8] Koichi Kato, Chief Cabinet Secretary of the Miyazawa cabinet, considered Watanabe's remarks to be in line with the current government's position that, as long as Moscow confirms Japanese sovereignty over all four of the disputed islands, Tokyo will be flexible over the timing, modalities and conditions of their return.[9]

Constraints and obstacles

Given that both Moscow and Tokyo have recently been showing some flexibility over the Northern Territories issue, can we then expect that they will shortly solve this long-lived territorial dispute? Unfortunately, such a conclusion would be premature. There are serious domestic constraints and obstacles in Russia and in the other former Soviet republics that prevent Moscow from making a bold concession to Tokyo on the territorial conflict.

First, the eruption of Russian nationalism, which was released by glasnost and which filled the vacuum created by the collapse of communist ideology in the USSR, has made solving the territorial dispute with Japan in some ways more difficult. The demands by many of the former Soviet republics and autonomous regions for a re-demarcation of their boundaries, many of which were arbitrarily drawn in the time of Stalin and Khrushchev, make it very hard for the Russian Federation to honour Japan's territorial request. Vitaly Tretiakov, editor-in-chief of the *Nezavisimaya gazeta*, for instance, told me that 'so long as Russia is quarrelling with Ukraine over the Crimea, Russia finds it extremely difficult to yield to Japan's request over the Northern Territories.'[10] It is well known that Valentin Fedorov, the head of administration on Sakhalin, is an enthusiastic flag-bearer of those opposed to returning any of the islands. One can enumerate many reasons for this, including the failure of Fedorov's radical economic reform experiment on Sakhalin. But the nationalistic, patriotic sentiments of the residents of the disputed islands and Sakhalin undoubtedly constitute the most important reason. Letters to the editor of *Sovetsky Sakhalin* reveal how nationalistic they are: 'We will neither sacrifice our own national interests nor lose face. If we did give up the islands to Japan, our prestige as a great power would be greatly damaged'; 'A unilateral concession would hurt our patriotic sentiments'; 'Our "small motherland" must continue to be a part of our sacred and inviolable territory as it has been'; 'We cannot sell our land under any circumstances'; and so forth.[11]

Second, the fragile political power base of the Yeltsin government makes a bold decision to yield the four islands to Japan very difficult. If Yeltsin dared to do this, he would provide his opposition with a convenient political instrument to exploit in their power struggle with his government. As demonstrated vividly during the sixth session of the Congress of Russian People's Deputies held in April 1992, there are powerful conservative forces in the Russian parliament. Many conservatives criticize even the idea of receiving financial aid from the G7 advanced Western capitalist countries in exchange for successful implementation of the Yeltsin–Gaidar radical economic reform plan, which is not only supported but also partly administered by the International Monetary Fund (IMF). These forces would not endorse any plan that seemed like selling land to Japan for money. Thus, even if Yeltsin signs a peace treaty or other document with Tokyo, in which he agrees to return the islands, there is a good chance that such an agreement would not be ratified by the Russian Supreme Soviet.

Put simply, it was previously the Soviet leadership but now it is both conservative opposition forces and nationalistic public opinion, particularly in the far eastern part of the Russian Federation, that Japan has to contend with. In this regard, it is interesting to note that in October 1991 Russian Foreign Minister Aleksandr Kozyrev said to his Japanese counterpart Taro Nakayama, 'Let us *jointly* work together to achieve our *common objectives*' (author's emphasis).[12] One example of such a Japanese–Russian joint effort is an agreement reached by the two Ministries of Foreign Affairs concerning the publication of a volume of historical documents and materials on the Northern Territories. It was a pleasant surprise for the Japanese side to learn that the Russians agreed not to include in this volume 'Nishimura's Reply to the Diet,'[13] in which Kumao Nishimura, Director-General of the Department of Treaties at the Japanese Foreign Ministry at the time, stated in 1952 in the Japanese Diet that 'Kunashiri and Etorofu belong to the Kurile islands that Japan renounced in the San Francisco Treaty.' In the past the Soviet Union had never failed to cite this statement in contesting Japan's legal arguments.

Yeltsin's scheduled visit to Tokyo

In the light of the positive and negative changes recently in Russia, what could be Yeltsin's choices when he visits Tokyo on 13–15 September 1992 (when this volume will be in the process of publication)? He has four theoretical options. He could propose to Japan a return of: (1) none of the islands; (2) two islands; (3) two islands plus alpha; or (4) all four islands. Let us examine each of these options.

Should Yeltsin pursue the zero-island option, he would have done better to postpone his visit to Tokyo: it would not be very different from Gorbachev's visit in April 1991, which was a great disappointment to Japan. Yeltsin is expected by Tokyo to do more than Gorbachev, not least because this will be his second visit to Japan. During his first, albeit unofficial, visit, Yeltsin proposed a 'five-stage solution to the Northern Islands'.[14] This helped make him rather unpopular in Japan because his proposal advocated that the final disposition of the islands be determined by the next generation, which would have shelved the dispute for many years. Since then, Yeltsin has often repeated that his 'five-stage solution' must be accelerated; the first and second stages have already passed and we are now on the third stage.[15] Yet it is highly unlikely that Yeltsin will choose the fourth option, the reversion of all four islands, if only because of his domestic situation. The above-mentioned constraints and obstacles, which could have increased by mid-September, make attempting such a breakthrough in Russo-Japanese relations extremely difficult.

Logically, then, the options open to the Russian government and specifically to Yeltsin during his official trip to Tokyo in mid-September are the 'two-island' or 'two-island plus alpha' formula. The pessimists in both Japan and Russia tend to think Yeltsin is more likely to choose the former, whereas the optimists are inclined to anticipate the latter. The two-island option means that Yeltsin would confirm the validity of Article 9 of the 1956 Soviet–Japanese Declaration, in which the Soviet Union promised to hand over the Habomai and Shikotan islands. This option would not be warmly received in Japan, because even in 1956 the Tokyo government under Prime Minister Ichiro Hatoyama rejected the return of only two islands (which accounted, moreover, for only seven per cent of the entire disputed territory). Since that time, Japan's national strength has expanded phenomenally, and Tokyo has become much more confident in its bargaining position. Since 1956 the Japanese government has assumed that the territorial controversy actually revolves around the remaining larger islands of Kunashiri and Etorofu. It is therefore unthinkable that Japan would now agree to something it did not agree to 36 years ago.[16]

The two-island option would not necessarily be a wise idea for Yeltsin either. In 1956 the USSR wanted to conclude a peace treaty with Japan, which would have been a diplomatic achievement at that time. What Russia seeks from Japan today, however, is not simply the conclusion of a peace treaty, but also the development of a 'full-bodied' relationship between the two nations. Russia wishes to obtain the active and willing cooperation of the Japanese government, business community, and general public. It is not an exaggeration to say that both positive endorsement of the G7 aid programme and actual assistance from Japan are critical to the success of Russia's radical economic reforms.

On balance the approach most likely to be taken by Russia in the near future will be the 'two-island plus alpha' formula, of which there are many versions. When alpha equals zero, the formula becomes the 'two-island' plan; when alpha equals two, the formula becomes the 'four-island' plan. Therefore, 'alpha' equals more than zero but less than two. However, alpha cannot possibly be one, that is to say a 'three-island' formula, because it would create the impression that both Japan and Russia would accept a deal which incorporated compromise but not principle.

Since a viable numerical solution to the 'two-island plus alpha' option is not apparent, the option left for Yeltsin involves a qualitative alpha. For instance, he could agree to handing over the two smaller islands when a peace treaty is signed and make a statement in Tokyo that his government promises to conduct serious negotiations with Japan on the other two islands – although the Japanese government would then be concerned that such a promise could serve to postpone the solution indefinitely. For its part Tokyo will try hard to force Yeltsin to clarify the direction and the specific time framework for negotiations over the two remaining islands. Japan will insist that the alpha be concrete enough to give Japan confidence regarding eventual reversion. The Japanese will also press Yeltsin to say what he will do if there is a deadlock, while Yeltsin will probably want to make his commitment to negotiate over the two other islands as vague and abstract as possible. Thus a key issue during Yeltsin's visit to Tokyo will be the firmness of Yeltsin's commitment on the last two islands. Although the Japanese cannot force the Russians to do anything, particularly in light of domestic situations facing the Yeltsin government, the more concessions the Russian government makes, the more it will obtain from Japan in terms of economic cooperation and assistance.

Future prospects

What are the longer-range prospects for Russo-Japanese relations? To offer a bold conclusion, I predict that all four disputed islands will be returned to Japan by the year 2000. There are several grounds for this belief.

To begin with, the military-strategic reason why the former Soviet Union clung so adamantly to its physical occupation of these four tiny islands (i.e. the Soviet military regarded them as absolutely necessary for its 'bastion strategy' in the Sea of Okhotsk) has lost its significance as a result of the end of the cold war. Economically, the region surrounding the Northern Territories is rich only in fish, which the Russians do not value as highly as do the Japanese. Moreover, Russia urgently needs Japanese economic assistance and cooperation, particularly for the development of its far eastern region.

The chief remaining obstacle in a settlement of the Northern Territories issue seems to be psychological. Many Russians, particularly in the far eastern region (including the residents of the disputed islands themselves), still oppose the transfer of the islands, regarding it as selling their holy motherland to capitalist Japan for money. There are also political forces that want to take full advantage of nationalist and patriotic feelings in their power struggles against Yeltsin's leadership. But eventually the economic and political gains to be obtained from Japan through the transfer of the islands will overcome this psychological and political resistance. Also over time the Russian people will come to understand that, from both the historical and the legal point of view, these islands did not belong to the former USSR. They will 'sooner or later'[17] be persuaded to return all four islands in an exchange for large-scale economic assistance and other types of benefits from Japan. Just as the Soviet attitude towards the Germans and unification of the two Germanies changed very quickly within a few years, the chances are that the Russian attitude towards the Japanese and the territorial issue will also change very rapidly. As Konstantin Sarkisov, director of the Centre for Japanese Studies, at the Institute of Oriental Studies in Moscow, has argued: 'The twentieth century was an era of territorial expansion and territorial conflicts. The twenty-first century should never repeat such experiences. Thus the territorial disputes initiated in the twentieth century must be settled within the century, so that the twenty-first century can be formulated in a completely new fashion.'[18]

Notes

1 For more details on Gorbachev's policy on the Northern Territories issue, see Hiroshi Kimura, 'Gorbachev's Japan Policy: The Northern Territories Issue,' *Asian Survey*, Vol. XXXI, No. 9 (September 1991), pp. 798–815; 'The Soviet–Japanese Territorial Dispute,', *Forum*, Vol. 2, No. 6 (The Harriman Institute, June 1989); 'Japanese–Soviet Relations: On the Frontier,' in Gregory Flynn, ed., *The West and the Soviet Union: Politics and Policy* (New York: St Martin's Press, 1990), pp. 156–93.
2 Kimura, 'Gorbachev's Japan Policy,' pp. 810–15; *Vizit M.S. Gorbacheva v Iaponiiu (16-19 apreliia 1991 goda)* (Moscow: Politizdat, 1991).
3 The Japanologist Khaim Eidus, for example, wrote in the 1960s, 'The victory of the Soviet army gave back to the people of our country the South Sakhalin and the Kurile Islands.' Khaim Eidus, *SSSR : Iaponia : Vneshnepoliticheskie otnosheniia posle vtoroi mirovoi voiny* (Moscow: Nauka, 1964), p. 9.
4 Quoted in Derwent Whittlesey, *German Strategy of World Conquest* (New York: Farrer and Rinehard, Inc., 1942), p. 95.
5 See, for instance, Konstantin Sarkisov, *Izvestiya*, 31 August 1990.
6 At the conference held in Tokyo on 30 March–3 April 1992, many Russian experts in Russo-Japanese relations expressed such a view. They included Vedren Martynov, the director of the Institute of World Economy and International Affairs, Russian Academy of Sciences (IMEMO), Valery K. Zaitsev, head of the Centre for Japanese and Pacific Studies, IMEMO; Sergei E. Blagovolin, head of the Security Department, IMEMO; Konstantin O. Sarkisov, Centre for Japanese Studies at the Institute of Oriental Studies; and Geli Batenin, Yeltsin's adviser on military affairs.
7 For example, *Pravda*, 20 December 1989.
8 *The Japan Times*, 22 April 1992, p. 1.
9 Ibid.
10 Interview on 14 February 1992. On the other hand, however, having been enlightened by a private briefing given to him by Russian Deputy Foreign Minister Georgii Kunadze, Aleksandr Rutskoi, the Russian Vice-President, reportedly said that 'when we get back the Crimea from the Ukrainians, we will give the islands back to the Japanese' (confidential source in April 1992).
11 *Sovetsky Sakhalin*, 17 December 1990.
12 *Asahi Shimbun*, 16 October 1991.
13 *Hokkaido Shimbun*, 18 April 1992.
14 Yeltsin's 'five-stage solution' programme calls for (1) an acknowledgment of the territorial issue by the Russians within two to three years; (2) a conversion of the islands to free trade zones in three to five years; (3)

demilitarization of the islands in five to seven years; (4) conclusion of a peace treaty in 15 to 20 years; and (5) the resolution of the dispute by the next generation.

15 A Japanese official quoted Yeltsin as explaining to Michio Watanabe on 4 May 1992 that the third stage of his five-stage plan was near completion as many of the troops were preparing to leave what the Japanese called their 'Northern Territories'; Kyodo News Service, 5 May 1992.

16 In this regard, Harry Gelman seems to be correct when he writes: 'The Japanese reaction would be negative ... It would be too late for such a partial concession; Japanese public opinion would no longer tolerate a deal that failed to return all four islands to Japan.' Harry Gelman, *The Soviet Military Leadership and the Question of Soviet Development Retreats* (Santa Monica: The Rand Corporation, 1988), p. 5.

17 Interview on 29 April 1992 in Moscow with Viktor Bosnuyk, Institute for the USA and Canada, Russian Academy of Sciences.

18 Interview in Moscow on 25 September 1991.

CHAPTER 6
THE IMPACT OF CHANGES IN THE FORMER SOVIET UNION ON THE COMMUNIST STATES OF ASIA

YOSHIAKI NAKAGAWA

The cold war is over. History has advanced into a new era. In East Asia, however, there remain strange exceptions to the world trend – namely, China, North Korea, Vietnam and Laos – which are typical and significant specimens of the few remaining communist regimes.* These four East Asian regimes insist on their legitimacy – and even sometimes their supremacy – each with its own justification. Common sense tells us, however, that no one nation can long deny the general tide of the times.

In this paper I shall examine, first, the origin of the impact of specific changes in the former Soviet Union (FSU) on the Asian communist states, and then the principal implications of these changes, assessing their probable political, economic and military consequences.

The origin of the impact
The failed Soviet coup of August 1991 had the effect of greatly accelerating the changes that had already been set in motion in 1985 with the beginning of perestroika. These changes are still in progress, and nobody knows what their final consequences will be. Transformations are occurring in many different areas of the FSU, at varying speeds. They will have differing impacts on the world at large. In discussing the implications that they carry for the Asian communist states, it will be useful to sort these changes into the following four categories: (1) changes relating to the dissolution of the Soviet-style centralized power structure; (2) changes concerning the dissolution of the Communist Party; (3) changes that occur due to the malfunctioning of the central command economy; and (4) changes in the FSU military power structure.

---

*Cambodia is considered by some to be under communist leadership; however, as it is now engaged in a peace process under the United Nations Transitional Authority in Cambodia, for the purpose of this chapter I will not include it among the Asian communist states.

Dissolution of the Soviet-style centralized power structure

The Soviet-style centralized power structure, which originated in the Tsarist empire, had two main pillars: the Soviet Union itself, and its satellite states. The secession of the satellite states from the centralized Soviet structure became irreversible as a result of the renunciation of the Brezhnev Doctrine, the 1989 East European revolution, and prolonged turmoil in the FSU. The possibility of coercing the satellite countries (including Mongolia, which has become an exception among the Asian communist states by embracing liberal democracy) to return to a Soviet-style centralized power structure appears quite unlikely, even if an authoritarian regime should emerge based on strong Greater Russian nationalism in the Russian Federation.

It is apparent that the process of dissolution of the centralized power structure in the Soviet Union itself has now gone beyond the point of no return. The two major elements of the centralized power structure apparatus, the Communist Party and the KGB, have been disbanded.

The potential role of the Commonwealth of the Independent States (CIS) remains uncertain but it is apparent that the CIS is in extreme turmoil. The existence of a common interest and basic needs, however, means that some form of central authority is quite likely to remain, with the assigned functions of managing the remaining Soviet nuclear arms and power plants, operating railway systems, and coordinating external relations. The CIS could be a candidate to become the next central authority. However, a central authority which is based simply on basic needs and common interest cannot become a simple substitute for the role that the Soviet communist government played. Therefore, the dissolution of the Soviet Union's centralized power structure can be judged now as conclusive and irreversible.

In its wake, the nationalistic sentiments and local independence movements that have been activated in the dissolution process can be expected to have an impact on the Asian communist states. Among the four countries mentioned, this impact will be greatest in China, next in Vietnam and Laos, and perhaps smallest in North Korea.

Dissolution of the Communist Party

The Soviet Communist Party has been disbanded. Its monopoly rule disappeared along with the FSU. Some traditionally communist organizations which remain, however, still possess a strong base, and certain ex-communist party elites continue to function as political and economic leaders. This is due in part to the fact that the best and the brightest in the Soviet Union usually entered the party system in order to rise to a status appropriate to their ability.

Therefore, total abolition of all remnants of the system is unrealistic if the society of the FSU is to be preserved.

It also seems unrealistic, however, to think that these leaders could reinstate the authority of Marxism-Leninism as the orthodox ideology. Ever since Stalin named the Second World War the 'Great Fatherland War', communism in the Soviet Union was gradually transformed into an instrument used to justify the Soviet-style centralized power structure, and thus to assure Russia's control over the entire Soviet Union. It is easy to understand, therefore, how the national movements activated in the republics of the FSU have so easily gained momentum, and have become a substitute for the communist ideology lost after the dissolution of the centralized power structure. In a sense, in the post-communist era we can now observe the reality of Soviet society. Furthermore, outside the Russian Federation, the nationalism that has arisen is inevitably opposed to the previous Greater Russian nationalism. It is becoming more and more difficult to imagine the reinstatement of the communist ideology which acted as a justification of the past power system.

The dissolution of the Communist Party in the FSU is irreversible. The CPSU was the first communist party in the world to seize power and had been the leader of the international communist movement. Its dissolution has direct impact on other communist parties which maintain monopolistic rule in their respective countries and is thus equally damaging to the Communist Parties of China, North Korea, Vietnam and Laos.

Malfunctions in the central command economy
Explanations of malfunctions in the central command economy in the FSU are almost too apparent to write here. In order to control the republics and the satellite states under the communist party within the Soviet-style centralized power structure, it was essential to maintain a central command economy. This type of economy was a useful political instrument for creating a one-party communist dictatorship and maintaining the privileges of the communist leaders. Therefore, it follows that the dissolution of the centralized power structure and of the communist party would result in the disappearance of the need to maintain the central command economy. The central command economy in the FSU is functioning no longer.

But, in actuality, the performance of the central command economy was poor long before changes began in the FSU, mainly due to an artificial division of labour which operated without having a market system as a coordinating tool. The need for reformation of the central command economy system was and is widely recognized by leaders in the communist states around the world and was the major reason why the Soviet Union began perestroika. Now the only way of revitalizing the FSU economy is to struggle along the road to a market economy. It is a risky, narrow path, fraught with many hazards, such as hyperinflation, extreme levels of unemployment, and marked inequality among the living standards of the people.

The experience of the FSU might lead us to expect that any reform of a central command economy which is initiated by the political leadership, backed by Marxist-Leninist ideology, is destined to fail.

The leaders of the East Asian communist states could dismiss the case of the FSU as one where the Soviet Union failed in hasty political reform which was basically irrelevant to economic reform. Nevertheless, these leaders must address the problems of economic reform in their own countries. And in addition to issues of reform, the East Asian communist states must in some way overcome three consequences of Soviet policy: cutbacks in aid from the FSU, a new trade policy that relies on hard currency, and a decrease in trade due to the current economic chaos in the FSU.

Changes in the military power structure
The largest and most powerful Soviet military forces have been gradually withdrawn from the global arena. The dissolution of the centralized power structure and the ensuing economic chaos have significantly restricted the military power projection capability of the FSU.

Most of the CIS member states are establishing military forces of their own, but pledge to use these forces only for self-defence and the enforcement of internal order, and not for external deployment. The Russian Federation is an exception, as it possesses a strategic nuclear force: it will operate according to a different principle, while remaining defensive in nature. Because of the inevitable global implications of a nuclear force, the Russian Federation may retain limited external deployment capability.

The sudden decrease in the Soviet military threat to the north has resulted in a fundamental change in the geopolitical situation of East Asia.

Implications for the East Asian communist states
China
The dissolution of the Soviet-style power structure has revealed prevalent nationalism and local independence movements among ethnic minorities. Such developments are very alarming to China, which has been faced with internal disputes in Tibet and other regions inhabited by ethnic minorities.

More significant than this, however, is the fact that China wishes to unite Hong Kong and Taiwan, where the people already enjoy a high level of economic prosperity, with itself. Furthermore, China's new neighbours in Central Asia, the republics of the former Soviet Union, are hotbeds of ethnic nationalism and local independence movements. They are geographically adjacent to the areas where China's potential problem ethnic minorities live.

The difficulties China faces in managing the ethnic problems that have arisen are shown by its controversial use of force internally: such use of force definitely affects Chinese attempts at unification. The dilemma of maintaining internal order while seeking unification with Hong Kong and Taiwan will grow even larger in the near future as a result of increasing ethnic group challenges to Chinese authority.

The dissolution of the Soviet Communist Party and the collapse of the Soviet central command economy has raised questions about the legitimacy of the present regime in China. Historically, the strong leadership of the communist party was a crucial factor in achieving China's national independence. This is one reason why the Chinese communist regime retains its power and claim to legitimacy even after the collapse of the Soviet Union. Further, it can appeal to the people's feelings of nationalism in order to support the present regime.

The Communist Party of China, however, now realizes the difficulty of maintaining its legitimacy via this ideology; indeed, long before the beginning of perestroika in the Soviet Union, the Chinese Communist Party realized the importance of economic performance in sustaining its legitimacy. Its efforts at economic reform have made the present economic situation in China far better than that in the FSU. The leadership can thus use the argument that a collapse in the social order, such as occurred in the FSU, would greatly jeopardize economic development and destroy the present standard of living, and further remove opportunities for a better life in the future.

This implies that the Chinese Communist Party will continue its double-track approach towards sustaining its legitimacy as a regime. This approach is characterized by tight political controls and calls for internal stability, accompanied by open economic policies to create a better standard of living for the people. The Chinese government is searching desperately for the best balance between a hardline domestic policy and an open economy. Though they may possess different views on specific matters, many party leaders believe that their present approach is the best and indeed the only possible choice if they are to manage China.

Gradually the question of whether or not China is still a communist state will become obsolete because the essence of Chinese-style communism is evolving. However, there are doubts about whether the Chinese Communist Party will continue to maintain its one-party dictatorship in the future.

The reality of the situation is that, though politics can be used to intervene in the economy, it cannot wholly control economic developments. It cannot even control political developments. The question remains as to whether or not the Chinese style of communism can coexist with an open economy. Undoubtedly, the political concerns of the Chinese Communist Party may seriously affect the economic development of China, as well as cause cracks in the legitimacy of the regime – just as the Gorbachev administration did in the Soviet Union.

To look at another aspect of the Chinese economy, a major problem lies with the decentralization of the economy under the open economic policy. The resulting growth of regional divisions and greater assertions of regional authority may imply that the communist party will remain the only effective national organization or political tool which can sustain the unity of China. The force of decentralization coming from economic development may have been reinforced not only by the massive size of the country and the lack of a unified market, but also by China's own economic policy.

The sudden decrease of the Soviet military threat from the north implies a great opportunity for China. First, China could eventually become the sole military force capable of power projection in East Asia, even though that capacity may be limited. China can use this situation as a political tool and it is understandable that Sino-Vietnamese relations have improved lately. Second, China may be able to obtain new weapons and weapon technology from a supplier other than the Western developed countries. The FSU can supply weapons and technology via many means, from illegal export to official military cooperation. For the republics of the CIS, military sales to and military cooperation with China could help in efforts to maintain their military industry and to foster economic development. Third, China could cut its own military force further. China had, however, already planned a reduction in forces, and is currently executing that plan. It will probably be difficult to persuade the military to accept further reductions, but it is useful and rational for China to try to do so in order to accelerate economic development.

North Korea
In North Korea, the implications for the legitimacy of the present regime are almost the same as in China. The major difference between China and North Korea is that the economic situation of North Korea is not good enough to

allow the government to assert its success in economic development. The North Korean leaders are thus seriously concerned about their hardline administration, fearing that it may be fighting a losing battle against the general tide of the times and may be destined to collapse in the near future.

The dissolution of the Soviet centralized power structure, however, may not have a direct, immediate impact on North Korea because of the country's relatively small size and ethnic homogeneity. By maintaining extremely strict control over information in the country, the present regime is able to cope effectively with any local uprisings.

The sudden decrease in the Soviet military capability implies that the importance of China has dramatically increased for North Korea. China can exert more leverage on North Korea than previously.

North Korea's intention to obtain nuclear weapons must be viewed in this context. As it watched the collapse of the Soviet Union, its strongest ally and the counterbalance to China's power in the region, North Korea rightly felt fearful of international isolation and has therefore intensified its efforts to obtain nuclear weapons as a political bargaining chip. These tactics seem to be working: very few states challenge the country's hardline policies and human rights restrictions because they are preoccupied with North Korea's potential nuclear threat. But while many fear the possible results of North Korea's nuclear programme, its economic difficulties, especially those related to a limited oil supply and a low operability in industries, have severely limited the country's capability to sustain a war.

Economic implications, as shown in Tables 6.1 and 6.2 at the end of this chapter, involve a dramatic decrease in the amount of economic aid from the (former) Soviet Union and a downturn in trade between the FSU and North Korea. Considering the fact that North Korea's industrial base was built by Soviet economic assistance and that North Korea has depended heavily for its energy supply on oil and coal exports at discount prices from the Soviet Union, the North Korean economy has been seriously damaged. The percentage of factories in operation has fallen below 50 per cent.[1] The decline in agricultural production due to unpredictable weather and the Soviet decision to set trade exchanges in hard currency have made the situation worse. At present, shortages of foreign exchange, food and fuel are major obstacles for North Korea. There is no way to overcome these other than to pursue, to some extent, the rapid implementation of an open economic policy.

Vietnam

The question of the legitimacy of the present regime in Vietnam in principle resembles that of China, but the dissolution of the Soviet-style centralized power structure has had no significant effect on Vietnam, as it is a relatively small country that does not contain the same number of ethnic groups as the FSU.

From a military standpoint, Vietnam's situation is similar to that of North Korea, and Vietnam too will continue to struggle in the shadow of China. For economic reasons described below, Vietnam will encounter difficulty in procuring advanced technological weapons, resulting in a weakened military force. We can predict that Vietnam will eventually lose its status as the greatest military power in Southeast Asia. In comparison with industrialized North Korea, Vietnam is basically an agricultural state and cannot produce its own arms, at least not in the near future.

As is shown in Tables 6.1 and 6.3 at the end of this chapter, the dramatic decrease in the amount of economic aid from the Soviet Union and the downturn in trade between the FSU and Vietnam will have a great impact. As with North Korea, Vietnam's industrial base was built by Soviet economic assistance, and the Soviet decision to conduct its foreign trade in hard currency has created a grave situation within the Vietnamese economy. The major difference in comparison with North Korea is that Vietnam is an exporter of food and crude oil. In 1989, it exported 1.4 million tons of rice to become the world's third largest rice-exporting nation, and sold 1.5 millions tons of crude oil to other countries.[2] Economically, Vietnam is in a more stable situation than North Korea, and may perhaps be considered second to China in economic wellbeing.

The leaders of Vietnam are currently attempting a program of economic reform, called *doi moi.*, which dates back to late 1986. Vietnam's efforts to create an open economy and to cooperate with the Western capitalist states have clearly helped it. The result can be seen in Vietnamese exports, where goods sold to the world's 'hard currency areas' have exceeded those sold to the 'non-hard currency areas' (mainly the Soviet Union and its satellite states) since 1989.[3]

Obviously, Vietnamese leaders realize that the only way to go beyond the economic stagnation that has plagued Vietnam is to cooperate with the capitalist West – in particular, with the United States. In fact, Vietnam is making overt attempts to improve its relationship with the US, including stepping up efforts to resolve the MIA (missing in action) issue. Ultimately,

Vietnam is looking for the US trade embargo to be lifted in order to improve its overall economic situation.

Laos

As regards the effect of the dissolution of the Soviet power structure on the legitimacy of the regime, the situation in Laos resembles that of Vietnam. The magnitude of the problems in Laos is greater, however, owing to the desperately poor condition of the Laotian economy and the lack of an intellectual class that could give rise to an internal democratic movement.

Since 1988, the present regime, led by the Laotian People's Revolutionary Party (LPRP), has continually made efforts towards economic reform. The leaders of the LPRP have not, however, shown any willingness to give up their party's dictatorship. They have apparently chosen to follow a policy similar to China's double-track approach.

The Laotian economy was in desperately poor straits even before the Soviet collapse. The gross national product per capita was US$200 in 1990.[4] Suspension of foreign assistance from the Soviet Union, coupled with the switch to a hard-currency-based trade, imposed even further burdens on this rice-producing, agricultural country. It has become difficult for Laos to sustain even marginal economic growth. Economic liberalization is necessary if Laos is to obtain aid, vital to its very existence, from the world's industrialized countries.

The consequences

Overall view

In general, the critical issue which will decide the future of the existing East Asian communist regimes is that of legitimacy. In any case, as these countries seek stable economic growth, critical to establishing the legitimacy of their regimes, they are in effect inviting the collapse of the traditional Marxist-Leninist one-party dictatorship. Therefore, their demise is only a question of time and manner.

It is probable that most – or perhaps all – of the East Asian communist states will progress towards authoritarian-pluralistic political systems[5] with developmental market economies, rather than towards the Western-style liberal democracy in the first steps of their evolution.

In fact, this general trend is obvious if we examine changes in China and Vietnam from the mid-1980s until now. Further evidence can be seen in the actions of North Korea in the 1990s, for example in its eagerness to undertake the Tumen River Project.[6]

From a military standpoint, the forecast for the near future for Asia is calm, except for some minor potential disturbances. As China and Russia devote themselves to internal reform, we can be assured that a major conflict in Asia will not break out. The use of military force will most likely be limited to specific areas where regional conflict or domestic disputes arise.

China
China is now poised at the edge of a era of uncertainty. In particular, a leadership change is imminent. At present, the Chinese leadership has given priority to tightening internal politics and fostering economic openness via a double-track approach. However, the dilemma of aligning the differing objectives of these two processes may well cause China itself to implode.

China is now greatly affected by two decentralized power sources – ethnic nationalism and the local independence movements – which were activated by the collapse of the FSU and the result of economic reforms in China.

The decentralizing process in China is irreversible. There are, however, certain counterbalances that may slow down or limit the process. First, China is ethnically dominated by the Chinese race, which comprises more than 90 per cent of the total population. Second, the introduction of economic reforms has had notable positive effects in rural agricultural areas. The prospects for persuading the people that it would be better to avoid rapid and extreme changes are fairly good. Therefore one result of the inevitable decentralizing process in China might be the development of a loose federation system. The future of the Chinese Communist Party is largely dependent upon its flexibility. Judging from its actions and policy in recent years, there is a great likelihood that it will be able to adjust to the necessary changes.

We must realize that the transformation of China involves risks. In the worst scenario, a mass migration of people to economically prosperous regions within China or even beyond its borders might result. This could seriously threaten the stability of the entire East Asian society and might have global repercussions.

Because of its huge size, the country's transition to a new authoritarian pluralistic political system will take a long time. The transitional period in China will be different from that of the FSU, but at present it is difficult to predict the process or results.

North Korea
North Korea now lags far behind its colleagues in East Asia. Even if it has demonstrated slight changes in economic policy, its overall progress is slow.

At present, the charisma of Kim Il Sung and his *chuche* ideology allows him to control the force of change in North Korea. As in China, however, the transfer of power to a new generation is imminent. The son of Kim Il Sung, Kim Jong Il, does not have his father's charisma; his power will be based only on the *chuche* ideology. As we have seen, though, ideology alone is not sufficient for maintaining a power structure. Once the leadership changes, the situation in North Korea will become very fluid.

It is unlikely that North Korea will pursue unification with South Korea. Even normalization of relations between the two Koreas, which would be the basis for unification, would at the same time allow greater exchange of information. Because the legitimacy of the North Korean regime is heavily dependent on the myth that North Korea's system is supreme in the world and especially is superior to South Korea's, it would be dangerous to allow the North Korean people to find out about the true situation of their southern neighbours. Of course, North Korea's rigid control of information and unbending stance toward South Korea is based on the desperation born of the need to sustain the regime at any cost, but in future this strategy may prove to be self-destructive.

We must consider a wide spectrum of possibilities in trying to predict the future configuration of the North Korean state, from a Romanian-type revolution to an ideological bastion – the last Stalinist communist state to survive in the twenty-first century.

Vietnam

Vietnam possesses the greatest flexibility with regard to its basic conditions. In general, the small size of the state will help the government to maintain its control but, lacking strong charisma, the present regime has already sunk very low in the eyes of the people. Therefore, economic performance will provide the impetus for change in the near future, regardless of the present regime's efforts to retain tight political control. Eventually, Vietnam will slip away from the ranks of the communist states.

Considering the dramatic economic policies carried out in recent years and the fact that there remain people well-trained in the workings of a market economy in the southern part of Vietnam, we may look to Vietnam as a possible leader in the transition process for the East Asian communist states.

If the leaders continue to be as rational as they have been recently in making efforts to seek the normalization of relations with the United States, it is almost certain that Vietnam will have the leading edge among the East Asian communist states.

Laos

Kaison Phomvihan, the present leader of the LPRP, will continue his dual-track approach to preserve the regime because there is no other option. Under the auspices of the IMF, Laos is relying on the industrial countries, such as Japan and the United States, to provide the financial aid which allows it to maintain some economic growth. Laos will remain the poorest nation among the four countries presented here, whether or not it embarks on a programme of political liberalization in the foreseeable future.

Conclusion

The full consequences of the global changes which were activated by the FSU have not yet developed and the speed with which each East Asian communist state will respond is variable. Because the leaders of these states have gradually come to realize that the economic success of their regimes is critical to their legitimacy, the general policy trend now evident in the remaining communist regimes is a double-track approach with two different objectives: first, a political tightening to ensure internal stability; and, second, open economic policies promising a better standard of living. Even if the efforts made in these directions could be considered vigorous and reliable, the prospects of success will be rather limited because politics will not remain the master of economy as time progresses, even in communist states. A nation's economy is of first priority to the lives of its citizens. In this regard, the natural human desire to seek a better standard of living can be recognized as a basic human right. Therefore, as long as there are differences in the economic growth of nations, pressures of migration will increase and may result in a mass outflow of people.

In the post-cold war world, there is a need to address what could be the next global challenge – a mass population outflow from the economically disadvantaged countries. In particular, in China, Vietnam, North Korea and Laos, this is an undeniable possibility because of the inevitable political changes that will occur in these countries in the near future. Should such mass migration begin, we may have to open discussions on controlling a potential 'population and migration bomb', rather than talking about the current issue of how to handle the nuclear arms of the former Soviet Union.

Table 6.1: Economic aid from the Soviet Union to the Asian communist states (in millions of $US)

Country	1984	1985	1986	1987	1988	1989	1990
North Korea	55	93	6	-33	-41	-16	0
Vietnam	1,040	1,160	1,325	1,575	1,365	1,110	585
Cambodia	87	98	128	134	137	159	110
Laos	77	100	74	94	86	75	70
Mongolia	785	918	905	991	987	995	965

Table 6.2: Trade between the FSU and North Korea (in millions of roubles)

Year	Total	Exports from FSU	Imports to FSU
1985	1,059.2	654.8	404.4
1986	1,207.9	757.2	450.7
1987	1,232.1	800.2	431.9
1988	1,601.7	1,062.2	539.5
1989	1,502.0	940.5	561.5
1990 (1–6)	778.9	481.0	297.9
1991 (1–6)	451.9	223.2	228.7

Table 6.3: Trade between the FSU and Vietnam (in millions of roubles)

Year	Total	Exports from FSU	Imports to FSU
1985	1,458.9	1,176.1	282.8
1986	1,612.7	1,318.4	294.3
1987	1,773.4	1,454.5	318.9
1988	1,782.2	1,393.6	388.6
1989	1,910.6	1,390.9	519.7
1990 (1–6)	1,176.3	847.6	328.7
1991 (1–6)	486.4	263.3	223.1

Note: All tables are taken from *Economic Relations between the Asian Socialist States and the Former Soviet Union and Eastern European States*, in-house report published by the Japan Association for Trade with the Soviet Union and Central-Eastern Europe, Tokyo, 1992.

Notes

1 *Asian Security, 1991–1992*, compiled by the Research Institute for Peace and Security (New York: Macmillan Publishing, 1992), p. 156.
2 *Economic Relations between the Asian Socialist States and the Former Soviet Union and Eastern European States*, in-house report published by the Japan Association for Trade with the Soviet Union and Central-Eastern Europe, Tokyo, 1992, p. 41.
3 Ibid., p. 20.
4 *World Development Report 1992* (New York: Oxford University Press, 1992), p. 218.
5 Robert A. Scalapino, 'The United States and Asia: Future Prospects', *Foreign Affairs*, Vol. 70, No. 5, Winter 1991/92, p. 23.
6 Sugimoto Takashi, 'The Dawning of Development of the Tumen River Area' (Tokyo: IIGP Policy Paper 75E, March 1992).

CHAPTER 7
THE IMPACT OF CHANGES IN THE FORMER SOVIET UNION ON EASTERN EUROPE

YVES BOYER

Between May and December 1989, forty years of communist reign collapsed suddenly in Eastern and Central Europe. After the surprise and euphoria of experiencing freedom, the task of reconstruction appeared immeasurable. Beyond the River Elbe towards the east, the texture of society has to be rebuilt, democratic institutions need to prove their capacities to harmonize conflicting views, ecological disasters have to be confronted, security concerns have to be totally reassessed and the economic mechanisms have to be radically transformed.

From the Baltic coasts of Poland to the Bulgarian shores of the Black Sea, six European countries (not to mention Albania and the former Yugoslavia) are in desperate need of restructuring. All have experienced fruitful but traumatic ruptures with the old order. Such revolutionary changes have left them with feelings of isolation after the collapse of such Soviet-controlled frameworks as the Warsaw Pact and the Council for Mutual Economic Assistance (CMEA) in the absence of immediate alternative options. The transitional period from political, security and economic subordination to Moscow's Marxist-Leninist rule to free-market societies, turned towards Western institutions, makes these countries very vulnerable.

In the economic and political arenas, two phenomena are closely linked. Internal change towards a free-market economy is an essential prerequisite to a reorientation towards the Western economic sphere. In return a political benefit is expected: integration into current West European institutions and particularly the European Community. For those countries such an objective is more than a question of economic advantage, it represents 'the safest means to guarantee the establishment of democracy and to find a definitive place for the people of countries whose existence has been threatened many times over the centuries'.[1]

In the political domain, many East and Central European countries will have to overcome centrifugal forces when various ethnic groups cohabit in the same country. In more homogeneous ethnic countries such as Poland or Hungary, there is less danger of an internal fracture. There is, however, the potential risk of involvement with neighbouring populations of Polish or Hungarian origin located in Romania, Ukraine, Slovakia and so on, giving birth to associated risks of a radical transformation of the geopolitical scene in the heart of Europe. Accordingly, the parameters within which the external security of Eastern and Central European countries should be established are now very difficult to define. Without exaggeration, one can apply to the whole of this part of Europe the remarks of a Hungarian observer about his country: that it is becoming 'militarily indefensible, economically vulnerable, and politically unstable'.[2]

When looking at the impact of changes in the FSU on Eastern Europe, one has also to consider the side-effect of the transformation of this part of Europe on the transatlantic relationship and particularly on the respective roles of the USA and Western Europe in the post-cold war era.

The economic depression
Three years after the 'velvet revolution' in Eastern and Central Europe, the transition from a state-controlled economy to a market system was proving to be far more complex and difficult than anticipated. In his 1991 New Year address to his fellow countrymen President Vaclav Havel recognized that 'the reconstruction...will take more time than we anticipated and will cost more than we initially thought....What appeared a year ago as a deteriorated system is, in fact, a ruin'.[3] A year later, the Czechoslovak president reflected a growing sense of disillusion in his country because economic progress had not followed political liberalization, when he asked : 'Why, at a time when no other power threatens us or interferes in our affairs and, for the first time in centuries, for us as a state and as citizens our fate is really in our own hands, why do we have hardly any reason for joyful happiness? What are the roots of our nervousness, confusion, impatience and often even of hopelessness?'[4]

The task of reconstruction in the eastern part of Europe is indeed appalling. Beyond the general consensus that these countries must gradually adopt the Western way of economic development, no comprehensive economic and societal model can be applied. There is clearly no single model of capitalism. Among Japan, the United States and Western Europe, and even among individual West European countries, there are more than slight differences regarding the functioning of economies and the mechanisms of social protection. To explain the successes of Western economies solely by the law of the market is an oversimplification of the complexities of the Western model of development. However, it is simply the market which is presented as a miracle solution to the citizens of Eastern and Central Europe. Up to now, unfortunately, they have experienced an aggravation rather than an improvement in their situation.

The economic depression is indeed very severe in Eastern and Central Europe. It began in the early 1980s when it was marked by a slowing down of economic growth, which fell from 4.2% per head in the 1970s to 1% between 1980 and 1985.[5] Real decline has accelerated since 1988. Between that date and the end of 1991, the volume of internal production has fallen by 25% on average.

All sectors of the economy have been affected. Industrial production declined in 1991 by 12% in Poland and 60% in Albania.[6] For the third consecutive year since 1989, agricultural production continued to decrease although the situation was already difficult in this sector. In Poland, for example, even with subsidies, agricultural outputs in 1989 were less than half those obtained in the EC.

These very bleak figures have to be offset against the consideration that the collection of statistical data in this part of Europe is undergoing a process of radical change. It is most likely that official statistics do not yet incorporate the very recent development of the private sector. In addition, it is almost certain that, during the communist era, firms tended to exaggerate their production in order to prove they had fulfilled their required quotas under the plan.

The capacity of East and Central European countries to invest in order to rebuild their industrial and agricultural production is essential for their economic recovery. However, there are still many obstacles to national or foreign private and public investments, ranging from weak economic performance to political instability and slowness in establishing legislation for a market economy.

Privatization of the economy is an immensely difficult task to manage, considering that before 1990 the public sector represented 65% of production and 70% of employment even in Hungary (the lowest percentage in the former CMEA); in Czechoslovakia (which had the highest percentage in the former CMEA), it was 97% and 85% respectively.[7]

Inflation is an additional burden for the leaders of Central Europe in their attempt to reorganize their economies: in 1991 it reached 44% in Poland, 78% in Bulgaria and 367% in Romania.[8] Unemployment figures are also appalling and the trend is very negative: in Poland, for example, unemployment rose from 0.3% of the working population in December 1989 to 6.5% in January 1991; total unemployment in Eastern and Central Europe more than doubled in 1991, to almost 6 million.[9]

In economic relations Eastern Europe and the former Soviet Union accounted for only 5% of world trade in 1989;[10] each East European country was then trading mainly with the former USSR even if, in some countries, trade was increasing with the European Community; for example, in 1988, 28% of Poland's external trade was with the EC.[11] In 1990, Moscow reduced by 40% its purchases from East and Central European countries, thus accelerating the pace of the recession. On the whole these cumulative difficulties have provoked what is described as 'shortagflation', a mixture of inflation, unemployment and shortage of goods.

The great hope that followed the 1989 upheavals in Eastern Europe has now given way to a far more sober appreciation of the economic and political problems of these countries. The transformations they will have to achieve are enormous and will take many years to bear fruit. This is the paradoxical legacy of the transformation of the FSU for Eastern and Central Europe: the collapse of Soviet control led to the establishment of free democratic institutions but at the same time to deadlock in the economic development of these countries. Reconstruction will take time and, during that period, the structural economic adjustments will have serious consequences in terms of unemployment and standards of living. This uncertain transition, with its high social costs, may have a heavy political impact on both the internal and the external stability of the region. This is all the more worrying at a time when there is a security vacuum in the heart of Europe as the result of the demise of the Warsaw Treaty Organization.

The political uncertainties
Among the many political uncertainties surrounding the progress of democracy, two are of particular importance for the peaceful development of the transition period: the functioning of democratic institutions and the ethnic problem.

The capacity of the newly democratic regimes to implement the urgent reforms towards modernization are highly dependent on the correct functioning of political institutions. These institutions will be tested to their limit in forging an enduring consensus to fulfil the task of renovation necessary in each country. The situation of the three members of the 'Visegrad Triangle', i.e. Poland, Czechoslovakia and Hungary, will be of particular importance because of their weight and the potential stabilization effect they can have in *Mitteleuropa*.[12]

In these three countries the seeds of discord are already sprouting. In a well-established democratic regime the problems could easily be solved; in the very volatile and fragile situation prevailing in Central Europe, they may prove to be far more difficult to overcome.

In *Poland* instability has characterized political life since the establishment in September 1989 of the first government inspired by Solidarity and led by Tadeusz Mazowiecki. His successors have as yet been unable to forge a minimal consensus among the new Polish political elite. The respective powers of the president, the government and the parliament remain undefined, and this has contributed to the deepening, enduring political crisis in Warsaw. The conflict between President Walesa and Defence Minister Jan Parys of the Olszewski government over control of the armed forces revealed in early 1992 the uncertainties which bear upon the proper functioning of democratic institutions in Poland. The crisis took a new course when on 26 May 1992, Lech Walesa asked the parliament to designate a new government since 'the relationship between the government and the president has reached an unprecedented level of crisis ... and the destabilization of the structures of the State has become so acute since irresponsible measures were taken in external affairs'.[13] The political crisis lasted five weeks and ended with the appointment of the fifth prime minister in Poland since the communists lost power in 1989. The elected prime minister, Mrs Suchocka, a member of the Democratic Union party, led a coalition of seven parties among the 29 represented in the Sjem, the Polish lower chamber. Faced by so many political parties, one wonders whether Poland does not run the risk in the long term of being both ungovernable and untransformable.

In *Czechoslovakia*, relations between the Czechs and the Slovaks have been very delicate and seem likely to lead to a partition of the Federal Republic. Since the adoption in December 1990 of the law organizing the division of competencies between the Federation and the two Republics, the future of the federal state has been on the agenda. Advocates and opponents of the unity of Czechoslovakia were struggling for the success of their respective causes. The movement for secession was particularly strong in Slovakia. In July 1991 a leader of the Slovak Christian-Democrat party, Jan

Carnogursky, even proposed, the creation of a national Slovak army.

The difficulties between the two republics have been exacerbated by economic differences. Heavy industries are concentrated in Slovakia, where 80% of the arms industries are located. The crisis in these specific sectors explains why 12% of the working population are unemployed in Slovakia, against 4% on average in Czechoslovakia as a whole. Federal and national parliamentary elections held on 5 and 6 June 1992 finally stimulated negotiations which envisaged the partition of the Federation into two independent republics by the autumn of 1992. The electoral campaign revealed the splintering of the new political life in Czechoslovakia: more than forty political parties appeared on the scene. The movement for a democratic Slovakia (HZDS), led by Vladimir Meciar, won the election in Slovakia. After being nominated prime minister of Slovakia, Meciar began talks with his Czech counterpart, Vlaclav Klaus. After the failure of their talks both leaders announced together, on 19 June, an agreement to split Czechoslovakia in two. Then events accelerated. The new federal parliament in Prague did not re-elect former president Havel, whose mandate comes to an end in October 1992. Havel immediately presented his resignation on 17 July, on the same day that the Slovak parliament voted a declaration of sovereignty, leading to the end of the 74-year-old republic of Czechoslovakia. Both Meciar and Klaus went onto agree a peaceful division of the federation, with a law to be voted by the parliament on 30 September 1992. Although in areas like foreign and defence affairs both leaders wanted to maintain privileged contact between the two republics and declared that they would accept the international agreements signed by Czechoslovakia, some issues may become a bone of contention, such as the question of Czechoslovakia's $9.1 billion net foreign debt.

In *Hungary*, the political situation has up to now evolved more smoothly than in the two other countries of Central Europe. Budapest, however, is burdened by several internal problems. One is linked to the control of the armed forces. There is a creeping struggle between the civilian authorities and an 'old guard' of officers still attached to the old order and seeking to preserve its control. Despite the offer of resignation by the Chief of Staff, General Kalman Lorinz, to President Arpad Göncz in July 1991, the issue is not yet resolved. A second question concerns the very slow progress towards economic recovery despite the plan launched in September 1990 by the democratically elected government of Prime Minister Jozsef Antall.[14] The growing dissatisfaction of a larger segment of the population may force Antall, a moderate leader, out of power. This may open the way to a populist leader building a constituency on the dissatisfaction stemming from the economic situation as well as the irredentism of a large part of the Hungarian population.

This third issue is of growing importance in Hungary, where the Trianon Treaty of 1920, which deprived the country of two-thirds of its historical territory, is still disputed by part of the population. Eighteen per cent of the 13.3 million Hungarians live outside Hungary. About two million live in Romania, where the elimination of the Ceaucescu regime eased the situation of the Hungarian minority in Transylvania. However, a growing divergence in economic development between the two countries may rekindle the aspiration of the Hungarians living in Romania to become part of their former country. This could take the shape either of a mass emigration or of demands for the reintegration of Transylvania into Hungary. The Hungarian minority living in Vojvodina (Vajdasag in Magyar) is also of concern for Budapest since its autonomous status within Serbia is questioned by the Milosevic government. With the independence of Slovakia the situation of the Hungarian minority there (0.6m) may be exacerbated. Slovakia was part of the Hungarian monarchy for 1,000 years and Bratislava, under the name of Poszony, had been for 150 years the capital of Hungary. At present, Budapest and Bratislava have divergent views about the construction of a dam on the Danube. Budapest is questioning the relevance of continuing the project, decided in 1977, which appears now irrelevant for economic and ecological reasons. The issue is now becoming a bone of contention between the Hungarians and the Slovaks and may exacerbate tensions if the Hungarian minority's interests are ignored or neglected by the new independent Slovak republic. This may even led this minority to press Budapest for protection if not renegotiation of the borders between Hungary and Slovakia, thus starting a process of destabilization of Central and Eastern Europe.

Other minorities issues in Eastern and Central Europe are undoubtedly arising: Russia even accuses the Romanian authorities of giving weapons to the Moldovans. In Yugoslavia events arising have degenerated into a dramatic civil war. Difficulties began in Yugoslavia soon after the death of Tito; in 1981 the Albanian population from Kosovo provoked unrest, feeling their rights were being neglected by the Serbs. The economic crisis in Yugoslavia during the mid-1980s exacerbated tensions between the various republics of the federation. In January 1990, at the 14th congress of the Communist League of Yugoslavia (CLY), the Slovene representatives were unable to win acceptance for their proposal for a democratization of the CLY. This opened a split within the party and, in the April 1990 elections in Slovenia, democratic forces in favour of independence won a majority. Similar events occurred in Croatia. Only months later, in February 1991, both republics declared they favoured the dissolution of Yugoslavia into sovereign and autonomous states. A referendum held in Croatia in May 1991 gave a huge majority for independence, the polls having been boycotted by the Serbian minority. Five weeks later, on 27 June, fighting began in Yugoslavia; in 1992 it spread from Croatia to Bosnia-Hercegovina. The EC tried hard through its mediator, Lord Carrington, to find a solution. The situation was so deadlocked that the CSCE too proved to be rather ineffective. The UN Security Council passed resolutions condemning Belgrade, organizing a boycott of Serbia and Montenegro and trying to find a solution. One such move was Resolution 743 (21 February 1992), which created a peace-keeping force of 14,000 blue helmets (UNPROFOR) to guarantee the many ceasefires that had been declared and violated between the Serbs and their opponents. However, despite the internationalization of the crisis it remains doubtful that any country (or group of countries, such as the members of the WEU) wishes to become deeply entangled in rivalries for which no solution is readily at hand. The widespread view is that, besides humanitarian aid, the best plan is to establish a cordon sanitaire to avoid any spread of the conflict into other countries.

Attempts at reconstruction in East and Central European countries

After their emancipation from the USSR, East and Central European countries went through a series of different adaptation phases. Whether they aimed at reorientating their economic development or, particularly after the coup in Moscow, somehow finding a solution to their search for security, they definitely turned their backs on Moscow and headed towards Western institutions.

As early as the summer of 1989, the leaders of the G7, during their annual meeting,[15] realized the urgent need to help economic reform in those countries in Eastern and Central Europe which were initiating changes, at that time essentially Poland and Hungary. A mandate was given to the European Commission to coordinate assistance to both these countries. In order to increase this aid, it was agreed to work with specialized institutions (OECD, IMF, World Bank, etc.) and to open the coordination programme to other states. A group of 24 OECD countries (the G24) is now working to assist Eastern and Central Europe. The EC Commission launched a comprehensive aid programme for restruction in Poland and Hungary, the PHARE programme (Poland and Hungary: aid for economic reconstruction), which was later extended. The EC Commission also negotiated agreements for association, first with Poland, Hungary and Czechoslovakia in the autumn of 1991 and later with Romania, Bulgaria and the Baltic states.[16] These agreements are for an indefinite period. They have four components: to organize commercial, economic and cultural cooperation and to develop the political dialogue. In the preamble to the agreements, the parties recognize that the ultimate objective of the associated countries is to become members of the European Community. A transitional period for application of the agreement is organized in two stages of five years each.

In addition the European Bank for Reconstruction and Development (EBRD) was created in May 1990, following a French initiative supported by the European Council held in Strasbourg some months earlier. The aim of the EBRD is to help the reconstruction of economies in the former Soviet bloc, provided that the recipient countries respect democratic principles and restructure along market economy lines. These goals have also been incorporated in the association agreements currently being negotiated between the EC Commission and Romania and Bulgaria.

Individual countries have also participated in the reconstruction of Eastern Europe, particularly through investments. The Federal Republic of Germany has the greatest share, as indicated in the tabulation below, which shows estimated foreign investment in Eastern Europe and the FSU between January 1990 and April 1991, in millions of ecus.[17]

FRG	556	France	178
Austria	447	Switzerland	141
USA	445	UK	120
Italy	333		

For a short time the countries of Central Europe hoped that, after a relatively rapid period of association, they could become fully-fledged members of the EC. The first disappointment was a declaration by President Mitterrand that 'accession to the EC by East and Central European countries cannot occur for decades'.[18]

This matter reflected in large part an internal EC issue, in which those who favoured widening EC membership were motivated by a wish to obstruct the further deepening of integration among the existing EC members. London particularly favoured widening and Paris deepening. Germany appeared to be oscillating between them but seems to have grown closer to the French view in recent months, as was highlighted by the declaration of the minister of state from the German Foreign Ministry that 'Poland, Czechoslovakia and Hungary would have a realistic possibility of joining (the EC) around the year 2000'.[19] At the same time Chancellor Kohl underlined the fact that Germany had reached the limit of its capacities to help the ex-Soviet bloc countries and asked for a greater contribution, particularly from Japan.[20]

The task of integrating even the most developed countries of Central Europe will prove to be a real challenge for the EC since there are still huge economic differences between the two parts of Europe. In 1989 the per capita income (in 1980 dollars) was $4,700 on average in Eastern and Central Europe, half that of the EC as a whole. This disparity had been increased by the recession of 1990–92, which has relegated them more than ever to the periphery of the prosperous core of Europe.

In the security field, the adaptation of Eastern and Central Europe has taken various forms. The first one was the initiation of a restructuring of the armed forces which involved a purge under the pretext of reducing their strength. This is why, for example, in Poland 9,460 officers have left the services; this purge has been, however, far more difficult to implement in other countries, particularly in Hungary. The reshuffle of the armed forces also took the form of a territorial reorganization as well as the adoption of new concepts such as the Czechoslovak doctrine of 'reasonable defensive sufficiency', which may continue to be the doctrine of both the Czech and the Slovak Republics.

The second dimension of the changing security situation of the Central European states has been the development of bilateral treaties or agreements, particularly but not exclusively with their eastern neighbours. For example, Poland signed a treaty of friendship with Russia in May 1991, Hungary did the same with Ukraine, and Czechoslovakia with Germany in January 1992. Many of these agreements incorporate a provision guaranteeing respect for the rights of minorities. This has been the case, for example, in the Polish–Ukrainian Declaration of Friendship of October 1990, the Polish–Belarus agreement of October 1991 and the Hungarian–Ukrainian Joint Communiqué of April 1992. Many agreements have been also concluded with West European countries regarding the exchange of military personnel and regular meetings between Chiefs of Staff.[21]

More politically-oriented regional rapprochement initiatives have also proliferated (such as the Visegrad Triangle, the Pentagonale, the group of Danube States, the Alpen-Adria group, the Baltic Pact).[22] The most important of them has undoubtedly been the cooperation process between Poland, Hungary and Czechoslovakia initiated at the Visegrad summit in Hungary on 15 February 1991. Later on, at their Prague summit, the leaders of the 'Triangle' published a Declaration[23] in which they disclosed their long-term goals: 'They stress that the deepening and the widening integration (in the EC) are compatible with each other and emphasize their interest in using the European Agreements on Association with the EC to prepare their respective countries for fully-fledged membership of the European Union.' They also reaffirmed their long-term commitment to becoming members of NATO. At the same meeting, the leaders of the Visegrad group sent a message to the Group of Seven (G7) suggesting 'that the role and the interests of the countries of the Visegrad Triangle be taken account of during the Munich summit', so demonstrating the current links between economic and political questions.

These measures are not considered in many circles to be sufficient in themselves to guarantee the security of the Central European countries. According to the former Polish defence minister, Polish sovereignty could only be protected by cooperation and ties with Western countries, not through internal organizational changes in the armed forces. This largely explains the decision taken by the former Soviet bloc countries to get as close as possible to NATO using a step-by-step approach. This was considered with great interest by the NATO allies. Many leaders from the new democracies were invited to Brussels to address the North Atlantic Council. President Vaclav Havel was the first Chief of State from a former Warsaw Treaty Organization country to deliver a speech in which he expressed the hope that his country might soon become a member of NATO.[24] NATO began to develop a comprehensive policy towards the former Eastern bloc at the London summit in July 1990 when the Alliance invited the USSR and its allies to establish a political liaison with it. At the NATO meeting in Copenhagen, in early July 1991, it was decided to launch a policy of 'partnership with the countries of Central and Eastern Europe'[25]. Months later, at the Rome summit, and taking into account the aborted coup in Moscow, NATO went further in proposing the creation of a North Atlantic Cooperation Council (NACC), which held its first meeting in late December with foreign ministers and, in April 1992, with defence ministers. Membership of NATO is undoubtedly the focus of a struggle regarding which political forces will become pre-eminent in Eastern and Central Europe. On that matter – following the divorce between the Czechs and the Slovaks – one may be witnessing the emergence of a group of countries (Poland, Hungary and Slovakia) willing to create a kind of common market and developing closer collaboration in the field of foreign and security affairs, but less integrated into Western institutions than was initially thought in the early 1990s. The Czechs, because of their relatively higher standard of living, for their part would become more or less absorbed into the Western sphere of influence.[26]

East and Central European security and Western attitudes

The collapse of the Warsaw Pact and the radical changes in Eastern and Central Europe have made the current security architecture in Western Europe virtually obsolete. NATO and probably the WEU in their present forms will need drastic adjustments. Already, tensions can easily be distinguished in the Western camp between the need to preserve the current arrangements because of the stability they guarantee and the temptation to modify them to take into account the new international deals and the modified equilibrium stemming from the collapse of the Soviet order and the strengthening of the EC structure.

There are already clear signs of the way in which the United States and some West European countries intend to adapt the Atlantic alliance to the new geopolitical situation. The French authorities have, for example, expressed their reluctance to see the NACC overextending itself beyond its present function, that of a forum of exchanges and consultation. Backed by Germany and Russia, they have argued in favour of a transformation of the CSCE into an international organization with effective powers.

Gradually two views of security developments in Europe are emerging. One is the American vision based on the concept of 'interlocking institutions'. NATO will continue to function as a security guarantee for its members; the European Union will constitute at last the European pillar of the Alliance; as for the CSCE, it may see its powers reinforced by NATO. This should give birth to a strategic axis spreading from Vancouver to Vladivostok,[27] largely controlled from Washington. An alternative view is, however, considered in some West European countries. It consists of developing a narrower pan-European framework of cooperation within the Atlantic Pact. At the heart of this architecture lies the EC, which will initiate defence policy through growing links with the WEU. Thus, from Brest to Brest-Litovsk, a European confederation will emerge. In this conception the Euro-American connection will exist under the aegis of a stronger CSCE.

Which of these models will develop is a function of many factors; what is certain is that the role of Eastern and Central Europe will be crucial in forwarding the existence of either. If these countries desperately seek immediate protection, they will move towards establishing the closest possible links with NATO as it stands today. If the current transition period were to be succeeded soon by a modicum of stability, they may find more advantage in gradual participation in the West European institutions, including those aimed at preserving security.

Notes

1. Jerzy Lukaszewski (Polish ambassador to France), 'Europe: l'attente des pays de l'Est', *Le Figaro*, 28 April 1992.
2. Rudolf L Tökés, 'From Visegrad to Krakow: Cooperation, Competition, and Coexistence in Central Europe', *Problems of Communism*, November/December 1991.
3. Vaclav Havel, speech published in the *New York Review of Books*, 7 March 1991.
4. Vaclav Havel, quoted in *IISS Strategic Survey 1991–1992*, p. 28.
5. North Atlantic Council Economic Commission, Interim Report of the Subcommittee on East–West cooperation and economic convergence, 'Retrospective des relations économiques Est-Ouest de l'après-guerre. Réforme économique en Hongrie: Bilan', Norbert Wieczorek, November 1990.
6. UN Economic Commission for Europe, 'Evènements récents dans la région de la CEE'. UN Press Communiqué, 24 March 1992, United Nations Information Service, Geneva, Switzerland.
7. Figures from *L'Economie mondiale 1990-2000: l'impératif de croissance* (Paris: Centre d'Etudes Prospectives et d'Informations Internationales [CEPII]/Ed. Economica, 1992), p. 521.
8. UN Economic Commission for Europe, op. cit.
9. Ibid.
10. CEPII, op. cit.
11. David Marsh, 'Central Europe surveys an imperfect pact', *The Financial Times*, 11 May 1992.
12. Those three countries represent about 65 million inhabitants (Poland: 38.2m, Czechoslovakia: 15.7m, Hungary: 10.6m) and are of direct concern to Western economic and security interests. Bulgaria (9m) and Romania (23.6m) are at a different stage of development and their potential entry to the EC is even more remote.
13. Lech Walesa, quoted by *Le Monde,* 25 May 1992: 'M. Walesa demande à la Diète de constituer un nouveau cabinet'.
14. In 1989 Hungary had an external debt of $21bn, which made it the highest per capita debtor in the region.
15. 'Sommet de l'Arche', Paris, 14–16 July 1989.

16 Czechoslovakia was the first country from Eastern and Central Europe to ratify the agreement, in March 1992.
17 'Les coupables hésitations françaises', *Le Figaro*, 15 April 1992.
18 François Mitterrand, interview, Radio France Internationale, 12 June 1991.
19 'Germany grows Cool to Entry of Ex-East Bloc States into EC', *International Herald Tribune*, 14 May 1992.
20 'Kohl plead for Aid to the Ex-Soviet Bloc', *International Herald Tribune*, 6 May 1992.
21 During his visit to Hungary, Sir Michael Quinlan, then Permanent Under-Secretary at the British Ministry of Defence, concluded various agreements with his Hungarian counterparts, such as the training of Hungarian officers in British military academies. Such agreements have also been concluded with other West European countries.
22 On this question see Libor Roucek, *After the Bloc: The New International Relations in Eastern Europe*, RIIA Discussion Paper No. 40, 1992.
23 6 May 1992.
24 21 March 1991. It was decided in Budapest on 25 February 1991 to dissolve the military structure of the Warsaw Pact by 31 March 1991; in Prague the political structure was dismantled on 1 July 1991.
25 Statement issued by the North Atlantic Council meeting in ministerial session in Copenhagen on 6 and 7 June 1991.
26 This, at least, is a view put forward by Meciar. See 'Un entretien avec le premier ministre slovake', *Le Monde*, 7 July 1992.
27 See James Baker's speech in Berlin, 18 June 1991.

CHAPTER 8
THE SECURITY IMPLICATIONS OF CHANGES IN THE FSU FOR WESTERN EUROPE

TREVOR TAYLOR

Introduction: the established impact of the Soviet Union on Western Europe's security policies

Politicians and academics in the field of international relations in the 1990s are constantly challenged to find new and striking language which does justice to the continuing change in the European security situation since President Gorbachev's UN General Assembly speech of December 1988. Moreover, European security remains in a state of transition and it is not clear what its next stable condition will be.

To assess the impact of change in the former Soviet Union (FSU) on West European security policies, it is important to recall the influence of the old Soviet Union in such matters. During the cold war, the military threat to Western Europe posed by the Warsaw Treaty Organization (WTO) was real and pressing. Even in the mid-1980s the Soviet High Command was still making the massive preparations meant to give it a capability to invade and quickly overrun Western Europe. We do not know if the Soviet political leadership was ever even tempted to use its armed forces against the West. We do know that it sought to maintain the option of being able so to do.[1] This made defence and deterrence of the Soviet threat a priority task for the West, indeed the foundation for West European security and defence policies was the Soviet challenge at the heart of Europe and in the wider world. The chief problems for West Europeans were to get the nuclear and conventional elements in their capabilities in an appropriate relationship, and to make a sufficient contribution to the overall effort for the United States to remain engaged in Europe. In retrospect, few significant military or political problems could have been expected had all West Europeans been willing to spend perhaps four per cent of their national product on defence.[2]

The confrontation with the Soviet Union also coloured many West

European attitudes towards security issues in the wider world, beyond the NATO area,[3] where the recent collapse of their empires had made many West European states reluctant anyway to contemplate serious military action. The pressing nature of the Soviet threat in Europe meant that few European resources could be spared for out-of-area activities, and even Britain and France had to devote a steadily larger share of their defence resources to the defence of Europe. Also, since much of the developing world was affected by the global competition for influence between the two superpowers, UN requests for substantial European forces to intervene in a region of conflict were unlikely. On the other hand, to a limited degree, the forces which the West Europeans designed to defend against the USSR had the potential to operate elsewhere. Britain demonstrated this during the Falklands war. While France continued to operate some small, light professional forces mainly for use in its former empire in Africa, from the mid-1980s it planned its Force d'Action Rapide, a 40,000-man force designed for use either in the NATO area or beyond. The 1991 war against Iraq finally demonstrated what happened when well-prepared Western forces, designed with the Soviet Union in mind, took on even the large forces of a developing state. In brief, while the weight of the point should not be exaggerated, the confrontation with the USSR meant that Western Europe developed some forces which could be used in other contexts.

By early 1992 that confrontation was over. The Warsaw Pact had been disbanded, most of the former Soviet Union had become the fragile Commonwealth of Independent States, CIS forces had left the Czech and Slovak Federal Republic (CSFR) and Hungary and were on target for a scheduled withdrawal from Germany and Poland by the end of 1994. Yet much remained to be settled. None of the political systems in place in Eastern Europe (including the FSU) appeared assured of survival and, despite the commitments made in the Paris Charter of November 1990 not to change borders by force, the territorial limits of several new states were in question. Ethnic struggles were proliferating and no acceptable principles were apparent to shape their solution. Finally, no former communist state had succeeded in making the transition to a growing market economy. Thus a dangerous but straightforward condition of confrontation had been replaced by one dangerous in different ways and infinitely more complicated. While Brezhnev was in power in the Kremlin, the West needed to pay little attention to the cultural characteristics of the Uzbeks or to the political aspirations of the Chechens.

Immediate Western reactions: adjusting to a diminishing threat

Between 1990 and 1992 West European states, acting individually and through NATO, adjusted their collective posture to take account of the diminishing threat from Moscow. The goal was to maintain prudent defences against residual capabilities controlled from Moscow while ensuring that militaristic forces in Russia did not feel unnecessarily provoked or pressured. NATO worked to reassure its own populations that their defence was being provided and to reassure Moscow that NATO had no aggressive or hostile intent.

What was the nature of the residual Moscow-based threat? Even in early 1992 there were still more than 200,000 Russian/CIS troops in Germany which could cause considerable damage. Fundamentally, forward-based Russian/CIS forces were incapable of sustained aggression without the support of their former WTO allies, with the CIS conscription in disarray, and with the Russian/CIS defence industry deeply disrupted by cuts in procurement spending and by Ukrainian independence. The Russians in Germany had considerable potential (though happily not the inclination) for crime and terrorism. By 1994 Russian/CIS forces should have withdrawn completely from Germany and Poland. Also, in mid-1992 it seemed unlikely that CIS conventional forces would persist for long, even in name. Ukraine, other republics, and from May 1992 Russia itself were intent on establishing their own armed forces. Thus, if all goes well, NATO will have a substantial territorial buffer between itself and Russian troops by 1994.

On the nuclear front, the situation was different in that Russian capabilities certainly would remain extensive and there was the added possibility that Ukraine, Belarus and/or Kazakhstan might try to acquire control of the nuclear forces based on their territory. Fundamentally, West Europeans could do nothing to prevent a successful nuclear attack against them should Russia (or another former Soviet republic) decide to launch one. So long as it remained a coherent state, Russia would remain a nuclear superpower with thousands of warheads at its disposal. On the other hand, it was hard to imagine the political circumstances in which Russia or any other former Soviet republic would find it rational to launch such an attack.

Between 1990 and 1992 the states of Western Europe were able to adapt their national political postures and conventional military capabilities so as to match the changing situation in the East. National defence budgets were cut on a unilateral basis, with countries generally spending around two per cent a year less on defence. Equipment spending was particularly cut back and projects were consequently deferred or stretched.[4] At their London summit in July 1990 the states of NATO took the political initiative by announcing that the states of the still-existing WTO were no longer to be treated as adversaries and that a process of political liaison would be established. Political liaison was further reinforced in November 1991 at the Rome summit when NATO states agreed to establish the North Atlantic Cooperation Council (NACC), on which all the states of the by then defunct WTO could be represented.

A comprehensive review of NATO's posture was inaugurated. The first fruits of this came in the spring of 1991 when, recognizing the changed threat situation, NATO announced the end of its eight-corps, 'layer-cake' force structure in the Central Region and the introduction of a new force structure. Emphasizing the defensive, non-provocative orientation of this structure, NATO forces were divided into three classes:

- *Immediate and Rapid Reaction Forces* consisting mainly of the Allied Command Europe (ACE) Mobile Force, the Standing Naval Force in the Mediterranean and a new Allied Rapid Reaction Corps to be commanded by a British officer. It emerged that this corps would consist of eight divisions drawn from a range of countries, to be available on two weeks' call. However, it was envisaged that only four such divisions would be deployed in any single crisis.
- *Main Defence Forces* made up of the 'bulk of forces needed to ensure the Alliance's territorial integrity and unimpeded use of their lines of communication'. It was planned that there would be five, largely multinational, corps, which would include some 'Ready Manoeuvre Forces' kept at a high level of manning and readiness.
- *Augmentation Forces* which were 'means of reinforcing existing forces in a particular region'. They would be mainly but not exclusively North American and would include active and reserve units.

NATO stressed the shaping concepts of multinationality, flexibility and mobility behind this force structure.[5]

NATO also amended its command structure both to simplify it and to lay somewhat less stress on the central region of Europe. The Major NATO Commander (MNC) post of Commander-in-Chief Channel (Cinchan) was abandoned. Two MNCs were retained for the Atlantic (Saclant) and for Europe (Saceur). Under Saceur were three Major Subordinate Commands for the Southern, Central and Northwest Regions, the latter absorbing some of the former Cinchan's roles. Planning was initiated for each of these regions to have Principal Subordinate Commands and in the Central Region the number of such commands was reduced to two (for Land and Air Forces) to replace the five geographically-based commands previously in operation.[6]

Finally, at its Rome summit in November 1991, NATO agreed a New Strategic Concept which gave up the strategy of flexible response but did not replace it with any clear-cut commitment not to initiate use of nuclear weapons: 'nuclear weapons make a unique contribution to rendering the risks of any aggression incalculable and unacceptable'.[7] NATO continued to insist that non-strategic nuclear weapons should be based in Europe with dual capable aircraft 'which could, if necessary, be supplemented by offshore systems'.[8]

NATO could reasonably claim that it had moved effectively to modify its positions to take account of change in the East, but it could also be argued that NATO had not yet faced up to the most difficult problems which could be anticipated.

One such problem was whether the force structure agreed in 1991 would seem appropriate once Russian troops had left Germany and Poland, especially if Belarus and Ukraine had become established sovereign and non-nuclear states by then. With Russian forces back in Russia, Germany was unlikely to seem a threatened member of NATO in direct terms and thus the justification for stationing large numbers of foreign forces there might well not be apparent. Doubt must be expressed as to whether the US will want to keep 150,000 troops in Europe, the number envisaged in 1991 plans, and as to whether Germany will want the bulk of them deployed on its territory.

A second problem arises from the consideration that, as the Russian threat diminishes and literally disappears over the horizon, West Europeans will need to pay ever more serious attention to the 'reconstitution' dimension of their defence capabilities, to their ability to build up their forces once more should an assertive, militaristic and aggressive government come to power in Moscow or a major new threat arise elsewhere. Western Europe's challenge will be to ensure that its defensive capabilities can be built up faster than offensive capabilities can be generated elsewhere. This will mean, among other things, that the industrial dimension of defence policy will need more attention. To date, neither NATO as a whole nor the West European sector of it has addressed defence industrial issues on a collective basis with any success. In 1992, the US was paying more attention to the maintenance of its defence industrial capabilities at a time of shrinking defence budgets, but its concerns were national rather than alliance-based.[9]

A third issue yet to be explored fully in Western Europe was whether the region should rely entirely on deterrence to handle the nuclear capabilities of others or whether it should give a role to active ballistic missile defences. Such defences should be most effective against perhaps the most likely forms of missile attack – an authorized launch by a small nuclear power, or an unauthorized launch of a small number of missiles by renegade officers, or accidental launches. The United States, for its part, was continuing to develop its GPALS (Global Protection Against Limited Strikes) concept and technology.

Clearly, in preparing defences to manage the residual Russian/CIS threat, West Europeans needed to avoid alarming Moscow. The ceiling (of 370,000) which the unified Germany voluntarily placed on its armed forces played a major part in this task, as should the formal and informal arms control agreements concluded between East and West. Implementation of these agreements was needed, of which the most important were the Conventional Forces in Europe (CFE) Treaty of November 1990, the Strategic Arms Reduction Talks (START) Treaty of 1991, the reciprocal commitments of Presidents Bush and Yeltsin in the autumn of 1991 largely to give up non-strategic nuclear weapons, their agreements of June 1992 on strategic weapons ceilings in the 3,000–3,500 range, and the Open Skies agreement and the Confidence and Security Building Measures (CSBM) in the spring of 1992. Significantly, although the republics concerned had difficulty in agreeing among themselves the equipment entitlements of the former Soviet Union under the CFE Treaty, they still recognized the value of the Treaty and wanted to see it come legally into force. At the Tashkent summit in mid-May 1992 they reached agreement on entitlements. The distribution of actual equipment, however, remained to be settled.[10]

Adjusting force structures in Europe to reflect the diminishing threat from Moscow will not be easy and the prospect that US forces might be withdrawn from Western Europe causes varying degrees of concern in different states. But the decline of the Russian/CIS threat is generating a new set of issues. These focus on the question of what should form the new bases for West European defence and security policies.

West European security policies without a threat from Moscow
There are at least four broad, fundamental questions which will need to be debated and for which no definite answers were in sight in the early 1990s.

Issue 1: What to do about Eastern Europe

What sort of security system should the West promote in Eastern Europe including the FSU, and for how large a region should Western Europe make a formal security commitment? As the Warsaw Pact collapsed, the states first of Central Europe (Poland, the CSFR and Hungary) and then of Eastern Europe as a whole began pressing for membership of Western security organizations, particularly NATO and the Western European Union, as well as for places in the European Community. The Soviet Union under Gorbachev and then Russia under Yeltsin made it clear that if NATO was indeed an alliance of pluralistic democracies with market economies, Moscow would be interested in joining in the foreseeable future. The feeling in much of Eastern Europe was that the collapse of Soviet domination had left the region in a security vacuum. This vacuum had a strong psychological element, in which governments and peoples had no clear sense even of threats, let alone sources of reassurance.

Whatever the cultural unity of Europe, the end of the cold war certainly left two Europes in place. In the West was a group of states which, for reasons not well understood, formed a pluralistic security community where the threat and use of force played no part in their international relations. This security community included the neutral and non-aligned members of mainland Europe, such as Sweden and Switzerland, as well as the members of the EC and NATO. The members of NATO and the Western European Union, on the other hand, were also protected against the outside world by firm security guarantees that others would come to their help if they were attacked. The only significant flaw in this rosy picture concerned the uneasy relations between Greece and Turkey, both NATO members but with Greece also being in the EC.

In Eastern Europe, on the other hand, there was no defined pattern of international relations and it was more than conceivable that some version of power politics would become the predominant model. As Robert Jervis wrote:

> the eastern part of the continent ... is not filled with stable, democratic governments that have learned to cooperate and have developed a stake in each other's well-being. Nationalism and militarism are dangerous and grievances abound, especially those rooted in ethnic and border disputes ... The traditional sources of international strife are sufficient to lead relations among these states to be permeated by the fear of war.[11]

Understandably, this was not an attractive prospect for many states in the area, which preferred to belong to the Western system through membership of Western organizations.

The European Community and NATO adopted rather different but at least initially complementary approaches before the Maastricht summit of the EC introduced a discordant element. The EC took the view that East European states could be brought into the Community as soon as they were ready in economic and political terms. The EC differentiated among members of the former WTO according to their political and economic progress, and in particular judged during 1991 that the three Central European states had made sufficient advance, and offered sufficient promise, to become associate members of the EC. Full membership was envisaged for around the end of the century. EC membership was seen on both sides of Europe as a stabilizing element for democracy and economic progress, as it had been in Spain and Portugal, as well as promoting cooperative interstate relations. As other states, such as Bulgaria and Romania, developed politically and introduced the macroeconomic frameworks needed for a market economy, they too could be considered for associate membership. Using the reasoning of Karl Deutsch,[12] as the states of Eastern Europe were integrated economically, socially and politically into Western Europe, they too would be absorbed into the wider security community. Their governments, affected by the reality of the interdependence of their economies and the mutual empathy of their populations, would recognize that the threat and use of force in their relations had become unthinkable.

NATO, in contrast, adopted a posture from the London Declaration of July 1990 which involved not differentiating in any formal sense among the members of the former Warsaw Pact. All were offered and took up the opportunity for political liaison, and all (including the successor states of the former Soviet Union) accepted membership of the NACC from the end of 1991. NATO's approach was mirrored in the CSCE, which also admitted all the new states of the FSU in late 1991.

NATO's approach was in part related to the problem discussed earlier in this chapter: how to amend NATO's defence and political posture so as to take account of change in the FSU and to avoid provoking reactionary developments in Moscow and elsewhere. NATO used political liaison and the NACC to reinforce arms control and to make sure that force restructuring in East and West could proceed without either side feeling threatened or exploited. Thus an early concern of the NACC was to work for a division of the CFE entitlements of the FSU among the new states so that the treaty could be ratified and brought into force. But NATO was also concerned to promote a peaceful pattern of international relations in Eastern Europe based on the principles of the CSCE's Paris Charter. For NATO, commitment to such principles was the focus of effort, rather than the economic and other forms of interdependence seen at the heart of the established North Atlantic security community.

These approaches could be seen as different but complementary since NATO's drive was meant to achieve immediate results and to prevent power politics being re-established in Eastern Europe, while the EC's effort in many ways was more long-term, aiming at gradually absorbing more and more of Europe.

There were many questions about both approaches. Scepticism was expressed about whether, inside a CSCE or a UN framework, collective security action could reliably be generated against an aggressor[13] or whether there was much that the West could do at all to influence the shape of international relations in the East.[14] On the EC's role, it may prove extremely difficult to promote the change in the East that would make even the Central Europeans viable members, and an enlarged Community should make more elusive the existing members' goal of building a common foreign and security policy (CFSP). Finally it was not clear how the Community envisaged dealing with Russia's belief that it too was a part of Europe. European Community enthusiasts were reluctant to contemplate Russia as an eventual member; yet, without a secure Russia, it was hard to see how there could be a secure Europe. Presidents Havel and Walesa both recognized the need to integrate the then Soviet Union into Europe when they visited NATO in 1991.[15]

But the EC Maastricht summit decisions threatened this dual approach through the agreement, made largely but not exclusively on the insistence of Greece, that any member of the European Community should be eligible to join the Western European Union (whose members provide one another with a firm security guarantee). This raised the prospect that, when the three states of Central Europe joined the EC, they could then claim membership of the WEU. They would also be in a good position to argue that, as WEU members, they should be allowed to join NATO.

This would shatter the NATO policy of not differentiating in a formal sense among former WTO states. It could lead to feelings of resentment and even alarm in Moscow that a zone of differential security was clearly being formed in Eastern Europe. If the Central Europeans were provided with firm

Western security guarantees, other democratic market economies in the East would demand the same or be offended by the reasons why such guarantees could not be given. Interestingly, the immediate reaction of several West European states after Maastricht was to argue that WEU membership was not an automatic right of EC members and to assemble an *acquis* of WEU policy and regulation which new members would have to accept before they could be admitted. However, this was a way of deferring rather than solving the issues raised by the Maastricht approach to WEU membership.

The Maastricht summit enhanced the possibility that Western alliances would be expanded in a rather uncontrolled manner. But the alternative possibility was that growth in EC membership would be held back. The danger remained that existing EC members would prove unwilling to grant membership to Poland, the CSFR and Hungary, despite the economic, political and security benefits which would result for Central Europe,[16] because West Europeans would be unwilling to make the firm security guarantees that would have to be given when the Central Europeans claimed WEU membership.

Issue 2: NATO and West European security cooperation
A second issue was what sort of coalition basis for defence should operate in the West itself. One forecast was that the end of the Soviet threat would generate the withdrawal of US forces from Europe, the end of NATO, and the dissolution of the West European security community, the return to power politics throughout Europe,[17] and a pervasive need to offset German power. While this view was rejected by many who felt that European integration had proceeded much too far to collapse,[18] certainly the continued effectiveness of the West European/North Atlantic security community should not be taken for granted.

One point of consensus in Western Europe was that defence should continue to be organized on some sort of coalition basis, at least as far as the major states were concerned. Politically, it is of little consequence that Switzerland is neutral. It would matter a great deal should Germany adopt this status. No one wanted to see what could be called the 're-nationalization' of defence.

However, opinions differed as to how best to achieve this. On the one side were those led by the British who felt that NATO should and could remain the principal defence organization and that the US military presence in Europe was a positive contribution to stability in the continent as a whole. European security cooperation could be endorsed as a desirable activity so long as it did not alienate the United States; indeed some such cooperation was seen as encouraging the US to stay in Europe, since it showed West Europeans to be taking defence seriously and to be making resources available for it. Italy and the Netherlands were often associated with the British position.

On the other side was an unlikely grouping led by France of both those who believed the US commitment to Europe to be rather fragile and those who saw it as rather robust. Both could see much intensified European defence and security cooperation as justifiable. For one group it was preparation for the imminent day when the United States abandoned its commitment. For the other group, intensified European cooperation would mean coherence and so influence in dealings with the United States. All these calculations were reflected in the phrasing of the NATO New Strategic Concept and the Maastricht Treaty, and in the differing national views of and reactions to the plans for a Franco-German corps.[19]

There was one multi-faceted problem for those who felt that NATO could be kept as the predominant defence and security body. There was some credibility in the view that the United States would stay interested in NATO only so long as it was a politically important organization. If NATO remained essentially a defence body for Western Europe against external aggression, it would probably have little immediate prominence, given that such aggression was extremely unlikely. Also, once the Soviet conventional threat had gone, and once the NACC had done most of its work of promoting the civilian, democratic control of defence policy and of securing East–West arms control, there seemed no external danger which West Europeans alone could not handle other than the unlikely possibility of nuclear threats or attack. Therefore it could be said that unless NATO took on significant new tasks, it would gradually fade in importance in the public eye.

In 1992 two new possible tasks were on the agenda for consideration as a means of sustaining NATO's importance and relevance. One was to take formal responsibility for additional territory in Eastern Europe by accepting new members, where the risks were perhaps greater. The other was to become a coordinating body for West European–US military activities beyond the NATO area.

Neither of these was an entirely welcome prospect. Taking on new members would mean taking on new problems as well. Such a step would probably be divisive in the Alliance since France, at least, was clearly opposed to what it saw as allowing the United States to expand its influence into

Eastern Europe. France appeared even unwilling to participate in activities of the NACC which involved military personnel. Expanding NATO's membership would mean acquiring allies whose behaviour was not entirely predictable and which had significant problems among themselves: during the 1990s, for instance, Hungary might be drawn to protect Hungarian minorities in neighbouring states. Expanding NATO's membership could alarm Russia and strengthen the position there of extreme nationalists and militarists who could cite the encroachment of the domineering West. Broadening NATO's membership could also be a difficult process to control. If the three Central European states were allowed in on grounds of their introduction of pluralist, democratic political systems and market economies, other states which also brought in such changes would demand entry. Russia had made clear its wish to join.[20]

A further potential problem where a US rather than a European lead was unavoidable concerned the possibility that Kazakhstan and/or Ukraine might develop seriously the position that they would want firm security guarantees from the West as the price of giving up the nuclear weapons on their soil. The West would prefer that they be content with the security assurances to non-nuclear states given by the nuclear powers in association with the Non-Proliferation Treaty.[21] However, the Ukraine and/or Kazakhstan may insist on a guarantee against any attack rather than just nuclear aggression. The pressures for NATO to expand its membership and so become more a collective security rather than a collective defence organization were clearly building up in 1992.

Turning NATO into a body for coordinating US and West European out-of-area military intervention activities was also limited in appeal. Historically, in conflicts as varied as Suez, Vietnam, Grenada and Panama, out-of-area interventions had often been a source of friction in transatlantic relations. Few European countries would relish their NATO membership if it might require them to become involved under American leadership in out-of-area conflicts. As the logic of the European common foreign and security policy commitments implied, West European states would want to choose for themselves whether to get involved in such conflicts. Making out-of-area activities a basic task for NATO might well discourage European states from making available and preparing defence resources for such activities, which would then cause further American disillusion with the West Europeans.

NATO's decision of May 1992 that NATO forces and facilities could be used for peace-keeping operations in Eastern Europe[22] could prove a positive step so long as not too much is expected of it. It should mean that NATO would act only under the mandate of a wider body such as the CSCE or the UN. It should also mean that, when the United States wants to add to a European conclusion that a peace-keeping mission can usefully be sent to an area of tension by itself making a contribution, such a mission can be given some kind of NATO badge. If, however, Europeans do feel deeply that such a mission should be sent and the US argues to the contrary in NATO, the Alliance will be weakened. Also the May 1992 agreement referred only to peace-keeping forces and did not cover peace-making or peace-enforcing missions against aggression.

Keeping NATO going after the disappearance of political confrontation and the conventional military confrontation with Moscow will not be easy. It will clearly have a major role in the tasks outlined in the first section of this paper, involving the measured running down of defence capabilities, but thereafter things will become more difficult to balance. However, it will be militarily and politically essential for West European and US forces to practise sufficiently together to be able to work well together when needed, as was the case in the Gulf in 1991. In this context, it is NATO standards, procedures and cooperative habits rather than command structures which need to be sustained.

Issue 3: What will be the core West European foreign policy thinking to guide security policy?

The third broad question facing West European security and defence planners looking at the rest of the decade and even beyond is what foreign policy guidelines will affect military capabilities.

Some observations and brief predictions can be offered in 1992, at least as a stimulus for further reflection. Even among the 12 of the European Union a CFSP will not be easy to establish, as immediately became obvious in the months after Maastricht. It can be anticipated that common positions will be easiest to agree when they assert principles but do not call for risky or costly action and, at the other extreme, when major crises arise and a failure to act in common would clearly be costly. In international relations, however, it is intermediate situations which are rather more common. Thus, while the members of the European Union should find it possible to agree on an arms embargo against a clear aggressor, they will find it much more difficult to adopt a common export policy in general.

As the Treaty of European Union made clear, Western Europe will not have a pacifist foreign policy, so Germany must eventually and reluctantly accept that it should on occasions play a role in military activities beyond the NATO area which are endorsed by the CFSP (and preferably the UN). There will be a bigger demand for peace-keeping forces than in previous decades but peace-enforcing capabilities will also need to be generated. Although France will continue to argue that Western Europe should aim at autonomy by developing its own air and sea lift capabilities, space-based reconnaissance and intelligence assets, airborne tankers and global communications networks, nevertheless pragmatism will prevail, in that Europeans will procure those systems which appear affordable and particular value for money. Western Europe will be particularly concerned with the Mediterranean region and the Middle East, with which it is not easy to imagine harmonious relations being developed.[23] Of more fundamental significance, West Europeans will continue to feel uncertain as to whether individual regional orders can be sustained without a bedrock of world order activities. This alone will make it difficult for Western Europe to go beyond the praiseworthy but vague statements on the objectives of the CFSP laid out in the Treaty of European Union.[24]

As in the past, financial considerations will play a big part in defence and security preparations but, unlike in the cold war period,[25] the 1990s will offer few guidelines as to 'how much is enough?' as regards defence expenditure. Although Representative Aspin has argued that the United States should maintain the capability simultaneously to fight at least one war of the kind conducted against Iraq and to conduct the sort of operation involved in the invasion of Panama,[26] such thinking finds no echo in Europe. Moreover, given West Europeans' belief that their security and defence problems will be much reduced if they can promote prosperity among their neighbours, there will be much more scope for arguing that in security policy economic aid is a viable alternative to defence expenditure.

Finally West Europeans did not have in 1992 a clear response to the demands of groups calling themselves nations who demanded statehood and who sought to incorporate more or less all their group in the one state. West Europeans in principle supported the CSCE positions that minorities in states can be protected through the introduction of group rights, and that the boundaries of states should not be changed by force. West Europeans reluctantly accepted in the cases of Yugoslavia and the FSU that existing states could break up, but only if they used as international borders the internal borders which had previously applied. For Serbs, Armenians, and perhaps many Russians and others, this was an unacceptable principle. In 1992 boundaries were being changed by force in Azerbaijan and the former Yugoslavia, and the European Union had no clear sense as to what firm action was needed or feasible.[27]

Issue 4: How are nuclear weapons to be regarded?
A final fundamental issue for West Europeans in general and Britain and France in particular was to reconsider their fundamental attitude towards nuclear weapons in the new situation where the Moscow-based conventional threat was fast disappearing, where East–West ideological hostility had gone and where many more states in the international system had acquired or would acquire the capacity to develop their own nuclear weapons. Arguably the predominant problem for the West had become to restrict proliferation rather than to deter Moscow.

Radical policies for nuclear weapons must encompass the United States, and Russia as well, but Britain and France had some scope for initiative. They could, for instance, promote the view that the only justifiable use of nuclear weapons was to deter a nuclear attack and that the environmental consequences of nuclear explosions mean that they should not be used even to stave off conventional defeat. Such a 'no first use' approach, although it would mean changing NATO strategy yet again, could give guidance to prospective nuclear weapons states which are considering such weapons as just another weapon of war and it could also provide reassurance to some states, especially in North Africa and the Middle East, who might fear becoming the targets of Western nuclear weapons. Certainly NATO's traditional case that it needed nuclear weapons in case of defeat in a conventional war could be adopted by many states as a justification for deploying nuclear forces.

A second radical policy might emerge should West Europeans start to work on the basis that nuclear weapons could in practice be taken out of world politics over time.[28] This is in contrast to current Western wisdom that nuclear weapons cannot be disinvented. Trying to take nuclear weapons out of world politics would not only stimulate minimum deterrence relations at low levels of warheads through unilateral action and multilateral arms control, it would also open possibilities for discussions on ever lower levels of readiness. This is an issue which Britain and France must face once START I has been implemented and if Russia and the United States seek to cut their warhead levels once more, below the 3,000–3,500 total agreed by Presidents Bush and Yeltsin in June 1992. At such a stage, the two West European nuclear states would find it very difficult to keep out of further arms reduction talks.

In mid-1992, however, Britain and France remained keen on the continued operation of what they insisted was a minimum deterrent force. A specific cause of concern, which in the long term could threaten the viability of the European deterrents and render NATO virtually meaningless, was the possibility that the United States might adopt Russia as a virtual partner in the ballistic missile defence area. Russia was clearly tempted to press for extensive information and technology sharing as a price for accepting substantial modification of the ABM Treaty, whereas elements in the United States were drawn by sectors of Russian technology. Britain was very wary of US–Russian cooperation in this field and indicated clearly that its own definition of minimum deterrence would depend on Moscow's ballistic missile defence capability. Even in the middle of 1992, Britain insisted it might want to mount eight warheads on each of its Trident missiles.[29]

Conclusion

This chapter has argued that West Europeans initially adjusted successfully to changes in the FSU. On a national level, defence expenditures were cut prudently rather than recklessly. NATO was reformed with a new conciliatory political posture towards the East, a new Strategic Concept, and an amended force and command structure. The Rome summit of NATO and the Maastricht summit of the EC successfully produced forms of words which showed that the members of both organizations wanted both sets of cooperative activities to be maintained.

But all this was in a context in which Russian forces were still in Germany and the former Soviet nuclear arsenal remained large and under uncertain final control. The world could and should look quite different in 1994, especially if only Moscow in the FSU controls nuclear weapons and if a reasonably stable, elected government is in place there. Only with such developments will the true impact of change in the FSU on West European security begin to be seen.

In 1992 it was possible to see only what would be areas of uncertainty after 1994. There was recognition in Western Europe that security and defence should be sustained on a coalition basis, that such matters should not be re-nationalized. But to the West there was doubt as to whether NATO could survive without a clear enemy and therefore whether the West Europeans should not base their cooperation on an assumption that the United States would probably not be engaged in Europe for much longer. To the East, there was pressure to expand the membership of Western security organizations, a pressure which provoked reluctance in the West. There was perhaps a rather misguided sense in Central Europe that membership of NATO and/or the WEU would bring partipation in a zone of order, while the East European and FSU states, not having such membership, might well find themselves in a zone of chaos.

Optimistically, if a successful transition is achieved in the FSU and Russia becomes a market-based democracy without regional domination ambitions, new bases for West European security and defence policies in the future will be needed. Without a major threat from Moscow, West European defence and security policies will have to be reshaped from the bottom up. Documents agreed to date in CFSP give little guidance for such a progress.

For clear reasons relating to oil, geographic proximity and migration concerns, Europe's immediate major security and even defence concerns could increasingly focus on the Mediterranean and the Middle East. In such a context, West European nuclear policies could play a significant role. But to guide their overall path, West Europeans will need overarching principles so that aspirations for national self-determination can be absorbed without massive conflict and disruption, not just in the former Soviet empire, but in the world as a whole. They will also need a clearer sense of the sort of international order which can be built, and what West Europeans can do to promote it, in the military sector and elsewhere.

Notes
1 See, for instance, Lothar Ruehl, 'Offensive defence in the Warsaw Pact', *Survival*, Vol. 23, No. 5, September/October 1991, pp. 442–50, on Warsaw Treaty Organization plans revealed after the unification of Germany.
2 In fact the states of NATO Europe tended to spend only around 3.5% of their GNP on defence in the 1980s, while the non-aligned states of Europe spent only 2.3% of their GNP on defence. NATO membership could thus be seen as stimulating higher defence spending for Europeans; see US Arms Control and Disarmament Agency, *World Military Expenditures and Arms Transfers 1990* (Washington DC: USGPO, 1992), pp. 48–9.
3 The original Article 6 of the North Atlantic Treaty said that 'an armed attack on one or more of the Parties is deemed to include an armed attack on the territory of any of the Parties in Europe or North America or the Algerian departments of France, on the occupation forces of any Party in Europe, or the islands under the jurisdiction of any Party in the North Atlantic area north of the Tropic of Cancer or on the vessels or aircraft in this area of any of the Parties'. Inclusion of Algeria was abandoned when it became independent in 1962; see *The North Atlantic Treaty Organisation: Facts and Figures* (Brussels: NATO, 10th edition, 1981), p. 265.

outside the integrated NATO command. However, under the corps plan, the first French Armoured Division of about 10,000 people would remain stationed on German soil. It appeared that the force eventually would come under the wing of the WEU. The participation of other European states in the corps was being sought so that it could have a total strength of around 35,000: see 'The Franco-German initiative on Political Union' of 14 October 1991, released by the French Embassy in London on 18 October 1991; 'European corps units to remain separate', *The Financial Times*, 21 May 1992; 'Mitterrand and Kohl to set up Europe Corps', *Independent* 21 May 1992; 'Paris and Bonn to present plans for a "European army"', *Independent*, 6 April 1992; and 'A Joint Force For Europe', *International Herald Tribune*, 18 March 1992.

20 For an expanded version of these arguments, see T. Taylor, *NATO and Central Europe* op. cit.

21 The United States, the USSR, France and Britain gave pledges in 1968, approved by the UN Security Council, to take action in accordance with the UN Charter to support non-nuclear states threatened with nuclear weapons; see J.H. Barton and L.D. Weiler, *International Arms Control: Issues and Agreements* (Stanford: Stanford UP, 1976), p. 301.

22 The May decision needed confirmation by foreign ministers at their June 1992 meeting; see 'NATO ready to step outside its borders', *The Financial Times*, 22 May 1992.

23 I am struck particularly by the growing wealth differentiation between the northern and southern shores of the Mediterranean, by population growth pressures in many Muslim Mediterranean states, and by the growth of Islamic political influence in the south, which will conflict with the Western secular approach to politics and much of social life.

24 Article J.1, para. 2 of the treaty states that 'the objectives of the common foreign and security policy shall be:

- to safeguard the common values, fundamental interests and independence of the Union;
- to strengthen the security of the Union and its Member States in all ways;
- to preserve peace and strengthen international security, in accordance with the principles of the United Nations Charter as well as the principles of the Helsinki Final Act and the objectives of the Paris Charter;
- to promote international cooperation; and
- to develop and consolidate democracy and the rule of law, and respect for human rights and fundamental freedoms.'

25 During the cold war, although the temptation for states to pay less than their

reasonable share ('to free-ride') in the Alliance was always there (see for example Gavin Kennedy, *Defence Economics,* London, Duckworth, 1983, Ch. 2), West Europeans knew that they should spend what was needed to generate a robust conventional defence against the WTO and to keep the US content that they were at least close to carrying their fair share of the overall defence burden.

26 See 'A Strategy for Rethinking National Security Policy', 6 January 1992; and 'An Approach to Sizing American Conventional Forces for the Post-Soviet Era', 24 January 1992, from the Office of Rep. Les Aspin, Chairman of the Armed Services Committee, House of Representatives, Washington DC.

27 By the summer of 1992 the EC had moved to obtain UN-based sanctions against Serbia.

28 See, for instance, Ken Booth, 'Security in anarchy', *International Affairs*, Vol. 67, No. 3. July 1991, p. 542.

29 *Statement on the Defence Estimates 1992*, 1981 (London: HMSO, July 1992), p. 28.

CHAPTER 9
THE SECURITY IMPLICATIONS OF CHANGES IN THE FORMER SOVIET UNION FOR ASIA AND JAPAN

SATOSHI MORIMOTO

Introduction

The international community is facing its most significant turning-point in recent history. In particular, 1991 was an unprecedented year which saw the conclusion of two major wars. The first was the Gulf war, in which a coalition formed by members of the international community fought to restore the international order that was damaged by the Iraqi military invasion of Kuwait. The second was the cold war, which resulted in a victory for solidarity and deterrence by the nations which share the common values of democracy, freedom and a market economy. The United States has insisted that the end of the cold war marks a victory for its containment strategy, but Japan still has a major territorial dispute with Russia dating from 1945. In Europe, significant political and economic changes have been caused by the transformation of the Soviet Union and the collapse of the framework of the Eastern bloc. While the entire world, and especially Europe, has been exploring a new security architecture, reality has often got ahead of wisdom. It is to be hoped that wisdom will soon be able to lead reality.

The international community will continue in its uncertain and unstable state until a new order can be built. Regional conflicts, ethnic tensions, and religious fundamentalism have mushroomed owing to an explosion of the discontent and friction previously contained by East–West tension. *Coups d'état* and regional conflicts broke out in Eastern Europe, Africa, the Gulf, South Asia, Latin America and the former Soviet Union (FSU) only months after the end of the Gulf war.

The direction taken by the FSU will significantly affect the security and stability of the international community. Although the future of the FSU military structure cannot be predicted exactly, Russia's conventional military strength will remain overwhelmingly superior to that of any other republic, and it has a strong grasp on the command and control of the unified strategic military forces. Russia, however, is in the difficult position of grappling with an austere defence budget, restructuring its military industry, and scaling down its military forces.

To date, the security of the West (broadly defined) has been successfully ensured by the containment of the former Soviet Union on two sides: by NATO on the European front and through the US–Japan security arrangement on the Asian front. A significant consensus was achieved at the Williamsburg summit of the Group of Seven states (G7) in 1983. There it was agreed that, because Soviet SS-20 missiles could have been transferred from west to east of the Urals (and back again), the only acceptable arms control arrangement for the G7 as a whole was for a zero deployment of the Intermediate Nuclear Forces. This was the arrangement negotiated in the 1987 INF Treaty.

The impact of changes in the FSU on Asian security

The relationship between the security of Europe and the security of Asia has become closer with the end of the cold war era. The main reasons for this change are the political and military transformations within the FSU. Especially significant is Moscow's change in attitude towards Asia. Security implications for Asia and Japan can be assessed under three headings.

(a) The impact of European security and arms control on Asian security
At present, European security is not maintained by a single security structure. European nations are still exploring new security systems that could be valid within the changing strategic environment. Europe is still trying to secure stability and peace by developing the existing frameworks of, for example, the EC, NATO, WEU and CSCE. These organizations are all seeking to extend and expand their original roles. However, they have had difficulty handling internal conflicts within Europe – such as the ethnic civil wars in Yugoslavia and in certain FSU republics. It must be hoped that the EC will strengthen its political and security roles, and that the WEU will organize its own military and security structures in order to manage stability in Europe. NATO is changing the nature of its military organization and expanding its political role by promoting its relationship with Eastern Europe and the FSU. The relationship between NATO and the FSU will become stronger than in the past, although for the time being it is not expected that republics of the FSU will join NATO. The North Atlantic Cooperation Council (NACC) includes the Asian republics of the FSU. In terms of exchange of information, security

dialogues, mutual visits and personnel exchanges, NATO European members are currently closer to their former Eastern bloc adversaries than to Japan.

The CSCE, too, is expanding its area of influence and is in the process of extending into Asia. In particular, security and arms control in the CSCE will be extended from west of the Urals to include the Far East, and Asian republics of the FSU have already joined the CSCE. In the new round of arms control, the Asian region cannot be disregarded.

This geographical expansion of security interests must necessarily have a serious impact on Asian security. The new security framework to be constructed in Europe, and the way in which the Western nations proceed with arms control, from now on will also have a direct influence on Asia. This presents problems. It is neither realistic nor effective to apply European arms control measures in Asia. However, if the trend towards greater arms control in Europe is extended to Asia, serious political pressure will be put on the Asian nations to conduct negotiations to create an arms control policy in their own region.

Secondly, Japan has a unique relationship with Russia which includes the conflict over territorial issues. Japan has held back on arms control and confidence-building measures (CBMs) with the FSU to a certain extent, using them as leverage to encourage the FSU to be more flexible over the Northern Territories issue. At the Helsinki summit in the summer of 1992, the CSCE members decided to invite Japan to participate in discussion on topics where it had a direct interest or wanted to contribute. Japan intends to take up such invitations: it hopes to represent Asian concerns and interests and to impress upon the European nations how CSCE decisions on certain issues will have a direct impact on Asia and Japan. On the other hand, even though Japan will join the CSCE, it is not reasonable or realistic to apply the same CSCE framework directly to the Asia-Pacific region.

(b) The impact of the changes in the FSU military on the strategic environment of Northeast Asia and Japan

In the past three decades the Soviet Union consistently built up its forces in the Far East, in terms of both quality and quantity. During this period, there were two significant turning-points.

First, in the early 1970s, intensified military confrontation with China and the territorial conflict on Damanskiy Island triggered the reinforcement of Soviet ground forces along the Sino-Soviet border.

Then, in 1979-80, the Soviet Union began to build up a strategic posture at the Sea of Okhotsk from which to confront the US military threat. The existing strategic posture was established at this time.

The Soviet Union wanted the strategic capability to attack the North American continent using SLBMs launched from the Sea of Okhotsk. Extensive Soviet conventional forces were deployed to defend Soviet ballistic missile submarines and the overall Soviet strategic position. In essence, the USSR sought to establish a sanctuary for its forces in the Sea of Okhotsk. However, one part of Northern Japan is located within the Soviet inner defence zone, and thus the Soviet forces in the Far East imposed a serious military threat to Japan. Consequently, the US–Japan security arrangement and Japan's Self-Defence Forces were used to counter the threat from Soviet forces.

Simultaneously the Soviet military forces in the Far East introduced modern equipment, such as the Kiev-class air-carrier, Backfire bombers, Delta-III-class nuclear-powered strategic submarines, Ivan Logov-class amphibious ships, and SS-20 missiles (subsequently destroyed under the INF Treaty). Previously, such equipment had never been seen in the Far East theatre. Also, for the first time in its history, the Soviet Union established a headquarters for the command and control of all its units in the Far East.

The last Soviet build-up was right at the start of the 1990s. Since then, Moscow has scrapped some equipment (most of which was obsolete) but continued to deploy more modern equipment in the Far East, though Russian activities overall have been relatively low-key. In other words, the Russian forces in the Far East have been reduced in quantity but have increased in quality, while the overall strategic stance has remained basically the same.

How will this posture change in the future? It is risky to speculate, but clearly the major factors affecting any change are what kind of new military structures and doctrines Russia and perhaps the CIS will develop, and how Russia will establish strategic relations with the US. It may take a few years to determine what stable form Russian military forces will take. However, some suggestions can be offered, taking into consideration the historical background against which the Soviet military forces developed.

First of all, Russia is inheriting most of the former Soviet military forces, and is assuming command and control of nominally CIS strategic forces. This will make Russia a military superpower in comparison with the other republics. For the present, it may well give greater priority to achieving political stability and overcoming its serious economic problems than to sustaining any military build-up. In order to achieve this, it is obvious that

Russia must attach more importance to cooperation with the US so that a more beneficial relationship may be created.

Yet Russia has no choice but to maintain its strategic nuclear arsenal and a strategic posture of virtual equality with the United States if it is to secure its status as a superpower and thereby counterbalance the strength of the US.

However, Russia cannot easily compete with the US in terms of the strategic balance owing to the devastated state of its economy, the slowdown in military production, and its failure to convert military industries to civilian production. From the diplomatic standpoint, the Soviet style of expanding political influence in the Third World through military aid will inevitably disappear.

In assessing these elements, four conclusions are possible. First of all, Russia will continued to develop a new military doctrine, placing a higher priority on the defence of its territory. It will seek to restructure its forces and improve the condition of its troops' training, social welfare, housing, wages, employment and education, rather than build up military hardware.

Secondly, although Russia must significantly reduce its strategic forces, it will continue to develop a residual strategic force with its limited resources. It will maintain its strategic stance towards the US. This has been confirmed by the Bush–Yeltsin agreement of June 1992, under which both the US and Russia will scale down to comparable arsenals of 3,000–3,500 warheads.

Thirdly, with an efficient and effective reorganization, involving significant reductions and the scaling down of military equipment development and production, Russia would be able to create a compact conventional force.

Lastly, Russia will try earnestly to implement its arms control agreements and will proceed with additional arms control talks.

How will these likely developments affect the defence and security of Japan? The most serious threat to Japan would occur if Russia increased its conventional forces in the future, though its strategic forces will be reduced by START and other agreements. Russia's strategic forces are deterred by the US strategic counterpart, but its conventional forces pose the main military threat to Japan.

On the one hand, a continuing reduction of FSU military forces in the Far East has resulted from the dismantling of old equipment, but on the other hand, this has helped to speed up modernization. Large numbers of weapons have been transferred from the European front to east of the Urals. These weapons have not all been moved to the Far East, but significant quantities have been used to modernize Russian forces in the region. However, because of the CFE treaty, Russia can no longer deploy additional equipment on the European front. Therefore, production in the defence industry has been scaled down, and it may well assign and deploy in the Far East the additional weapons which have been produced.

Russia may also deploy parts of the Black Sea fleet in the Pacific, even if a successful compromise over this fleet is reached with Ukraine.

Eventually, strategic forces in the Far East will be reduced by START and other agreements and the strategic implications of the northeast Pacific region will become less important to the superpowers. This will have a positive impact on the territorial dispute between Japan and Russia, because the disputed land will have lost its military importance for Russia. On the other hand, Russia's conventional forces will not be reduced at the same pace as its strategic forces. Conventional forces may actually be strengthened to some extent by the transfer of equipment from other areas, which again will have a serious impact on the security and defence of Japan. Political pressure has been exerted on Russia to encourage it to reduce its defence budget and defence forces, so that it may enjoy a peace dividend.

(c) The impact of the changes in the FSU on the security environment of Asia
The special features of the security environment of Asia contrast with the security environment in Europe. Europe has mainly been preoccupied with the reduction of military tension, while the Asia-Pacific region has been concerned with economic development. Also, while the East–West tension of bipolar confrontation between NATO and the Warsaw Pact has dominated Europe, the Asia-Pacific region has been influenced by a variety of factors, including the presence of communist China and the mainly bilateral relationships between the various political powers of Asia.

The differences between the security environments of Asia and Europe have decreased owing to changes in the FSU and in Europe. While most alliances are bilateral in the Asia-Pacific region, most Asian nations are slowly working towards creating new political and security frameworks based on multilateral cooperation.

A consensus on strengthening political and security dialogues was reached at the ASEAN summit meeting in January 1992. This was a significant development. Although this approach is still moderate and slow in comparison with the progress of the EC, it is an indication of a new security direction for the Asia-Pacific region.

The United States has introduced a new defence strategy in answer to the changing international situation and new threats to its national and security interests. It is now shifting the emphasis of its strategic military posture in the Asia-Pacific region from Northeast Asia to Southeast Asia because it no longer needs to counter the Soviet military threat in the Sea of Okhotsk. The US is also trying to take up a new role as 'the glue' for the nations of the Asia-Pacific region through the reinforcement of defence and security relationships. By pre-positioning equipment, maintaining a forward presence, conducting joint exercises that promote the access of US military to these nations, and offering security assistance, military exchange and dialogues, the US will secure its position.

The FSU military has been withdrawn from Cam Ranh Bay and the Pacific Ocean. This will lead to a power vacuum in the Asia-Pacific region, as previously the superpowers kept the balance. Currently, threats to the West come from within the area, not from outside. Security for the West, therefore, must be such that it can respond to these new threats which have resulted from the end of the cold war.

Russia has two faces, one looking towards Europe and the other towards Asia. Confusion and disorder in Russia will have a serious impact on both sides. The US–Japan security arrangement plays an important role in countering this threat through its strong political and security framework. Yet it is still necessary to promote exchanges and dialogue on security between Russia and the countries of the Asia-Pacific region. Japan has already entered into a dialogue with Russia at the level of policy planning staffs, and has been trying to probe the extent of the transparency of the Russian military.

China does not seem to have changed its military approach; it continues to modernize its defences. It is steadily increasing defence expenditures, expanding its presence and improving its operational bases in the Spratly and Paracel Islands.

There have been some positive improvements in the relationship between South Korea and the Eastern bloc nations. North Korea is, however, suffering from a stagnant economy and from the problem of an imminent crisis over the succession of its current leader. The possibility that it may develop nuclear weapons poses a serious threat to the security of the Asia-Pacific region as a whole.

Some of the changes that have occurred in the Asia-Pacific region have derived from changes in the FSU. The main factors for ensuring peace and stability in the Asia-Pacific region are retaining a US military presence and fostering economic development. Of these two, a positive American presence in the region has become increasingly important and, consequently, the US–Japan security arrangement remains vital to securing a safe and stable region.

CHAPTER 10
DISARMAMENT AND ARMS CONTROL IN THE POST-COLD WAR WORLD

RYUKICHI IMAI

Introduction

Most of what was achieved in the US–USSR nuclear arms control negotiations in the 1980s could have been foreseen had it been possible to look into Gorbachev's mind as well as to fathom the full extent of the deterioration in the Soviet economy and society. Achieving nuclear parity with the United States virtually destroyed the main fabric of the Soviet military-industrial complex. (The American GNP during the cold war was probably three to four times greater than the Soviet equivalent and the United States spent around 6.5% of its GNP on defence.) Gorbachev tried very hard to disengage his country from this military competition, and especially from what he perceived to be the challenge to start a new technological competition in outer space, namely SDI. The joint communiqué of the Geneva summit of 1985 contained the now famous statement, 'a nuclear war could never be won and must never be fought'. Another summit followed in Washington in 1987, at which the INF Treaty was signed. Then in 1989, the Malta summit served to tie up the efforts of those years.

A critical issue in the area of nuclear disarmament is to define the entity that will succeed the Soviet Union in, for instance, ratifying the START treaty signed by Gorbachev in July 1991 'on behalf of the Union of the Soviet Socialist Republics'. In addition to legal problems, which the clever negotiators of the May 1992 Lisbon Protocol probably can find ways around, there are also substantive problems. The body that ratifies the treaty should have full control of the entire fleet of strategic nuclear forces including ICBMs, SLBMs, Blackjack- or Backfire-mounted ALCMs as well as the entire C^3I system, including early-warning satellites and large phased-array radars. The Russian Federation does not seem to be in that position, and neither does Kazakhstan. In fact, as of June 1992, it is far from clear how the destruction of giant SS-18 ICBMs or their conversion (to single warheads or other activities) can be managed to meet the promises made in the Bush–Yeltsin accord. Unless sufficiently convincing steps are taken in terms of the strategic arsenal, it is very difficult to proceed seriously and credibly with the elimination of tactical weapons. Even within the United States, tactical warheads pose complicated problems among the air force, army, navy and marine corps regarding who has control over which nuclear weapons. With the future of the former Soviet armed forces by no means clear, one should expect similar problems within their ranks.

The former Soviet Union will itself remain a problem. Already, there is concern about the disposition of the alleged 27,000 warheads which were dispersed, at least until last year, in all fifteen republics as well as in East Germany, Czechoslovakia and Hungary. Tactical weapons may have all been brought back to Russia as announced, but it is difficult to confirm because, for one thing, tactical weapons movements cannot be verified through satellite observation. Weapons might have been stolen, or sold on the black market, perhaps finding their way to places like Libya. Transporting and dismantling nuclear weapons is a difficult and complicated operation. If mishandled they may explode; and even if there is no nuclear detonation, they could each spread some five kilograms of plutonium, seriously contaminating the environment. It has already been widely recognized that production of the military-oriented industries which employed 6.4 million people in 1988 will have to be converted to market economy-oriented consumer goods. Otherwise, it is entirely possible that those in charge will find it easier to continue current operations and produce weapons for the foreign market. Finally there are questions about what would happen to former Soviet nuclear weapons should they become involved in civil war in the FSU.

Overall, nuclear disarmament will become very different if Russia and the United States arrive at a new equilibrium of deterrence with 3,000-3,500 strategic warheads each, and an uncertain promise to bring tactical warheads to zero in due course. The Helsinki CSCE, whose major objective has been to deal pragmatically with the East–West confrontation, will need to redefine its purpose.

One thing is sure to happen in the arena of multilateral disarmament. The traditional Western, socialist, and non-aligned country groupings will cease to be effective in the UN First Committee (concerned with political and security issues) and in the Geneva Conference on Disarmament. New rules and practices will have to be devised, whatever the game may be.

Nuclear disarmament negotiations in the 1980s

Much has been written about the Geneva process which produced the INF and START treaties, as well as the proceedings in Vienna and Stockholm which ended in the CFE Treaty of 1990. The flavour of the negotiating atmosphere under Reagan on the one hand, and Gromyko and then Gorbachev on the other, has been extensively described by *Time* magazine's Washington bureau chief Strobe Talbott in his books *Deadly Gambits*[1] and *The Master of the Game*,[2] by Don Oberdorfer (*Washington Post* White House correspondent) in *The Turn*,[3] as well as in numerous testimonies of others. It would be superfluous to give more details here. Suffice to say that as soon as Gorbachev took over it became evident that his target was to disengage from the expensive nuclear competition with the United States. Figures 10.1 and 10.2 indicate how and why the Soviet Union under Brezhnev had gone full steam ahead to catch up with and overtake the United States in the number and yields of nuclear warheads.

When the 1963 Test Ban Treaty was being negotiated, it seems that Khrushchev was not aware of the wide gap that existed between the nuclear arsenals of the United States and USSR. Otherwise, it is difficult to believe the story that he and Kennedy came close to achieving a comprehensive test ban (reaching agreement on all but the number of on-site inspections). Although it is obvious that matters were not as simple as that, it seems that both sides were negotiating seriously. Kennedy was probably very aware of the size of the US arsenal, and personally horrified by the idea of similar escalation throughout the world; this accounted for his efforts towards a test ban and non-proliferation, which included Israel.[4] It was well into the 1970s before the Soviet Union achieved numerical parity with the United States, and not until the 1980s that (at least in US eyes) qualitative parity was reached, and such issues as 'window of vulnerability' could be raised in real seriousness. From the point of view of the US strategists (and equally in the eyes of Soviet strategists), what counted was the accuracy and reliability of missiles and warheads, as well as their numbers. When one thinks of the extent of maintenance required to keep liquid-fuelled ICBMs and SLBMs in readiness, along with problems of the safety and reliability of MIRVed warheads, it is not too difficult to see that maintaining qualitative parity must have been an extremely demanding job, given the level of quality control in the Soviet arms industries.

After the confrontational breakdown of the Geneva negotiations in 1983, the Soviet Union had no choice but to accept Pershing II deployment as a

Figure 10.1: Nuclear warheads in the US and the USSR

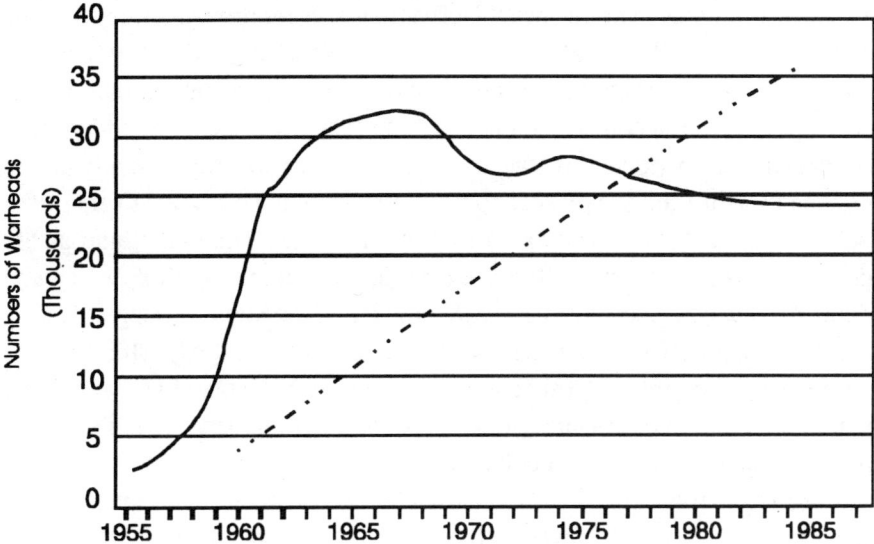

Figure 10.2: Nuclear yields of the US and the USSR (in thousand megatons, TNT equivalent)

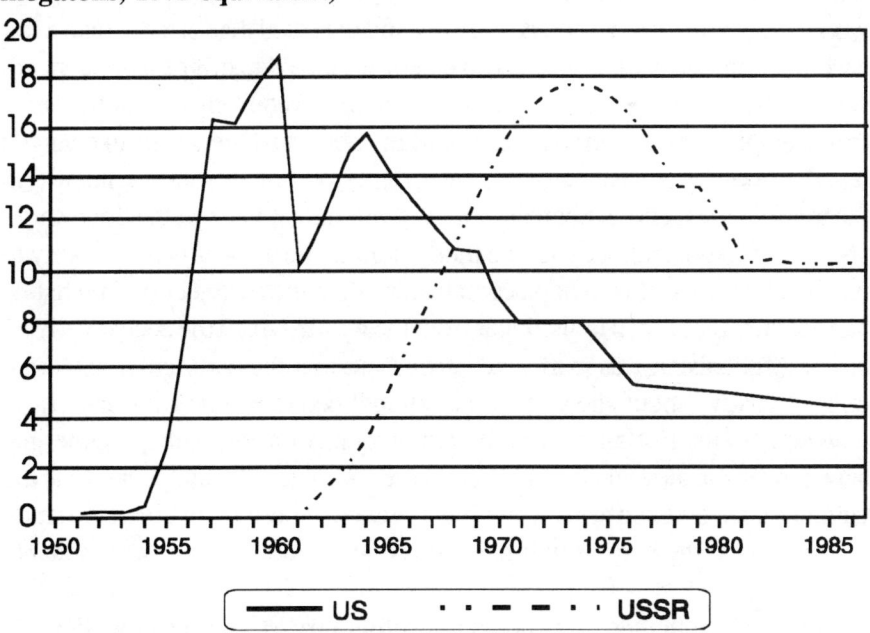

Source: Thomas B. Cochran et al., *Nuclear Weapons Databook vol. IV: Soviet Nuclear Weapons* (New York: Ballinger for the Natural Resources Defense Council, 1989), pp. 26, 43.

reality and to look for the best possible compromise in order to make these missiles impotent. This is what Gorbachev's compromise achieved. The problem with the Pershing IIs was not that they could reach Moscow (whether they could or not was not clear) or that they made decoupling unreal (which was not a trivial accomplishment), but the fact that precision-guided, medium-range army nuclear warheads could allegedly destroy instantly all the choke points for the Soviet second echelon to move west in the event of the outbreak of a third world war. In addition to their strategic value at the doctrinal level, the Pershing IIs created practical problems for the Soviet game plan. What was worse, the entire world knew that the Soviet strategy of using the Western peace movements to prevent deployment of the Pershing IIs had failed. It was possibly to Gorbachev's advantage that he faced a US president who was far from being a nuclear strategist, but who happened to believe very firmly in a world free from nuclear threat.

Seen from that angle, it was worthwhile for Gorbachev to accept the zero-zero option, which in 1981 was nothing more than an opening bluff on the side of the US president. One can recall the extent of surprise within the Geneva disarmament community when the contents of the INF agreement were made known. People had been involved in studying things like the 'walk in the woods' formula of Nitze and Kvitsinsky and regarded that as more than a fair accomplishment on the side of the Western alliance. Japan's primary concern was to prevent the SS-20s which were to be removed from west of the Urals from being redeployed in the Far East. Many personal letters were exchanged between Reagan and Nakasone during that period.[5] It is not clear what was in the mind of the General Secretary of the Communist Party at the time, and if you ask him today about what he thought then, the answer is more likely to be his reflection of his own place in history than the recollection of what he had actually thought. It is also clear from the way in which the decision to pull out of Afghanistan was made and carried out that the party chief had other things to worry about and was least of all inclined to continue the arms race. It would be interesting to accumulate evidence on the perhaps huge gap between Gorbachev and his politburo over what stance to adopt vis-à-vis the United States over the arms control negotiations. Until more objective study is carried out, the subject will have to remain in the domain of reasonable guesswork.

In the same manner, it is not very useful to try to reassess how SDI was really perceived by the Soviet leaders: whether they regarded it as a technically viable proposal to guide the US defence strategy, or as a mere dream. It is on record that the Japanese ambassador to the Conference on Disarmament at the time thought that the project was not technically feasible and that he had conveyed his sentiments to his government at home. There were a considerable number of technically qualified people both in the United States and in Britain who shared his doubts regarding space defence.[6] It is difficult to comprehend that Evgeny Velikov, a fusion physicist and close adviser to Gorbachev, believed that a nuclear explosion-pumped X-ray laser in space was a distinct possibility, and thus did not stop the party chief from bargaining so hard with the Reagan administration 'to prevent SDI at any cost'. At least, as a part of the negotiating history up to the 1988 Washington summit, SDI served to reveal just how urgent was Gorbachev's need to come to terms with the United States.

Who succeeds the Soviet Union?
In answering the major question of who is qualified to ratify the START treaty, the previous US tactic of granting the Security Council seat to Russia (legally questionable in terms of Article 23 of the UN Charter) will not work. The problem is not only a legal one; it is deeply concerned with technical qualifications. The ratifying body must be in clear command of all the strategic nuclear weapons of the former Soviet Union (and preferably of the tactical weapons as well in order to be able to make meaningful progress). This command may or may not involve the capability to fuel the missiles (especially those with liquid fuel for ICBMs and SLBMs), and to carry out periodic maintenance on both the missiles and the warheads. Such control would also involve the ability to maintain installations such as Arzamas 16 and Chelyabinsk 70 (considered the equals of Los Alamos and Lawrence Livermore), along with other weapon component manufacturing and assembly facilities. This would extend to the capability to design and produce new weapons and to test them underground, which may be required as a part of the technical options. This has considerable arms control implications, and can make the issue of financial and other assistance to Russia all the more complicated for countries like Japan. Moreover, if tritium and polonium 210 (with well-known half-lives of 12.4 years and 138 days, respectively) are major ingredients of the weapon systems, these systems will require frequent maintenance and/or separate storage of the weapons detonation initiation system. Quite apart from the issue of credibility, the United States is officially on record in claiming the need for selective nuclear testing in order to maintain its weapons stock reliability.

In addition to these technical capabilities, the body that ratifies START has to have a credible command-and-control system in hand, and this would most probably require the need to keep under Russian control the large phased-array radars in Azerbaijan, Belarus, Estonia, Kazakhstan and Ukraine, as well as any satellite launch, recovery and control sites outside the Russian Federation, such as at Sary Shagan in Kazakhstan.[7] The purpose of this requirement is not only to prove that there is effective control of the weapons systems, but also to make sure that the party in question has the National Technical Means (NTM) to verify US compliance, an issue historically very close to the heart of US disarmament and arms control treaty negotiations.

It is clear that at present Russia has neither the control nor the technical capabilities outlined above, nor is it authorized to speak on behalf of the four republics which inherited different fragments of the ex-Soviet strategic nuclear capability. It is extremely important to find an appropriate party to ratify both START and CFE if arms control is to continue to have credibility in the international community.

The problem of succession will affect the future of the nuclear Non-Proliferation Treaty (NPT) as the time approaches for the crucial 1995 review conference. At this conference the length of the treaty extension will be decided by simple majority vote (according to NPT article 10 ii). Unless all the former Soviet republics join the regime, the transformation will not be complete. If Ukraine, Belarus and Kazakhstan join as nuclear weapons states on the grounds that they were in possession of such weapons on 1 January 1967, the number of nuclear weapons states will jump from five to eight instantly, provoking an outcry from non-nuclear weapons states. If the three republics join NPT as non-nuclear weapons states and subject themselves to IAEA safeguards, then obviously inspectors will find nuclear weapons. The only answer is to pull out all nuclear weapons from these republics and move them to Russia, a solution which neither Kazakhstan nor Ukraine seems to support. Another possible way out is to create a super-republican military entity to control the entire strategic nuclear system, but this would go against the basic logic of the 'sovereignty' of the newly independent republics.

It may be possible to negotiate a way out in the 1995 conference, but that would be putting at stake the long-standing objections by many countries (including even France and China, who very recently joined this group) to legitimizing nuclear weapons as a viable national policy option.

Tactical nuclear weapons of the former USSR

In a way, strategic weapons are relatively easy to handle. They can be counted, and the arrangements for counting have already begun as a part of the SALT process as well as under the START regime (even if strange counting rules have been applied in the case of ALCMs and even though the INF experience with mobile missiles has been a lesson in the possibility of miscounting). It is fairly easy to observe if warheads have been removed from very large missiles, such as the SS-19 or SS-24. (Even if satellite observation is difficult, there must be an NTM system that gives sufficient confidence in counting.) It is not so with tactical weapons. Known mating between warheads and delivery systems would make counting easier, but another lesson learned from INF is that missiles (or warheads as the case may be) can be recharged. A good example would be nuclear mines and the Soviet equivalent of 155mm or 203mm shells. It is not at all clear how the current numbers have been obtained other than through a human intelligence network. Even the most efficient updated KH-11 or KH-12 satellites would not be able to count 155mm shells, even if they were lying uncovered in an open field.

Suppose that ways have been found to locate and count all tactical warheads. (This seems to be the working assumption in the US–Russian talks on disposal of nuclear weapons, for which the Congress has allocated $400 million out of the 1993 defence budget.) Testimony before the US House Armed Services Committee seems to indicate difficulties in land transportation of the warheads (assumed to be by rail in the case of Russia). In order to find a solution to the transportation problem, one needs to know how many there are, and to where they are to go. How many will depend on the possible follow-up to the Bush–Gorbachev exchange (of 27 September and 5 October 1991) on tactical weapons abolition, and the Bush–Yeltsin exchange (of 28 and 30 January 1992). It has already been discussed that such a follow-up presupposes the capability to deal with the strategic weapons agreement (such as credible evidence to implement the contents of the Bush–Yeltsin agreement). The answer to the second question will depend on where in Russia it is possible to dismantle nuclear warheads, and with what speed. This will clearly be governed by the design sophistication and plutonium isotopic specifications of the existing weapons. This may or may not require remote handling of heavy metals involved, owing in particular to the gamma radiation level of americium 241 from some of the aged warheads reportedly remaining in the ex-Soviet nuclear arsenal. If such complications are involved, and the process is to be carried out remotely, then the capabilities will be extremely limited. It is conceivable that the only feasible method would be to put the warheads through their production process in reverse.

Other evidence suggests that a significant limiting factor for dismantling could be the end use, or storage capability, for highly enriched uranium or plutonium. Both substances are toxic heavy metals, requiring very large and expensive storage facilities. Common sense would suggest they should be converted before storage into a non-metallic, and probably mixed oxide, form to avoid corrosion and reuse in weapons. Potential end uses, too, create uncertainty. To release the entirety of the enriched uranium will certainly confuse the existing international market and cause considerable difficulties for the United States, France and URENCO.[8] Plutonium, high in 239 isotopic content, will somehow have to find a place in the world nuclear market. The existing fast breeder technologies around the world are based on reactor-grade plutonium (about 60% Pu239) and even they are not yet commercially viable.

If there is concern around the world about sea transport of reactor-grade plutonium, people should be worrying even more about an estimated one hundred tons of weapons-grade material becoming surplus in the FSU. The global total will be double that amount, because of the material from the US nuclear warheads as well. There is technical evidence that material with one-fifth heat generation, one-third neutron background, and one-third specific activity (in short, a relatively low total radiation level), with a smaller critical mass, a larger tolerance for implosion timing and a more predictable yield, would be the preferred material for any would-be weapons manufacturer. Given such possible dangers as civil war, the storage of the plutonium extracted from nuclear weapons deserves very careful thought. The disposition of plutonium is an important subject which is likely to be addressed in a continuation of the nuclear disarmament process. It can no longer be left to a system which leaves two countries and two heads of state alone to work out solutions in places like Reykjavik.

Non-aligned countries and the prospects for a multilateral forum

During the Gulf crisis and the succeeding war, Syria's President Assad was an interesting example of those who were quick to sense which way the wind was blowing. The US attitude to the $10 billion credit for the settlement of Soviet Jews in the West Bank is another example of how the situation in the Middle East may be changing; it shows that the United States feels less need to rely solely on Israel to protect its interests in the region.

A similar loss of importance applies to the entire non-aligned camp, which owed much of its political prestige to the East–West conflict. There may now be less need for its voice to be heeded, except possibly over non-proliferation. The non-proliferation of nuclear weapons technology, chemical weapons and missile technology could be a major North–South issue in closing or widening the technology gap. The same could be said about global environmental control. Those advanced countries of the North which have emitted vast amounts of carbon dioxide in the past to achieve their present status are now trying to curb the industrialization efforts of their former colonies. Rio de Janeiro 1992 could well be a replay of Cancun 1981 in that the differences in interests between North and South are not easily bridged by a large-scale public relations campaign alone.

There were many reasons for the strong non-aligned group in the United Nations and the Conference on Disarmament. This was by far the largest group and could always gain more than a simple majority. Often, influential sub-groups such as Latin America and Black Africa could sway the vote. Another interesting point is that, in the world of East–West confrontation (except for non-proliferation which was always a North–South issue), the non-aligned camp could always stress its cause of justice and peace, with both East and West having to concur. Another very important factor affecting tactical multilateral diplomacy is that the ambassadors of the non-aligned nations are rarely under instruction from their home governments on such general subjects as disarmament and arms control. The extent of flexibility available to them in the UN and other forums is always a cause for envy among ambassadors of other groups. Given the end of the cold war, it will be interesting to watch developments, for instance, at the First Committee of the General Assembly meeting in autumn 1992. Already, the number of First Committee resolutions is decreasing (from 68 in 1983 to 59 in 1989 to 41 in 1991), which may indicate a lessening of interest in working out compromise language for various worthy but ineffective resolutions.

Whether the changes in the ex-Soviet Union will affect China and North Korea, and if so, to what extent, will depend very much on the type of influence that existed before in the triangular relationship between Moscow, Beijing and Pyongyang, and that is not at all clear. The development of a nuclear armament programme in North Korea (if indeed one exists) was not the intention of the Soviet Union. In fact, there is evidence that Moscow refused to supply highly enriched uranium fuel to the upgraded research reactor, and that it also encouraged North Korea to join NPT. It is possible that Pyongyang did not fully realize the obligation it had undertaken under NPT. Confusion on the part of the Vienna agency which supplied the wrong draft agreement to North Korea also compounded the issue. For its past, China would obviously be interested in the fate of nuclear arms, particularly those warheads in the hands of its newly emerged neighbours, the Central Asian Islamic republics and autonomous states.

Conclusion

It is too early to draw conclusions on any of the problems discussed above. One very important issue concerns the ex-Red Army, whose options involve splitting up into fifteen pieces or staying together. If it is to split up, and political discrepancies can somehow be covered, a joint command called 'the military forces of the Commonwealth of Independent States', similar to that foreseen in Chapter 7 of the UN Charter, could probably be set up. If the military insists on sticking together, with all the implications that would entail, such as unified authority over strategic and tactical warheads, delivery systems and launching platforms as well as the command and control, then it is the CIS that will have to yield. Since the CIS is not a sovereign state, CIS armed forces with command over nuclear forces cannot be a credible entity. Another school of thought would stretch the concept of sovereignty of the republics so as to make their foreign policy and military decision-making a joint arrangement. If this is a concept of world government in reverse, it will be more than an interesting experiment on a grand scale. The alternative, which the United States seems also to be considering, is to make Russia in effect 'most equal' among equals. We all have to wait and see what happens. In any event, it will not be easy to find ways of financing any joint or separate nuclear command for the former Soviet Union. A nuclear superpower passing round the hat to the non-nuclear audience for help is difficult to conceive.

Notes

1 New York: Alfred Knopf, 1984.
2 New York: Alfred Knopf, 1988.
3 New York: Poseidon Press, 1991.
4 Seymour Hersh, *The Samson Option*, (New York: Random House, 1991).
5 Ryukichi Imai, *US–Japan Policy Interactions on Arms Control and Disarmament during the Reagan–Nakasone Era: A Personal Memorandum*, IIGP Report 51E, 1991.
6 Two published examples of such views are: Sidney Drell, Philip Farley and David Holoway, *The Reagan Strategic Defense Initiative: A Technical, Political and Arms Control Assessment*, 1984; and *Strategic Missile*

Defense: Necessities, Prospects, and Dangers in the Near Term, 1985; both published by the Stanford Center for International Security and Arms Control.
7 *Soviet Nuclear Fission*, Center for Science and International Affairs, JFK School, Harvard, 1991, discusses these locations.
8 An enrichment joint venture between the UK, Germany and the Netherlands.

PART III
PERCEPTIONS OF SECURITY AFTER THE COLD WAR

CHAPTER 11
EUROPEAN PERCEPTIONS OF THE NEW SECURITY SITUATION

LAURENCE MARTIN

There can have been few, if any, previous moments in history when West Europeans were more confused or uncertain about their place in the international security system than they are now. Indeed the end of the cold war, welcome though it must be, could scarcely have occurred in a manner more likely to render the transition difficult. First of all, the collapse of the Soviet Union happened with breathtaking speed and finality. Secondly, the process of reappraisal was almost immediately interrupted by the Gulf crisis, from which almost certainly overhasty conclusions were drawn. As a result, the ill-developed concept of a New World Order announced by President Bush was very widely understood, if at all, as being based upon the belief that the peace-enforcing coalition assembled for the Gulf war, with the assent if not the participation of the Soviet Union and China, could be perpetuated. This rather precipitate and simplistic conclusion has stimulated probably over-optimistic analysis of the much more fundamental question of what impact the collapse of European communism will have on the international system. Yet the failure of the August 1991 coup, which completed the disappearance of the Soviet Union, has made that the dominant change to which we must all accommodate.

It is now clear to all that the end of the cold war has replaced a system that enforced a high degree of stability with one that for the moment is in constant turmoil. The pattern of concentric strategic circles – central bipolar, nuclear confrontation between the United States and the Soviet Union, surrounding military blocs, and a further surrounding Third World – has dissolved. In disappearing, the Soviet Union has also destroyed 'the West' as we have long known it; for the West, and indeed the Third World, were defined and named by reference to 'the East'. While the world, and particularly Europe, are rich in security-oriented institutions, these are largely left over from the former era and have yet to acquire well-defined roles in the new context and to sort out their relations with each other. Meanwhile, the potentially catastrophic, but happily mostly latent, tensions between the East and the West blocs have been replaced not by harmony but by virulent, small-scale conflicts, many of which are manifesting themselves in actual warfare. Elsewhere, the context of Third World conflicts is more ambiguous. The hopeful developments with regard to 'good governance' and market economics in Latin America and parts of Africa are showing worrying if as yet minor signs of setback. Other areas, such as the Indian subcontinent, are simmering with potentially large-scale conflicts, some with a nuclear component.

In approaching this very fluid and ambiguous world, Europe faces another fundamental problem which, if not entirely unreplicated elsewhere, is certainly on a unique scale. This is the problem of identity: Western Europe simply does not know what it is at the moment. This manifests itself even in terminology. Increasingly the word 'Europe' is taken to mean the European Community or, more properly if and when the Maastricht Treaty is ratified, the European Union, one pillar of which embraces security and defence through the medium of Western European Union (WEU). Yet, for the moment, the only effective security and defence capabilities are in the hands of the nations, which differ widely in their approach to security matters and in their readiness to employ armed forces in an active mode outside Western Europe itself. Meanwhile the effective provision for the defence of Western Europe remains American-dominated NATO, which entirely outstrips any present or prospective alternative as a framework for practical collaborative military action.

In evaluating the new security context from within this muddled identity, West Europeans share the rather general uncertainty as to whether we are entering a hopeful era of relative peacefulness within a system of international law, momentarily disturbed by transitional frictions, or a period of endemic conflict frequently breaking the bonds of law and mechanisms for peaceful settlement. It is unclear whether we are back to the nineteenth century or the 1920s and 1930s, and whether that system may lead us to another 1914 or 1939–41, or whether at last we have now a third and now much more promising opportunity to realize the frustrated harmonious dreams of 1919 and 1945, based on collective security.

So far as European perspectives of their own continental security problems are concerned, these are now cast in terms of 'risks' rather than the long-familiar NATO planning basis of the 'threat'. This change in terminology originally began some five or six years ago as a public relations deference to the sensitivities of the West's opposite numbers in the detente process. Today it is justified by the prevailing uncertainty as to where any threats, if any, will arise and by the hope that some, perhaps most, of them can be averted by prudent political measures before they reach the 'military stage'. A 'risk', then, is something that may become a 'threat', in the sense of reaching a stage at which there is no alternative to making military provision – though not necessarily taking military action – against it.

If a serious and directly military threat is to arise against Europe in the foreseeable future there are probably only two forms that it could take. The first is a 'recidivist' Russia, resuming under some presumably illiberal regime a threatening military posture. For new geopolitical reasons, this threat would presumably now first manifest itself further to the East than before, against former components of the Soviet Union or Warsaw Pact, rather than against the present European members of NATO. A serious exception to this remoteness might arise in the South, where an increasingly important Turkey still borders closely on the former Soviet arena or, less probably, against Norway. While this prospect of a newly coherent Russia mounting a serious external military pressure in the near future seems unlikely, it would be wise not to forget the sizeable military power still in Russia's hands or the fact that a country with such a large educated population and rich natural resources could, if it pulled itself together politically, surprise the world by the speed of its recovery. Of course the hope must be that such a recovery would diminish the prospect of an authoritarian and expansionist regime coming to power.

The second potential direct threat consists of the danger of nearby Third World nations continuing their acquisition of long-range weapons with massive destructive capabilities. Such acquisitions could not conceivably give those nations a war-winning capability against Europe (unless the Europeans carried their disarmament to imprudent extremes) but it could introduce a novel element into the relationship between Europe and its Southern neighbours – a relationship hitherto characterized by frequent European intervention in Middle Eastern crises free of any of the inhibitions that the new balance of armaments more favourable to the South would introduce. The danger of direct attacks upon European homelands would have a quite different weight in interventionist calculations than the hitherto familiar weighing of the risks to be encountered by expediting forces. Given the many possible sources of dispute between Europe and the Middle Eastern or North African states, any future European defence policy clearly needs to take account of this possible new dimension. The question must also form a component in any more generalized approach to regional security through the medium of arms control and anti-proliferation systems.

These directly military, but hopefully remote, dangers have to be considered within a context of more immediate, but less well defined, security problems. Of these the two most widely perceived are the spill-over from actual and potential chaos in Eastern Europe and the former Soviet Union, the prime manifestation of which is thought likely to be refugees and reinforcement of economically driven migratory pressures, and a similar migratory pressure from the South, especially North Africa. To some extent, both threats are already manifest as a result of the Yugoslav conflict and the economic deterioration in parts of the Arab world. Some of the Balkan conflicts, however, also have a potential to extend actual warfare into the NATO area by involving Greece and Turkey.

Finally, and on the broadest scale of all, Europe obviously has an interest, as already suggested, in the general tone of international relations. In so far as respect for international law is 'indivisible' – and there is considerable controversy about this – then breaches anywhere, especially in the form of aggression, weaken structures and processes that might be relevant to solving European problems. At the same time vested economic interests, the safety of nationals overseas and simple humanitarian concern give Europeans some interest in the whole world security scene. Nevertheless this interest is already perceived to be much less general and compelling than during the cold war, when the fear of Soviet gains, of their extension by the 'domino' effect, and the urgings of the United States as head of the global coalition, compelled European attention to a wide variety of geographically remote events. One of the main uncertainties is to what extent the United States will try to keep up this pressure for global participation in the name of the New World Order, and one of the main questions facing the Europeans will be how they should respond. Already the Gulf crisis has provided a vivid, but almost certainly misleading, example.

It should be apparent from this brief account that one of the fundamental difficulties in adjusting European security and defence policy to the new circumstances is the vagueness and uncertainty that besets efforts to define the problems that have to be solved. To borrow a familiar metaphor from medicine, most of the problems can be regarded as 'elective' in comparison with the single, 'life-threatening' challenge that Soviet communism constituted. The result is an elusive substantive basis from which to approach the dilemma of choosing appropriate institutional frameworks for response.

Unlike Asia, Europe is provided with an almost embarrassing wealth of security-oriented institutions. All European governments without exception pay respect to NATO as the senior of these and advocate its retention. NATO is, of course, an organization at the military end of the extending spectrum of security instruments, linking the United States to Europe in order to deal with direct, external military threats to a clearly defined area. The general desire to maintain NATO as an insurance policy against the re-emergence of a serious direct threat arises from a wide range of attitudes and expectations. To some, particularly France, the insurance is valued only against a remote contingency: a so-called alliance of last resort if the diplomacy and crisis management of affairs within the newly extended Europe, handled on an exclusively European basis, should fail and produce a crisis the Europeans could no longer manage. The French attitude is apparently based partly on a simple anti-American, 'Europe first-ism' sentiment and partly upon a genuine fear, in which the actively hostile attitude is also often wrapped, that the US guarantee is in any case unreliable, weakening and therefore in need of replacement as rapidly as possible by a self-reliant European defence.

This view is naturally unwelcome in the United States and in those countries like Britain which favour the Atlantic tie, and which – partly but not solely for that reason – resist any rapid progress towards Europeanization. This viewpoint consequently encourages the extension of the NATO relationship into handling the new East–West relationship in Europe via the North Atlantic Consultative Council (NACC). Such an approach has the advantage that by common consent the lead in completing the CFE negotiations, and of course the bilateral START, can be taken only by the United States. Consequently, while the CSCE has developed as a source of rules of conduct calculated to enhance mutual confidence in security relations, NACC has become the channel for assisting and monitoring the demilitarization and civilianization of the former Warsaw Pact members.

Much of this is, however, only the unwinding of the past. The task of warding off any danger of revived aggressive threats or potential from the FSU seems less pressing than handling the chaos in the former Soviet empire and precluding its spill-over into Western Europe. Here, until very recently, the work of economic and political assistance, peace-keeping and adjustment of internal disputes was regarded as more the duty of CSCE, as an East–West forum, and of the European Union and its members as the effective actors. NATO thus saw the danger of being regarded as the most powerful possessor of the least relevant means – the military force – and the agent for handling the least pressing problems: direct threats to the Treaty area. Neither CSCE nor the European Union have, however, proved very effective in dealing with the initial challenges, particularly in Yugoslavia, as exemplified by the fact that the United Nations – once merely resorted to for legitimizing such coercive military measures as a maritime arms embargo – has had to assume the thankless, and perhaps in the circumstances even pointless, task of peace-keeping. Seeing an opportunity, NATO has offered its auspices for peace-keeping out of area when a CSCE mandate is available.

We should probably be cautious in evaluating this move. It is obviously intended to restore NATO's political relevance and to give its forces some practical work. On the other hand, NATO has survived perfectly well for decades without actual military operations under its own colours. More seriously, the political considerations underlying the hitherto strict interpretation of the area of responsibility still exist in many respects, and it remains to be seen whether the new initiative will take root as a policy and whether it will prove beneficent or harmful to the Alliance as actual peace-keeping operations are undertaken.

If the future of NATO on the European security scene is debatable, that of the European Union itself is scarcely less so. The Maastricht Treaty purports to establish a transitional formula. Being an effective economic union, the European Community cannot avoid a great deal of behaviour that by any definition constitutes a 'foreign policy'. Maastricht, building on former 'political cooperation', tries to institutionalize, extend and tighten this. Maastricht also assumes, correctly, that where there is a foreign policy, there cannot fail to be security-related issues, and consequently looks to closer coordination of national policies, including the possibility of qualified majority decision in areas to be specified. By a quirk of drafting dynamics, all the illustrative examples considered in the final treaty negotiations as possible topics suitable for common action are drawn from the security aspects of foreign policy. But security questions in reality are likely to prove divisive, both because of their intrusive nature, and because security brings Europe closer than many other issues to its controversial Atlantic dimension. The Maastricht Treaty also envisages the evolution of a common defence policy, by which it means the more military-dominated aspects of security, and acknowledges the possibility of a common defence, by which it seems to mean the joint maintenance and operation of military forces.

The whole treaty is, of course, a set of compromises, some drafted badly, some with deliberate vagueness. In no area was there more division of preferences than in security and especially defence. Those divisions included differences over the degree of exclusiveness in the European identity, especially vis-à-vis the United States, and the extent to which defence questions were to be treated instrumentally as a route for advancing European integration, or as practicable military solutions. The three major powers, France, Germany and Britain, are incongruently divided on these issues: France and Germany more prepared to sacrifice military logic to political atmosphere than Britain; Germany and Britain less prepared to alienate the United States than France. Moreover, for the future, a third asymmetry will be significant. France and Britain, on the one hand, are nations still politically prepared for undertaking hostilities, even – perhaps especially – out of area. Germany, on the other hand, is historically, politically and constitutionally inhibited. Maastricht handled all this by putting defence in the separate pillar of WEU and leaving it to the coming months or years to work out answers.

The description given so far in this chapter of what has occurred and in what context is probably uncontroversial. To predict the future leads one inevitably more into personal judgment. It seems likely that while the process of international coordination of security policy in the European Union will continue, the move towards the integration, as distinct from coordination, of defence policy has peaked. A commonality of problems and a shortage of resources will continue to promote processes of collaboration, not least in the area of procurement, given the twin stimuli of shortage of resources and the impact of harmonization and integration of European civilian industry. But this is likely to remain in many important respects an intergovernmental process.

This is so for two reasons. First, as reactions to the Persian Gulf and Yugoslav crises have reminded us, defence, with its costs, risks, bloodshed and need for speedy decisions, is best handled, can probably only be handled, by political communities with a much greater sense of solidarity and common interest than the European Union is ever likely to muster. Second, the Maastricht Treaty itself, in dealing with precisely the issues of security, has made the emergence of any such solidarity much less likely. For, partly in a reckless concession to Greece, appropriately enough the Achilles heel of Europe on so many issues, the Treaty provides that members of the European Community automatically become eligible to join WEU. Unless typically loose drafting permits this being construed as meaning members at the time of signing – and such a construction would be politically awkward, if not legally strained – then WEU faces the prospect of being joined over the next few years both by erstwhile Warsaw Pact countries, themselves within the ethnically flawed East Central region of Europe, and by the former neutrals of EFTA which, though relieved of the aversion to joining one side in the cold war, still have pacifistic, alliance-averse characteristics. It passes belief that a community of some twenty security-independent nations, embracing such a wide range of temperaments, would constitute an effective defence community in the foreseeable future.

A community of such a size might indeed serve a useful security purpose, but would have to do so by 'being' rather than 'doing': that is, it might defuse internal European animosities and foster an atmosphere of mutual reassurance but would be exceedingly unlikely to play an active external role. Thus, if Europeans are to play such a role at all, the agents will have to be the existing nation-states unless, of course, an inner core of defence-minded partners emerges.

One of the major determinants in this process will be the evolution of German attitudes to military questions: whether Germany will emerge from its present inhibitions and match a robust military policy to its increasingly forceful diplomacy and how, if it does, such a development will be received by its partners and neighbours. As Europeans look beyond their subcontinental preoccupations to the wider world, they ask similar questions about the role of Japan, for that must also be a major factor in determining the future world order.

The optimism that underlies the tendency to give the phrase New World Order capital letters arises from the hope that, with the decline of communism, democracy and the market will make the external behaviour of nations law-abiding and peaceable, extending globally the sense of a 'security community' that has fairly certainly established itself in the North Atlantic world. A less sanguine but more plausible belief suggests that such good behaviour will at least be sufficiently widely dispersed to permit enforcement of international law on law-breakers through the United Nations and other mechanisms of collective security.

Events since the reunification of Germany and the break-up of the Soviet Union signalled the definitive end of the cold war have surely convinced any rational observer that, if international goodwill based on the improved domestic character of states is spreading at all, it is not doing so at a pace sufficient to obviate the need for such a process of enforcement. Moreover, most agree that, while the UN-sponsored operation in the Gulf signalled a considerable revival of the United Nations, that conflict featured far too many special, favourable circumstances to constitute a reliable precedent.

As the new UN Secretary-General has pointed out, the United Nations still has no coherent intrinsic enforcement capability of its own once military force is called for, even if the potential of economic and political sanctions does seem to be enjoying increased respect. For forcible action, the United Nations has so far only licensed operations by well-disposed nations. Although the subject is one that has already inspired volumes and still requires much further study, it seems fairly obvious that democratic nations afford such support only when the case in question strikes an appropriate balance of moral justification – or, if one is cynical, moralistic plausibility – and self-interest. In the Gulf case the blatancy of Iraqi aggression provided the former and oil the latter for many participants.

There is, however, a third prerequisite, or in prudence ought to be, and that is practicability: the enforcement operation proposed should have a plausible prospect of re-establishing respect for law and resolving the underlying conflict at a reasonable price. At present, as in Yugoslavia, the international community has shown considerable caution in one category of dispute that is already proving a frequent phenomenon in the post-cold war world: that is, civil, usually ethnically based, conflicts. Experience shows that these are hard to arrest and even harder to resolve. The veto instituted in the United Nations Charter envisaged another type of intractable quarrel: that in which the disputants are too powerful to yield readily to even concerted international action. Into this category might well fall a future confrontation between, say, India and Pakistan. Moreover, in this context we must reckon with the possibility that China or even Russia might one day again exercise its veto or at least demand an excessive political price for not doing so.

The implication of all this is that it would be premature to assume that an effective and acceptable collective security system is about to emerge from the ruins of the cold war. Moreover, we should perhaps be cautious in assuming that such a system would necessarily be one to welcome. However benign may be the intentions of those who are intent on intervention in Yugoslavia or elsewhere, the world is being carried on a wave of immediate post-cold war euphoria into deep inroads upon legal concepts of sovereignty, state recognition, successor state rights, and so on, which have been carefully and for sound reasons established over many years of evolution in international law. As yet the world lacks the degree of political consensus and homogeneity that would be needed to assure each and every international actor that such behaviour would always be acceptable to it, whether as subject or object.

The wiser as well as probably more likely future, therefore, is that the

United Nations, and other legitimizing agencies such as CSCE, will serve as *ad hoc* sponsors of peace-keeping and perhaps even of occasional peace-enforcing actions by such nations or groups of nations as are willing and able to undertake them. Only a few states have the capacity to do this on even a regional scale and perhaps only one, the United States, can do so globally. The greater powers that perform these roles will come to constitute a *de facto* 'directorate' even if they are not formally recognized as such.

Just as the composition of a group acting in one case need not be the same as that performing in another, there is no necessary reason why the contributions made need be similar. Indeed they cannot be so; one of the reasons why the United States must be predominant in many cases is precisely its possession of some unique capabilities. From this perspective the current wish in many quarters that Germany and Japan should become more normalized to other great-power behaviour, especially by widening their military role, should not be regarded as necessarily the most constructive way forward.

Finally, this outlook suggests that some crises and conflicts may not be amenable to peace-keeping or peace-enforcing action and may have to 'burn themselves out' on their own terms. It also suggests that the currently popular goal of 'stability' will not merely sometimes be beyond achievement but may, unless very generously interpreted, be counterproductive to the search for long-term pacification. It was not by accident or stupidity that the search for effective collective security and disarmament during the 1920s was accompanied by an earnest debate about the prerequisites for 'peaceful change' but that no satisfactory conclusion emerged.

None of this scepticism is intended to belittle efforts to reinforce international law and bolster the processes of peace-keeping and conciliation. On the contrary, it springs from a fear that only disillusionment at best and perverse diplomacy at worst would be induced by over-optimism and over-commitment. As so often, incrementalism seems preferable to utopianism.

CHAPTER 12
JAPANESE PERCEPTIONS OF THE NEW SECURITY SITUATION

SEIZABURO SATO

The security policy of the cold war period
The post-Second World War world was built upon two fundamental frameworks: one derived from the East–West confrontation and the other from the predominance of the United States within the Western alliance. Given the existence of these frameworks, Japan's military security and defence policy centred on the establishment of an effective deterrence system. This system consisted of a defensive conventional force that relied upon US forces, including the nuclear arms they possessed, for offensive capability. As long as the United States maintained overwhelming military and economic superiority and continued to possess the will and the ability to play a decisive role in safeguarding the security of the West, Japan's defence effort could safely remain relatively low-key. Based solely on conventional weapons, this effort was called 'The Defence-Only Strategy'. In view of the fact that Japan's neighbours, victimized by Japan during Second World War, were deeply apprehensive of Japan's rearmament and that domestically there existed a strong popular sentiment for peace, this type of approach was deemed suitable at the time.

Nevertheless, Japan's defence policy has undergone certain notable changes in response to changing international relations and the emergence of Japan as a powerful world economy. From the late 1970s, the strategic importance of the Japanese archipelago increased significantly as the Soviet Union turned the Sea of Okhotsk into an 'ocean bastion' by deploying and protecting its ballistic missile submarines (SSBNs). Soviet military strength was rapidly increased, especially in naval and air forces, in Northeast Asia and the Northwest Pacific. This was also when Japan grew into one of the world's principal economic powers while the US experienced a decline in its relative economic position. It therefore became necessary for Japan to assume a larger role in maintaining and modernizing its deterrence system against the Soviet Union. Japan did progressively reinforce its defence capabilities, especially in air defence and anti-submarine warfare. The US also made a great effort to strengthen its military forces, particularly during the Reagan administrations. As a result, the military balance in the region greatly improved. Since the Northwest Pacific was deemed to be of pivotal strategic importance in the East–West confrontation, strengthening the deterrence capability in this area was necessary not only for Japan's own defence, but also for the security of the entire Western alliance.

Japan's security policy was not limited to military aspects. Japan was determined to learn from the mistakes of the Second World War and chose to pursue a basic security policy that would ensure national security while making maximum use of non-military means. Indeed, during the postwar decades the cornerstone of Japan's foreign policy was an immense effort to maintain an intimate cooperative relationship with the United States, its principal ally, as well as with all other friendly nations. Further, it would endeavour in the meantime – insofar as it did not contradict such alignment policies – to relax the existing tensions and improve diplomatic relations with other nations that could directly affect Japan's security interests. In this respect, its economic capability was considered more important than military power as an instrument of foreign policy. When the world was shaken by the 1973 oil crisis, Japan became more keenly aware of the importance of the economic aspects of national security. The term 'comprehensive security', which is now widely used, was in fact first coined by Japan. By the end of the 1970s, comprehensive security had been formally adopted as the official policy of the Japanese government. In this sense, it can be said that during the cold war years Japan already possessed a security concept that would be readily applicable to the post-cold war period.[1]

Varying types of post-cold war threats
Both the East–West confrontation and the overwhelming superiority once enjoyed by the United States, which together had created a structure for postwar international relations, have ceased to exist. As I will stress again later, because Russia will continue to be a major nuclear power in the coming decades, we must be concerned by the possibility that a regime driven by xenophobic nationalism could emerge in Russia. However, the East–West confrontation between the Leninist-based Soviet Union, which advocated a fundamentally expansionist foreign policy, and the democratic nations of the West has most definitely passed into history. This was a result of the collapse

of the Leninist systems in the Soviet Union and the East European countries, as well as the disintegration of the Soviet Union as a unified state. When the Soviet Union fell, the United States was left as the only remaining military superpower. In the military sense, the United States is now even more predominant in the world. Meanwhile, however, it has become more and more obvious that the American economic position has, if only relatively, continued to decline. For the foreseeable future, the United States will maintain its status as the world's largest economy, while also retaining its status as the world's leading player in many fields of technological development. However, it is also certain that the absolute economic supremacy which it enjoyed under the peculiar circumstances after Second World War is unlikely to recur.

Japan's economic position has also gone through some fundamental changes during the past few decades. Japan, starting as a war-devastated vanquished nation, became Asia's first newly industrializing country by the early 1960s. It grew to become the second-largest economy in the world during the 1970s. In the 1980s, Japan emerged as the world's largest creditor nation with the largest trade surplus. In terms of its dramatic pace, Japan's economic development was even more phenomenal than the relative decline of the US economy.

Because of such enormous shifts in international relations – and, as a result of these, the swift transformation of Japan's position in the world – the security policy of Japan is now under scrutiny to determine what major readjustments are necessary. However, since the sea changes that are taking place are occurring so rapidly and on such a large scale, the Japanese government has not yet reached any clear conclusions as to how its national security policy ought to be reshaped. Among the Japanese people, a consensus on the subject is far from being reached. In the following pages, as a prelude to exploring Japan's new security policy options, I shall analyse the types of potential major crises in the post-cold war period and examine desirable policy alternatives for coping with them.

New threats from the former Soviet Union
What ultimate changes were wrought upon the former Soviet Union by the second Russian Revolution which followed the summer of 1991 still remain to be seen. As Russia's Foreign Minister Andrei Kozyrev has pointed out, 'daily newspapers and even CNN, let alone magazines, prove increasingly unable to keep up with the rapid pace of change';[2] conditions in the FSU are still in flux.

However, it has become evident that irreversible changes have already occurred, at least in two areas which are bound to have a significant impact on international relations as well as on the security of the West. The first is the collapse of the Leninist system. It is certainly true that many reformists, including Boris Yeltsin himself, were at one time or another communists. Also, in some of the republics which once constituted the Soviet Union, as well as in some East European countries, the former communist parties still continue to exist as governing bodies under a different organizational guise. There are numerous other instances in which leadership positions, both economic and political, are still occupied by former communists and their friends. This kind of situation can easily be understood, however, when we consider the fact that, with the exception of Romania, the successive revolutions that took place in Eastern Europe and the Soviet Union were quiet revolutions almost without bloodshed; in addition, most of the elite in these countries previously belonged to communist parties.

However, what has become obvious to most of the people who were living under Leninist regimes is that the Leninist system has turned out to be a 'grand failure'[3] in terms of improving the living standard of the people, in realizing social justice, and above all in protecting human rights. The fact that the collapse of communist rule in Eastern Europe and the Soviet Union was so sudden and complete is an indication that the legitimacy of Leninism had become 'hollowed out' long before the second Russian Revolution. For most East European countries, communist rule was something that had been forced upon them by the Soviet Union, and from the very beginning it failed to capture the hearts of their people because of their strong, if latent, anti-Russian nationalism. Under the prevailing circumstances, therefore, it is unthinkable that the seriously damaged Leninist ideology will regain any semblance of legitimacy or that communist parties will re-emerge overtly as governing bodies. In this sense, it is quite unlikely that the cold war will be revived in its previous form as a confrontation between the Eastern and Western camps, each side with its own political system and ideology.

The second irreversible change is the disintegration of the Soviet empire. As is often pointed out by Soviet specialists, neither the Tsarist Russian empire nor the Soviet empire, unlike the former British or French empires, was able to establish a position of cultural and economic superiority in relation to its colonies and peripheral countries. What functioned to ensure order in the empire was a colossal military force and a centrally controlled Party/State bureaucracy. In this sense, the Soviet empire was an empire without a metropolis, a 'bloated state of emaciated people' according to Vassily

Kluchevsky.[4] Therefore, when it became clear that the Brezhnev Doctrine had actually been renounced, the Soviet 'external empire' began to crumble, and later, in the process of the dissolution of the communist party organization, the Soviet 'internal empire' also collapsed with little resistance.

There is no possibility that the external empire will be reconstructed. In the first place, Russia itself does not seem to possess the will or desire. Moreover, any attempt at rebuilding an empire would certainly run the risk of total confrontation with the West. Russia could not bear the cost of this. The revival of the internal empire in any form which includes the three Baltic states is likewise inconceivable. Serious doubts exist as to how long and with how much substance the Commonwealth of Independent States (CIS), which includes most of the republics from the FSU, can survive. Even at the time of writing, the CIS member republics, including the Russian Federation, are experiencing a rapidly rising tide of nationalism that shows tendencies towards runaway independence. As the excitement of forging independent states subsides, it is nevertheless possible that some republics will opt to re-establish close ties with the Russian Federation for reasons of economic necessity and security. But it remains unlikely that a centrally controlled empire could ever be created again.

If these two changes are indeed truly irreversible, the Soviet threat of the cold war period has gone. It is true, however, that these changes are not as obvious in Northeast Asia as they are in Europe. In the Northeast Asia region there was no Soviet satellite state except for Mongolia, and the Soviet forces stationed there were never a source of threat to the non-communist countries in the region. Also, the former Soviet forces in the Far East have not been reduced in any substantive way since the end of the cold war. The transfer and redeployment of state-of-the-art weapons systems from Eastern Europe and the European side of the FSU to this region has actually accelerated the modernization of the Soviet forces. Despite this, however, the readiness and training level of the Russian forces which replaced the Soviet troops in the region have suffered from serious and inevitable deterioration. In addition, while the Russian Federation remains under pressure to cut deep into military expenditures in order to implement a wholesale civilian conversion of military industries, it will not be long before some significant consequences will become apparent in the east of Russia.

It is of course true that the FSU military threat has not completely disappeared from the world. In the foreseeable future the Russian Federation, *de facto* heir to the former Soviet forces, is bound to remain a world military power second only to the United States. More alarming is that it is a *nuclear* superpower and there is no guarantee that the Russian Federation will evolve into a peaceful democracy. It is quite conceivable that the vicious circle of economic difficulties and political chaos could give rise to an authoritarian regime in Moscow backed by armed forces, or that the country could fall victim to political extremism fanned by inflamed nationalistic sentiments. Even if it succeeds in revitalizing its economy, a Russia of vast land mass and abundant natural resources, with a high educational level for its citizens, is bound to assert itself as a major world power. But should that happen, such a new Russia would be a nation with its doors open to the outside world, an integral member of the world economy. Therefore, it would be a Russia that did not need external expansion by military force, and thus should constitute no military threat to the West.[5]

The Soviet threat of the cold war period arose from the fact that the Soviet Union possessed a vast military machine and vigorously pushed a policy of external expansionism. But the major current dangers from the Russian Federation and other former Soviet republics are different: for example, the possibility of an outflow of weapons of mass destruction from a politically confused and economically frustrated FSU into some dangerously ambitious developing nation; or crippling environmental damage caused by major accidents at nuclear power installations; or a mass migration of FSU refugees into the West resulting from internal wars and rebellions. All of these represent threats resulting not from the strength of the Soviet Union as demonstrated in the cold war years, but from the weakness and confusion arising from its disintegration.

Should the FSU fall into extreme chaos it would be profoundly detrimental not only to the people of its republics, but also to the rest of the world. Western Europe and Japan, located in close proximity to the FSU, would be particularly affected. Obviously, the efforts of the West and of Japan to provide timely and effective assistance programmes for the FSU member states are significant elements of security policy. Other new security tasks for the West are to continue to encourage Russia to pursue arms reduction efforts, to cooperate with FSU member republics in implementing safe storage and disposal programmes for all weapons of mass destruction, and to assist them in the safe management of their nuclear power plants. Obviously, however, external aid can be of only limited help to the Russian colossus and effective countermeasures to deal with new threats from the FSU will be nearly as expensive and difficult as was maintenance of the cold war deterrence system.

The time when the Western nations will be able to enjoy any kind of peace dividend is unfortunately still quite far away.

Trends of potential regional conflicts

The end of the cold war has affected the nature of conflicts among developing countries in complex ways. During the cold war years, the Soviet Union sponsored positive assistance programmes to various radical elements in the South with the aim of exploiting anti-Western nationalism in the developing nations and enhancing the Soviet sphere of influence. To contain this kind of Soviet action, the West itself often become involved in regional conflicts. Thus such conflicts often became virtual proxy East–West wars, rendering their resolution all the more difficult. For many of the developing nations, which lacked the preconditions necessary for viable development along Western market-economy lines, communism seemed the more attractive model until quite recently, and the Soviet Union was often able to use their admiration for communism as an instrument in promoting Soviet influence. However, as Russia now finds itself in no position to expand southward and the attraction of communism is now completely gone, it should become easier to find solutions to, or at least contain, regional conflicts in the South.

Most regional conflicts are caused by such factors as economic impoverishment, arbitrary state boundaries, religious conflicts and ethnic confrontations, none of which directly pertain to the East–West confrontation. It is becoming clear that the end of the cold war has not actually curtailed the number of local conflicts or cured their causes. On the contrary, chaotic conditions in the FSU and Eastern Europe have contributed to the increase in regional struggles and rebellions within these former communist countries, as is evident in the situation in Yugoslavia. As a result of the collapse of the Leninist system, many of the former communist countries have fallen into a state similar to that of the Third World. There is a significant danger that the nations of the North will cut the amount of assistance offered to the developing nations because of the diminishing Soviet threat. Should this happen, there is little that the Southern nations can do, at least for the time being. In the long run, however, further deterioration of the economic situation and political order in the South is bound to bring undesirable consequences with regard to global peace and prosperity.

To make things worse, the development and spread of military technology has made it much easier for developing countries to acquire dangerous weapons, including missiles. I have already pointed out that the chaos in the

FSU has vastly increased this kind of danger, but in addition there is now a real possibility that China and North Korea may sell on the weapons market because of their dire need for hard currency.[6] Should this happen, the damage inflicted on countries through regional conflicts is quite likely to become much more serious, as was shown in the Gulf war. Rigorous control of the international transfer of weapons of mass destruction, and a strengthening of the international system for management of arms transfers, are tasks which demand immediate attention.

Should the Western nations be pressured into force reductions that are too rapid and too deep in an effort to appease popular sentiment calling for a peace dividend, their ability to cope with continuing regional conflicts will be severely hampered. This may encourage further local conflicts.[7]

Communist regimes remain in power in certain East Asian countries such as China, North Korea, and Vietnam, and it is possible that such disruptions as have occurred in Eastern Europe and the FSU will also take place in these Asian countries in the not-so-distant future. It is highly likely that North Korea, which has fallen decisively behind South Korea in economic competition and yet continues to adhere to an extreme form of personality cult leadership and an isolationist foreign policy, will experience a sudden political breakdown. This may be triggered by factors such as the transfer of power from the current leadership to the next generation. In order for North Korea to overcome its serious economic crisis, an open-door policy is an absolute necessity, but such an option could be a direct cause of the collapse of the regime. For once the door is thrown open, the regime's legitimacy, which has precariously depended on the myth of North Korea's superiority in every way to South Korea, will be lost forever. Herein lies an insoluble dilemma for North Korea, leaving little possibility that the regime could successfully adopt a course of gradual and peaceful reform. Recently, North Korea has become interested in improving its relations with the United States and Japan, and also has been taking steps to relax the tensions between itself and South Korea. These moves seem to be motivated by North Korea's wish to attract outside capital and technology, and thus to find some way to ameliorate its economic difficulties. However, there is no sign that North Korea will adopt economic open-door policies similar to those of China and Vietnam; rather, it seems to be strengthening its measures of social control. If and when North Korea's regime collapses, the ensuing chaos could bring about a very grave situation on the Korean peninsula. It will be especially dangerous if North Korea is indeed developing a nuclear weapons capability.

Increased international pressure on North Korea for the suspension of its nuclear weapons development effort is thus an indispensable precondition for peace in Northeast Asia.

If China, the only remaining communist empire, should now also fall into great chaos, the sheer size of its land and population would mean that any danger from North Korea in terms of repercussions on the international situation in East Asia would be completely dwarfed. At present, the Beijing government's priority is economic development, and the country is truly in need of domestic political tranquillity as well as a peaceful international environment. As long as this condition holds, Beijing's foreign policy will remain non-expansionist and cooperative with the outside world. There is, however, no ready assurance that China's long-term foreign policy will continue in this way. China's recent strengthening of its military position has become a common concern of its neighbouring countries. China has increased arms expenditure by 14% in its 1992 budget, and is making positive efforts to modernize its forces by importing, for instance, 80 MiG-29s and 24 Su-27s from Russia.[8] If and when Chinese economic development faces grave obstacles, or internal destabilization becomes a threat, it is always possible that China may turn to a more hostile style of foreign policy. Even in such a case, however, China's capabilities will remain relatively limited for many years to come. For this reason, its threats may well remain less than global in scale. But for close neighbours such as Hong Kong and Taiwan, any threat from China could prove catastrophic. It should be noted that this is the very reason why the East Asian countries, including Japan, took a relatively conciliatory position by comparison with the Western nations over the Tiananmen incident.

The recent Philippine elections and the failed military coup in Thailand are indications that the economically viable non-communist East Asian countries are heading, if only slowly, in the direction of greater stabilization in spite of certain disquieting political events. It is expected that post-Suharto Indonesia may also be able to avoid any extreme political disorder.

However, the South Asia–Indian Ocean region, which provides important sea lanes connecting East Asia and the Middle East, is comparatively stagnant in economic terms. It is saddled with more deep-rooted problems that could result in regional conflict, and it runs a greater risk of nuclear proliferation; all in all, this region poses a much graver problem than East Asia. The collapse of the Soviet Union has caused significant changes in the external policy of India, the central power of South Asia. Not only has it lost its most powerful friendly neighbour, the Soviet Union, but it also faces an expanding Islamic influence. The fact that the Central Asian Republics have joined the Economic Cooperation Organization (ECO), whose principal members are Pakistan, Iran and Turkey, augurs ill for India. In fact, it is for this reason that India has been forced to improve its relations with the United States, Japan, China, Israel and the ASEAN nations. Also, it is probably to some extent a result of the failure of the Leninist system that India, along with other South Asian countries, is now partially abandoning its economic policy of socialist central planning and protectionist import substitution, and is beginning to adopt an export-led growth strategy by means of deregulation, privatization, and positive encouragement of foreign capital investment.

As I have pointed out, the end of the cold war has not always led to a situation in which regional conflicts can progress towards resolution. The Middle Eastern region, capable of major impact on the world economy because of its rich oil resources, will continue to be a region of special instability. But in Asia, and especially in East Asia, a continuing productive cycle of economic development and political stabilization can be witnessed; the region as a whole is surely beginning to move in a more peaceful direction.

Unconventional security threats
The termination of the cold war and the collapse of the Soviet Union have aroused new concerns over threats of an unconventional nature. Among such threats, the destruction of the global environment, the international spread of drugs and AIDS, and potential large-scale movements of political and economic refugees are most often cited. The most serious of all non-military threats, however, could be the possible dissolution of the Western alliance as a result of the disappearance of the common Soviet threat, and the resultant collapse of the open international economic order. In today's world, in which the United States has long since lost its towering economic dominance, the only way to provide the international public goods of peace and prosperity is for the principal advanced democracies to cooperate together, especially the G7 nations. Of course, it is also important to maintain close consultation and coordination with major powers like Russia and China as specific problems arise.

In terms of closeness of cooperation among its members and endurance (for almost half a century), the postwar Western alliance has been by far the most stable alliance in the history of international relations since the Peace of Westphalia in 1648. Moreover, within this stable cooperative framework, economic interdependence has greatly deepened. This network of international economic cooperation has included not only all of the advanced democracies, but also the newly industrializing economies (NIEs) and many developing countries, reaching out to all corners of the world. Since the end of the Second World War, overall economic growth has almost always lagged behind the rate of increase in international trade. Furthermore, in recent years, foreign direct investment has been growing at an almost unheard-of speed. The fact that the gross production attributed to such foreign direct investment had, for the first time in history, surpassed the value of total international trade during the 1980s is a clear indication of how intimately interwoven today's world economy has become.[9] This means, then, that the foundation for cooperation among the advanced democracies for providing such international public goods has become more firmly established than ever before.[10] However, the collapse of this open international economic order would deal a crippling blow to all the countries within this network.

On the other side of the coin of deepening interdependence are increased foreign dependency and economic vulnerability. An increase in foreign direct investment, for instance, can mean the decay of certain industrial sectors of the advanced nations as the production centres of such industries shift from country to country within a relatively short span of time. Therefore the expansion of the network which binds all countries together economically is bound to intensify international economic frictions. Under such circumstances the danger exists that countries which are allies could become preoccupied with mutual economic frictions and lose sight of their common interests. This could cause them to neglect their responsibility to provide adequately for the stable supply of international public goods.

In this respect, the fact that the EC and the US have become increasingly inwardly-oriented in recent years is of special concern for the countries of other regions, particularly those East Asian nations which have important economic ties with the West. The EC remains preoccupied with two gigantic and difficult tasks: achieving a deeper integration of the present member countries, and coping with the question of wider integration by bringing Eastern Europe and the countries of the FSU together into a Greater Europe. The United States faces a growing tendency at home for its own people to refuse to take on the burden of international responsibilities as their own domestic economic and social woes continue to worsen. Meanwhile the East Asian countries, including Japan (which now has the world's largest trade surplus), are not yet ready to take the initiative in constructing the new system of international cooperation that will be indispensable for ensuring a continued supply of international public goods. Russia and China, though permanent members of the UN Security Council, will remain recipients as opposed to providers of international assistance for a long time to come.

Therefore, if the EC and the US should continue to shift their attention towards internal affairs and Japan continues to hesitate in exercising greater world leadership, the possibility of the collapse of the existing multilateral cooperative system cannot be lightly dismissed. This could throw the entire world into chaos. It would become impossible then for the former communist countries to achieve a smooth transition to democratization and a market economy, and for the world to resolve regional conflicts or come up with effective measures for coping with the various unconventional threats. Human civilization, with its nuclear technology, might not survive such disorderly developments in international relations.

The new directions of security policies
Strengthening the system of international cooperation
As a result of the termination of the cold war, the UN has begun to take on its function as an international organ for peace, as originally intended. UN peace operations consist of peace–enforcing operations (PEOs), which demand that the aggressor country restores the *status quo ante*; peace-making operations (PMOs), which aim at securing the consent of the parties involved through resolution of conflict by peaceful means; preventive diplomacy, which endeavours to prevent conflicts from flaring into armed clashes and, if and when a clash occurs, to prevent its further spread; peace-keeping operations (PKOs), which recover and maintain peace after the end of hostile military activities; peace-building operations (PBOs), which prevent the future recurrence of conflicts and consolidate the foundations of peace once PKOs have achieved their objectives; and peace-creating operations (PCOs) which remove the causes of future conflicts.[11] The UN enjoys the strongest legitimacy and largest membership of existing international organizations, and we must endeavour to strengthen further this organ's peace activities. The contributions made so far by Japan have remained mainly limited to financial cooperation – reflecting Japan's postwar status in the international community. From now on, it must play a more positive role in other categories of peace activities. Public opinion in Japan is gradually shifting in favour of such commitment. The International Peace Cooperation Law was passed by the Diet in June 1992; it authorizes and stipulates the conditions for Japan's

participation in PKOs, including Diet permission for Self-Defence Forces (SDF) to be dispatched. Following this, the Japanese government is planning to send some 800 SDF troops (mostly corps of engineers and transport units) to Cambodia to join PKO activities by the autumn of 1992.[12] Japan's participation and cooperation in UN peace operations is expected to become more positive in time.

However, the UN member nations, now approaching a total of 180 countries, are of divergent backgrounds and have conflicting national interests. The existing permanent membership line-up of countries on the UN Security Council, which is charged with the special responsibility for the maintenance of global peace, reflects international power relationships as they existed at the end of Second World War and has in no real way accommodated the fundamental changes that have subsequently taken place in the world. For instance, the combined contributions of the Permanent Members of the UN Security Council (P5) represented 71 per cent of the total UN expense allocation in 1946, but the share had dropped to 47 per cent in 1990. The present rate of Japan's contribution is 12.45 per cent and is larger than the combined share (11.8 per cent) of three of the P5 members, Britain, France and China. The financial condition of the UN remains extremely weak, while at the same time the prospects for a new international consensus on how to create a greater fund are still dim. It will also be difficult to change the composition of the UN Security Council in the near future so that it is more in line with the prevailing power relationship among nations. For these reasons, therefore, the role that the UN is capable of playing in maintaining a peaceful world order is severely limited, making it necessary to look elsewhere at other international mechanisms.

For the purposes of maintaining an international order which guarantees peace and prosperity, the most effective approach at present is probably to strengthen the cooperative relationship between the P5 and the G7.[13] In order to do this, however, the expansion of the G7's role is absolutely necessary. So far, the G7's activities have remained primarily restricted to international economy and finance. It is my opinion that the G7 should be restructured so that its functions can be expanded to cover a full agenda of security issues as well.

In order to prevent or resolve regional conflicts, it will also be important to formulate and/or strengthen regional security frameworks. In this regard, Europe is far ahead of Asia. While there exist in Europe such functioning organizations as NATO, WEU, and CSCE, there are no comparable multilateral cooperative frameworks in Asia other than ASEAN and SAARC (South Asian Association for Regional Cooperation). Moreover, SAARC is still in its germination stage, and even in the case of the more successful ASEAN, there are no functioning fora in which major powers from outside ASEAN can participate, other than the ASEAN Post-Ministerial Conference (PMC), at which ASEAN foreign ministers meet their counterparts from the United States, Japan, Australia, New Zealand, Canada, the EC and South Korea. The Asia-Pacific Economic Cooperation (APEC) has recently been organized. Most of the principal countries of the Pacific region participate, including mainland China, Taiwan and Hong Kong, but its function remains no more than that of a forum for exchanging general opinions on economic issues of common concern. One of the major tasks facing Japan is to help develop a workable multilateral security framework in this region.

Strengthening the US–Japan alliance

Both in Europe and in Asia, the Western alliances already in existence, i.e. NATO and the US-Japan alliance, are critically important for the maintenance of regional order. The signatory nations of these pacts share the same basic ideologies and regimes, and possess a common interest in maintaining a peaceful and open international order. Moreover, these alliances have functioned well for nearly half a century. If they should collapse, there will be no means left of either strengthening the UN functions or assuring continued cooperation among the G7 nations. The postwar Western alliance was indeed first forged with the primary objective of building a deterrence against the Soviet Union. Yet in spite of the recent termination of the East–West confrontation and the ensuing disintegration of the Soviet Union, the continued usefulness of the NATO and the US–Japan alliance is still manifest.

In the Asia-Pacific region, in which both the US and Japan share vital security interests, there still exist not a few elements of instability. However, conditions are not yet ripe for the formation of a collective security system that will effectively cover the entire region. The only party which is accepted as 'honest broker' and capable of playing the role of maintaining the order in this region is the United States. There would be strong reactions against the expansion of an independent military role by any of the region's major players – Russia, China, India or Japan. Therefore, ensuring that the US maintains its forward deployment system intact is an almost absolute necessity for the stability of the region. It should also be added that stability and robust and continuous economic growth in the region are not only desirable for the countries involved, but are also critically important to the United States and Japan.

However, it is difficult for the United States – with an economy in relative decline and currently influenced by a strong inward-looking trend – to maintain forces in Asia even at a lower level than at present without the cooperation of the countries of the region. It should also be noted that even if US government policy remains in favour of such a commitment, adverse public opinion at home must still be contended with. Although nearly all the countries of the region desire a continued American military presence, only a limited few possess the will and ability to share the political and economic costs. In some countries, such as the Philippines and South Korea, rising nationalism and growing political instability tend to add fuel to popular sentiment against the local US military presence. In fact, only Japan may be able to provide the US with fully-fledged host-nation support. Japan's host-nation support of the US forces in the 1992 fiscal year reached 4 billion dollars, and Tokyo is expected to pay 70 per cent of the non-salary cost of the US forces stationed in Japan by the 1995 fiscal year.[14]

Japan is the only allied nation which provides a home port for a US carrier battle group, and the largest Marine Corps unit outside the continental US is stationed in Okinawa. The logistical support facilities which the US maintains in Japan are also among the largest outside the US mainland. These are indispensable services which Japan provides for the maintenance of the US forward deployment system, even without the need to deter a Soviet threat. Now that the American forces are definitely leaving the Philippines, the relative importance of the US forces and installations in Japan has increased in spite of the marked reduction of the Soviet threat.[15]

In the future when international crises similar to the Gulf war arise, Japan will be called upon to provide, in addition to host-nation support, expanded assistance in such fields as logistic support services (supplies, communications and medical care), and, if need be, reconnaissance and air defence activities. Given Japan's economic resources, it seems almost impossible in the long run to limit Japan's military role to host-nation support in coping with regional conflicts. During the years of the Soviet threat, nuclear deterrence was the decisive option, and it was predominantly the role of the US to provide it. In the case of regional conflicts, however, the role of conventional forces becomes much greater, and in this respect Japan's role must expand correspondingly. In order for Japan to play such a role, it will become necessary to revise the present official interpretation of the Constitution which makes it unconstitutional to exercise the right to collective self-defence. In the long run, therefore, the future of the US–Japan alliance will critically depend on when Japan will have a sufficiently strong leadership and mature public awareness to make these things happen.

The enhancement of cooperation in military technology is also considered to be an important task of the US–Japan alliance, and in a larger sense, of the Western alliance as a whole. Promoting cooperation among the world's technically advanced nations in the development of military technologies is important for achieving maximum cost efficiency within existing budgetary constraints. In particular, the development of a limited anti-missile defence capability such as GPALS (Global Protection Against Limited Strikes) will have a profound significance in preventing the occurrence and spread of regional conflicts as well as in promoting their early resolution.[16]

Restructuring the defence system

In order to undertake these new security tasks, it will become necessary for Japan to effect a systemic revision and restructuring of its existing defence system. First, Japan must establish a new organizational mechanism capable of developing and implementing a comprehensive security policy. For this purpose, the existing Cabinet Security Policy Division must be strengthened into a body comparable to the US National Security Council, and the liaison and coordination channels between it and the related government agencies such as the Defence Agency and the Foreign Ministry must be streamlined.

Secondly, as was already mentioned, Japan must undertake the task of changing the constitutional interpretation of the right to collective defence and participation in UN-sponsored collective security activities.

Thirdly, Japan must address the problem of a structural change in the Self-Defence Forces. There is a continued need for Japan to maintain the minimum force adequate for national defence. However, in the post-cold war era, there is some room for force reduction in the active service category. In addition, it will become increasingly difficult for Japan to maintain the present level of forces, owing to the expected population decrease in people of recruitment age. In order to cope with this situation, the reserve force system must be strengthened in order to develop the capability to deal with emergencies efficiently and competently. The present reserve force system of the Self-Defence Forces is too weak in both quantitative and qualitative terms, and falls far short of being an effective reserve force. To leave this system as it is and curtail the active force level would not be a wise policy for Japan's security.

The existing weapons systems of the Self-Defence Forces must also be revamped in order to meet the needs of the emerging international requirements, including logistic support services.

Fourthly, Japan must strengthen its development effort in military technology. By definition, the development of a new weapons system requires a long lead time, and it is crucial that the desirable effort level be maintained. For a country like Japan, in which a large military force is neither a realistic option nor a desired goal, the need to develop and possess state-of-the-art military technology is especially great. Such an effort will also substantially add, as I have already pointed out, to the reinforcement of the US–Japan alliance.

The end of the cold war and the rise of Japan as an economic superpower demands a fundamental shift in national security policy. In order to address this goal squarely, however, there are still formidable obstacles which must be overcome, including the prevailing conditions of Japan's domestic politics and the insufficient level of awareness among the general public. The most difficult tasks that Japan must address during this prolonged unstable transitional period are the strengthening of its national political leadership and the education of its populace in military security issues.

Notes

1 As regards the evolution in Japan of the concept of 'comprehensive security', as well as its influence on Japan's national security policy, see Tetsuya Umemoto, 'Comprehensive security and the evolution of the Japanese security posture', in Robert Scalapino et al., eds, *Asian Security Issues: Regional and Global* (Berkeley: University of California Press, 1988).
2 Andrei Kozyrev, 'Russia: A Chance for Survival', *Foreign Affairs*, Spring 1992, p. 1.
3 Zbigniew Brzezinski, *The Grand Failure: The Birth and Death of Communism in the Twentieth Century* (New York: Scribner, 1989).
4 Cited by A. Kozyrev, op. cit., p. 2. See also Martin Malia, 'Leninist Endgame', *Daedalus*, Spring 1992, p. 66.
5 As Susan Strange points out, the fact that the major nations of the world have lost their appetite for territorial aggrandizement is one of the most salient characteristics of the international relations in recent years. Susan Strange, 'The Name of the Game', in Nicholas X. Razopoulos, ed., *Sea-Changes: American Foreign Policy in a World Transformed* (New York: Council on Foreign Relations Press, 1990), pp. 239–40.
6 According to studies made by the US government, there are 15 countries

presently in possession of ballistic missiles, while 20 other countries are likely to join the club by the end of the present century. They also say there are nearly 20 countries which are capable of manufacturing chemical weapons. See Dick Cheney, Secretary of Defense, *Annual Report to the President and Congress*, February 1992, vi.; Kathleen C. Bailey, *Doomsday Weapons in the Hands of Many: The Arms Control Challenges of the '90s* (Chicago: University of Illinois Press, 1991), p. 58. As to the types of ballistic missiles owned or presently being developed by the countries of the South, see *Arms Control Today*, April 1992, pp. 28–9.

7 C. Fred Bergsten points out that a too rapid arms curtailment by the US will destabilize international relations, and thus runs counter to US national interests. The same can be said about all the Western countries as a whole; see C. Fred Bergsten, 'The primacy of economics,' *Foreign Policy*, No. 87, Summer 1992, pp. 14–15.

8 *Asahi Shimbun*, 3 July 1992.

9 Susan Strange, op. cit., p. 242.

10 Lester Thurow, who emphasized the possibility of an intensifying economic contest among the EC, the United States and Japan, points out that such a contest will be simultaneously competitive and cooperative, and these nations will remain friends and allies in spite of severe 'head-to-head' confrontations; see Lester Thurow, *Head to Head: The Coming Economic Battle Among Japan, Europe, and America* (New York: William Morrow and Co., 1992), p. 24.

11 Report of the UN Secretary-General to the General Assembly and the Security Council, *An Agenda for Peace* (17 June 1992), pp. 5–6.

12 See Address by Prime Minister Kiichi Miyazawa at the National Press Club in Washington, DC on 2 July 1991.

13 Stanley Hoffman pointed out that a 'polycentric steering' mechanism is necessary for the maintenance of the international order in a world without a hegemony state, and that it is desirable for the United States, the EC, Japan, Russia, and perhaps China to participate in such a 'central steering group'; see Stanley Hoffman, 'A New World and Its Troubles' in *Sea-changes*, op. cit., pp. 288–9. Also, Joseph S. Nye and others are proposing the establishment of a political 'P7' by adding Japan and Germany to the existing P5. Joseph S. Nye et al., *Global Cooperation After the Cold War: A Reassessment of Trilateralism* (Report to the Trilateral Commission, April 1991).

14 See Prime Minister Miyazawa's Address on 2 July 1992.

15 On 17 July 1992, the US government submitted to Congress a report including the plan to maintain the 'basic forces' now stationed in Japan until at least the beginning of the 21st century; see *Asahi Shimbun* (evening edition), 18 July 1992.

16 Report of the CSIS Study Group on Japanese Defense Policy cites the 'air and missile defenses' as the first item in 'Japan's procurement priorities' of the future. *Japan's Security Requirements in the Twenty-First Century* (Washington, DC: The Center for Strategic and International Studies, 1992), p. 7.

Also from the Royal Institute of International Affairs

Trade, Payments and Adjustment in Central and Eastern Europe
edited by John Flemming and J.M.C. Rollo
Published by the RIIA in September 1992

The choice of exchange-rate regimes, the choice of trade policy, the management of adjustment away from the trade and production patterns built up under communism – all these present pressing problems for the economies of central and eastern Europe. At the same time access to western markets, and to the EC in particular, is essential if exports and output are to grow. This volume of papers is an essential guide to the issues underlying these crucial areas of external policy.

Contents
Foreword by Jacques Attali, President, EBRD
Introduction – *John Flemming and J.M.C. Rollo*

Part I: International Trade and Payments Systems
1 A Post-Soviet Payments Union: Why and How – *Peter Bofinger and Daniel Gros*; 2 Trade and Payments Options for Central and Eastern Europe – *Oleh Havrylyshyn*; 3 How to Survive Trade Reorientation and Liberalization: The Example of Hungary – *Laszlo Csaba*; 4 Convertibility or a Payments Union? – Convertibility! – *Zdenek Drabek*; 5 Problems of Post-CMEA Trade and Payments – *Dariusz K. Rosati*

Part II: EC Trade Policy Towards Central and Eastern Europe
6 The Association Agreements between the EC and Central Europe: Trade Liberalization vs Constitutional Failure? – *Patrick A. Messerlin*; 7 Exports from Eastern and Central Europe and Contingent Protection – *Brian Hindley*

Part III: Trade Policy and Structural Adjustment
8 Towards the Establishment of a Continental European Customs Union – *Philippe Aghion, Robin Burgess, Jean-Paul Fitoussi and Patrick A. Messerlin*; 9 Trade Policy and Restructuring in Eastern Europe – *Gordon Hughes and Paul Hare*

About the editors
John Flemming is the Chief Economist at the European Bank for Reconstruction and Development and Jim Rollo is Director of Economics at the Royal Institute of International Affairs.

Also from the Royal Institute of International Affairs

Post-Soviet Business Forum

This forum was launched in January 1992 in response to the upsurge in demand for analysis of the emerging environment for investment and economic cooperation with the states of the former USSR. It brings together representatives of the business world with an international team of experienced researchers, specialists in key areas of economic and political change, and academics and officials from Russia and other CIS states. One outcome of its work is a series of special papers providing an up-to-the-minute account of particular aspects of change in the region.

Price and Currency Reform in Russia and the CIS
Brigitte Granville

A review of the price liberalization reforms of early 1992 and their impact. Particular attention is paid to the consequences for the currency systems of the ex-Soviet states. (Published June 1992)

After the Soviet Union: the International Trading Environment
David Dyker

An examination of the current situation and the prospects for access by exporters from the post-Soviet republics to the EC and other international markets. (Published June 1992)

The ex-Soviet States and the European Community
Perdita Fraser

An analysis of how the break-up of the USSR has affected and is likely to affect relations with the European Community and the EBRD, with particular reference to financial, technical and emergency assistance. (Published July 1992)

Post-Soviet Transcaucasia
Jonathan Aves

A study of political, economic and security developments in the three Transcaucasian states since independence, and an examination of emerging new international patterns in the region.

Economic Lobbies and Pressure Groups in the CIS
Peter Rutland
An analysis of the new politics of economic policy-making in the former Soviet Union, the role of economic associations, special interest groups and trade unions, and the impact on the operations of firms.

The Central Asian Economies after Independence
Michael Kaser and Santos Mehotra
An assessment of the prospects for economic development and international economic cooperation in Uzbekistan, Tajikistan, Turkmenistan and Kyrgyzstan.

The Economic Effects of the Dissolution of the Soviet Union
Michael Bradshaw
An examination of the regional economic legacy of the Soviet system, of the current state of inter-republican and foreign economic relations, and of the prospects for economic reintegration.

The Conversion of the ex-Soviet Defence Industry
Julian Cooper
A review of problems encountered in reorientating from military to civilian production and assessment of the likely outcome of current policies in Russia, the Ukraine and other ex-Soviet republics. Particular attention will be paid to the international dimension.

Systemic Change and Stabilization in Russia
Anders Åslund
A review of progress achieved during the first twelve months of the Russian government's drive for economic reform.

The Russian Energy Industry
Jonathan Stern
An assessment of attempts to renew the energy sector of the Russian economy, and of its role in the world energy economy.

Also from the Royal Institute of International Affairs

Discussion Papers

This series consists of brief, specialized and highly topical papers related to current research programmes.

No. 36: Enlargement without Accession: The EC's Response to German Unification
David Spence

One major consequence of German unification was the integration of the former GDR into the EC. This paper gives an account of how the institutions of the EC responded to German unification, specifically the role of the EC Commission in initiating and managing the process of integration. It questions the widespread assumption that the Community decision-making process is lengthy, bureaucratic and unable to respond effectively to challenge. Above all, the paper is a record of the issues posed for the EC by unification; it also considers briefly some of the political concerns of member states about the possible institutional implications of an enlarged Germany within the Community and more general fears about the balance of power in a wider Europe. (Published in November 1991)

No. 37: Japan's Security Policy in the Regional and Global Context
Kiyoshi Araki

Japan's role in international political and security affairs will grow larger in the coming decade, just as its economic strength has already made it a central player in the management of the world economy. How does Japan itself see its political and security role in the post-cold war world? What are Tokyo's priorities, and how does the changing security environment affect the domestic and international determinants of Japan's security policy? What constraints and difficulties affect what Japan can do in this area? With the dramatic changes in the Soviet Union and in the light of experience during the Kuwait crisis, these questions are of increasing importance. This paper outlines the past, present and future of Japan's security policy and analyses its limits and constraints as well as its implications for today's Europe. (Published in November 1991)

No. 38: The United Nations and the Gulf War, 1990–91: Back to the Future?
Paul Taylor and A.J.R. Groom

The United Nations today finds itself at the centre of questions of international peace and security. Since the Gulf war, the growing solidarity of the five permanent members of the Security Council, and their ability to carry the Council with them, have made themselves felt throughout the other organs of the UN. This paper focuses on the diplomacy of the Security Council associated with the 14 resolutions that it passed, from its condemnation of the Iraqi invasion of Kuwait to Iraq's acceptance of the settlement. The effect of these resolutions was to permit the coalition to restore the independence of Kuwait, and effectively to occupy part of Iraq. The paper also analyses the diplomacy of the specialized agencies as, in response to further resolutions, they struggled to cope with a flood of refugees from Kuwait, the trek of the Kurds to the Turkish border, the revolt in Southern Iraq at the end of hostilities and its brutal crushing, the fleeing of over a million refugees to Iran, and the suffering of the Iraqi people as sanctions continue to exacerbate their situation. The paper addresses some significant questions. Is the UN now America's poodle? Could it act on such a scale again? Is the network of humanitarian organizations, both in the UN and outside, able to cope with such huge man-made catastrophes? (Published in February 1992)

No. 39: NATO and Central Europe: Problems and Opportunities in a New Relationship
Trevor Taylor

The collapse of communism has transformed the security situation in Europe. NATO is widely seen in former communist Europe as the most successful security organization in the region, and this paper focuses on its achievements and potential with regard to Poland, the Czech and Slovak Federal Republic, and Hungary, and explores the problems associated with widening its membership. The paper is particularly supportive of NATO's rejection of any formal discrimination in favour of members of the former Warsaw Treaty Organization, and also identifies how NATO can positively assist the countries of Central Europe through aid programmes, technology transfer and other measures. After discussing the 'security shadow' that could be thrown over Central Europe by the European Community, and the significance of the principles of the Conference on Security and Cooperation in Europe, the paper asserts that a secure Europe is ultimately impossible unless adequate provision can be made for the security of the former Soviet Union. (Published in April 1992)

No. 40: After the Bloc: The New International Relations in Eastern Europe
Libor Roucek

Although there is much rejoicing in the countries of Central and Eastern Europe over the collapse of communism and the demise of the Soviet bloc, these events have also posed a fundamental question: what will the new international position of the region be? This study investigates the new pattern of relations that is emerging, focusing on Poland, Hungary, Czechoslovakia, Romania and Bulgaria. The author begins by assessing the relationship of Eastern Europe with the successor states of the Soviet Union, tracing the transformation of multilateral patterns into a network of bilateral relations. He then looks at the prospects for the development of different regional forms of cooperation, examining the growth of new multilateral groupings among the five ex-satellite states and their neighbours. He concludes that, given the situation in the ex-Soviet Union and the overwhelming power of attraction of the West, it is likely that the five countries will become more and more closely connected with the Western nations and their organizations. Just how close this association will be, however, remains to be seen. (Published in May 1992)

Forthcoming in October 1992

No. 41: The Western European Union and Central Europe: A New Relationship
Andrzej Podraza

A Polish contribution to the debate about the new security situation in Europe since the collapse of communism. The author argues in particular that the Western European Union should follow the EC in adopting the principle of differentiation in its relations with Central and East European countries, initially developing closer links with Poland, Hungary and Czechoslovakia because of their progress in pursuing economic, political and defence reforms.